ON CALL IN HELL

ON CALL IN HELL

A DOCTOR'S IRAQ WAR STORY

CDR. RICHARD JADICK

WITH THOMAS HAYDEN

NAL
CALIBER

NAL Caliber
Published by New American Library, a division of
Penguin Group (USA) Inc., 375 Hudson Street,
New York, New York 10014, USA
Penguin Group (Canada), 90 Eglinton Avenue East, Suite 700, Toronto,
Ontario M4P 2Y3, Canada (a division of Pearson Penguin Canada Inc.)
Penguin Books Ltd., 80 Strand, London WC2R 0RL, England
Penguin Ireland, 25 St. Stephen's Green, Dublin 2,
Ireland (a division of Penguin Books Ltd.)
Penguin Group (Australia), 250 Camberwell Road, Camberwell, Victoria 3124,
Australia (a division of Pearson Australia Group Pty. Ltd.)
Penguin Books India Pvt. Ltd., 11 Community Centre, Panchsheel Park,
New Delhi - 110 017, India
Penguin Group (NZ), 67 Apollo Drive, Mairangi Bay,
Auckland 1310, New Zealand (a division of Pearson New Zealand Ltd.)
Penguin Books (South Africa) (Pty.) Ltd., 24 Sturdee Avenue,
Rosebank, Johannesburg 2196, South Africa

Penguin Books Ltd., Registered Offices:
80 Strand, London WC2R 0RL, England

First published by NAL Caliber, an imprint of New American Library,
a division of Penguin Group (USA) Inc.

First Printing, March 2007
10 9 8 7 6 5 4 3 2 1

Copyright © Cdr. Richard Jadick with Thomas Hayden, 2007
Map by G. W. Ward
All rights reserved

NAL CALIBER and the "C" logo are trademarks of Penguin Group (USA) Inc.

LIBRARY OF CONGRESS CATALOGING-IN-PUBLICATION DATA:

Jadick, Richard.
    On call in hell: a doctor's Iraq War story/Richard Jadick, Thomas Hayden.
    p. cm.
    ISBN-13: 978-0-451-22053-0
    1. Fallujah, Battle of, Fallujah, Iraq, 2004. 2. Iraq War, 2003—Personal narratives, American.
3. Jadick, Richard. 4. Physicians—United States—Biography. I. Hayden, Thomas. II. Title.
DS79.766.F3J33 2007
956.7044'342—dc22   2006028936

Set in Fairfield
Designed by Ginger Legato

Printed in the United States of America

PUBLISHER'S NOTE
The views expressed in this book are solely those of the author and do not necessarily reflect those of the
Department of the Navy.
    While the author has made every effort to provide accurate telephone numbers and Internet addresses
at the time of publication, neither the publisher nor the author assumes any responsibility for errors, or for
changes that occur after publication. Further, publisher does not have any control over and does not as-
sume any responsibility for author or third-party Web sites or their content.

This book is dedicated to the families of the twenty-one brave Marines who gave their lives with the First Battalion, Eighth Marine Regiment in Iraq between June 2004 and January 2005. Your Marines sacrificed all so that we may live in freedom and security, but you, the Gold Star families, continue to sacrifice every day. We will never forget: Corporal Nathan R. Anderson, Corporal Kirk J. Bosselmann, Lance Corporal Demarkus D. Brown, Sergeant David M. Caruso, Lance Corporal Travis R. Desiato, Lance Corporal Bradley M. Faircloth, Lance Corporal Dimitrios Gavriel, Corporal Todd J. Godwin, Lance Corporal Michael J. Halal, Lance Corporal Jeffery S. Holmes, Lance Corporal David B. Houck, Corporal Romulo J. Jimenez II, Sergeant Richard M. Lord, Lance Corporal Joshua E. Lucero, Lance Corporal Cesar F. Machado-Olmos, First Lieutenant Dan T. Malcom Jr., Corporal Gentian Marku, Lance Corporal William L. Miller, Lance Corporal Bradley L. Parker, Sergeant Lonny D. Wells, Corporal Nicholas L. Ziolkowski.

CONTENTS

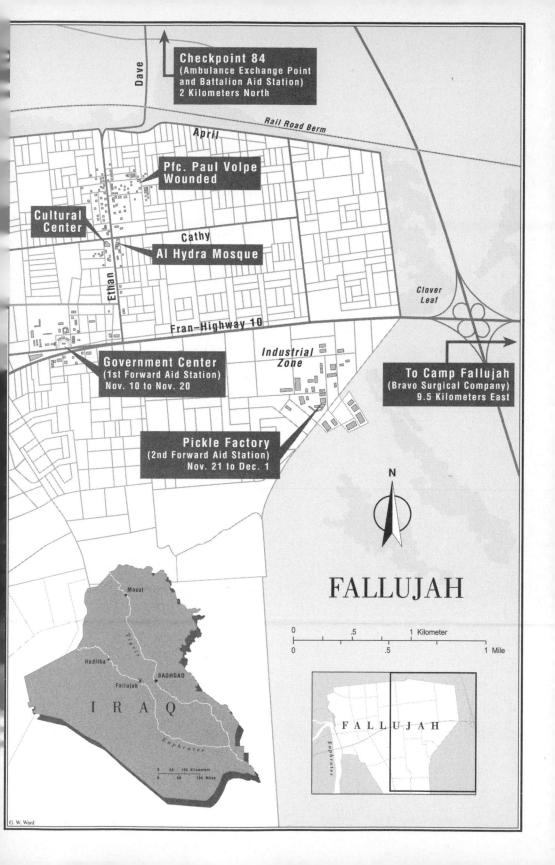

Checkpoint 84
(Ambulance Exchange Point
and Battalion Aid Station)
2 Kilometers North

Dave

Rail Road Berm

April

Pfc. Paul Volpe
Wounded

Cultural
Center

Cathy

Al Hydra Mosque

Ethan

Clover
Leaf

Fran—Highway 10

Industrial
Zone

Government Center
(1st Forward Aid Station)
Nov. 10 to Nov. 20

To Camp Fallujah
(Bravo Surgical Company)
9.5 Kilometers East

Pickle Factory
(2nd Forward Aid Station)
Nov. 21 to Dec. 1

N

FALLUJAH

0   .5   1 Kilometer
0   .5   1 Mile

Mosul

Tigris

Haditha

BAGHDAD

Fallujah

I R A Q

Euphrates

0   50   100 Kilometers
0   50   100 Miles

FALLUJAH

Euphrates

G. W. Ward

PROLOGUE

I t has been two years now since I returned home from Fallujah. All told, I was in Iraq for just seven months. But the time I spent there, the men I served with, and the people we saved, these things will stay with me forever. I have been in the military for almost all of my adult life—I started out as a seventeen-year-old Marine ROTC midshipman at Ithaca College in upstate New York in 1983, and after graduating I served over six years as a United States Marine Corps officer before finally leaving the Corps in 1993. But not long afterward, I was back, this time with the Navy. I had entered medical school at Long Island's New York College of Osteopathic Medicine, and I took a Navy scholarship with the idea that I would become a Navy medical officer and later retire to life as a civilian physician. I have served my country as a Marine, as a Naval officer, and as a doctor, and in civilian settings I've treated everything from gunshot wounds in inner-city Baltimore to prostate cancer in Augusta, where I am currently a urology resident at the Medical College of Georgia. But there is nothing in my life that has marked me in quite the same way as my time in Iraq.

As I write this, some 132,000 American servicemen and -women are stationed in Iraq—many on second or third tours—and another 22,000 or so in Afghanistan. Since September 11, 2001, more than 1.3 million Americans in uniform have shipped out to those theaters and elsewhere, putting their lives on hold—and on the line—to fight in the war on terror. I'm just one man, and I did only two combat tours. But I had the privilege of serving with 1,000 of the finest U.S. Marines and Navy hospital corpsmen this country has ever produced. My story—of my life, of my tour, and of the incredibly intense Battle of Fallujah, in November 2004—is just one of many in this book. And I hope that my own experiences reflect those of the hundreds of thousands of men and women who make the American military what it is—the most powerful and effective fighting force in the world.

In some ways, I had been preparing for Fallujah for most of my life. From my earliest days, I had wanted to join the military and I had wanted to be a doctor. Every step of my training, both military and medical, contributed something to the success our medical team had in Iraq, from my experiences as a communications officer with the Marine Corps to my background in trauma medicine and my several previous deployments as a Navy medical officer with Marine units. And the central idea behind the aggressive approach to battlefield medicine we used in Fallujah had started to percolate years earlier. As a young Navy doctor, I had come to believe that the system was in need of some serious changes. The medical infrastructure had traditionally been tucked away at the rear of the war zone with the headquarters elements—safe, and far from the fight. To me, that meant too much time lost in transporting injured troops back to base, precious moments that could have been spent stabilizing the wounded warriors and perhaps saving their lives. I first started to develop these ideas about far-forward medicine with my fellow battalion surgeon Will Dutton, and worked out many of the details with my good friend Joe Langholtz, now the command master chief of the II Marine Expeditionary Force (II MEF). The concept was simple enough: move the doctors, corpsmen, and aid stations as far forward as we could—we had to follow the fight. But it took Fallujah to turn theory into practice and to demonstrate the effectiveness of our approach. You'll see many of the results in the chapters that follow. The one that means the most to me and to all those who made it possible is that an estimated thirty Marines who otherwise would have perished in Fallujah were able to make it home to their families.

This wasn't a role I had been expecting to fill. At thirty-eight, I was considerably older than most battalion surgeons, who are generally young doctors, not long out of their medical school internships. As a lieutenant commander, I had already paid my dues, and was stationed at Marine Corps Base Camp Lejeune, North Carolina, while waiting for a spot to open up in a urology residency. But then in the spring of 2004 a different opportunity arose—the chance to deploy that summer with the First Battalion, Eighth Marine Regiment, the 1/8. I had missed the First Gulf War as a Marine officer, and regretted losing the opportunity to serve in a war zone. More recently, while working in Liberia as surgeon in charge of a Marine Expeditionary Unit, I had a group of Marines under my care come down with malaria—and I didn't want that to be the last major incident on my field service record. It would mean leaving my wife and our newborn daughter behind, but I jumped at the opportunity to put my two decades of military training to the test with the 1/8 in Iraq.

The First Battalion, Eighth Marine Regiment is a remarkable unit, with a history of honorable service stretching back to April 1, 1940. The battalion fought its way through the Pacific theater, from Guadalcanal to Okinawa, during World War II, and played a significant role in Cold War battles and confrontations in the Mediterranean and Caribbean, including the Cuban Missile Crisis in 1962. But it was at 6:22 Sunday morning, October 23, 1983, that the 1/8 earned its nickname—the Beirut Battalion. The Marines were stationed at that city's airport as part of a multinational force trying to keep the peace during Lebanon's brutal civil war, when a large yellow Mercedes truck loaded with twelve thousand pounds of explosives rammed into their barracks and exploded. It was one of the first modern suicide bombings and, with 220 Marines killed (along with 18 Navy Sailors, 3 Army soldiers, and an elderly Lebanese custodian), the deadliest single day for the Marine Corps since the Battle of Iwo Jima in 1945. The 1/8 recovered and has continued to serve America in war and in peacetime as well, including a 2005 deployment to New Orleans in the wake of Hurricane Katrina, where the battalion brought much-needed aid and security to the devastated city.

Camp Lejeune is home to the Second Marine Division, of which the 1/8 is one battalion. The Second Marine Division makes up the ground combat element of II MEF, one of the Marine Corps's four primary fighting forces. (I MEF is in Camp

Pendleton, California; III MEF is in Okinawa; and IV MEF is the reservists.) I MEF and II MEF have been alternating the fight in Iraq since the war there began on March 20, 2003, but in mid-2004, the 1/8 was assigned to augment I MEF's forces in the restive al-Anbar province. (This sort of augmentation is fairly common since Marine Corps units are designed to be inter-changeable.)

From May 2004 until January 2005, I served as battalion sur-geon for the First Battalion, Eighth Marines—the 1/8. As the senior medical officer for the battalion, I was essentially the primary-care doctor for roughly one thousand Marines, ultimately responsible for everything from keeping them hydrated in the desert to keeping them alive in the heat of battle. We didn't know when we first deployed to Iraq in late June of 2004 that we would eventually play a central role in the Battle of Fallujah; the 1/8 spent our first four and a half months patrolling the city of Ha-ditha, a hundred miles or so up the Euphrates River, to the north-west. Then, on November 8, 2004, the 1/8 took its place in the historic fight to free Fallujah from the deadly grasp of the Iraqi insurgents and foreign jihadis who held the city captive. As Ma-rines have been doing ever since the founding of the Corps on November 10, 1775, the men of the 1/8 took up the challenge, and performed their duty with courage, honor, and, often, tre-mendous personal sacrifice.

The Battle of Fallujah—dubbed Operation Phantom Fury by the Department of Defense, and later Operation al-Fajr ("Dawn" in Arabic) by the Iraqi Defense Minister—will go down as one of the most important battles in the current Iraq war. It was a decisive victory over the insurgents, and helped pave the way for the critical national elections held in January 2005. The city's solid, bunkerlike houses, narrow alleyways, and long, straight boulevards—and the fierce resistance we met—made almost every block a killing zone. Fallujah was the site of the most brutal urban warfare Americans had faced since the Marines retook Hue City from the Vietcong after the 1968 Tet Offensive.

The four Marine battalions and two Army battalions, as well as Iraqi Security Force elements, pushed south, and then swept to the east and west and back north again, clearing thousands of insurgents, foreign fighters, and their weapons caches from houses, mosques, and buildings throughout the city. The first eight days were the most intense, but our brave warriors fought on, not just through the November tenth Marine Corps birthday and Veterans Day on the eleventh; they fought on through Thanksgiving and stayed in the city past Christmas as well. They fought on through heat, rain, cold, and the near-constant threat of snipers, booby traps, and roadside bombs. During that time, my medical team and I pushed forward into the city with our Marines, and established a Forward Aid Station in the heart of the battle zone. We came under significant enemy fire in the process, but we believed it was our duty to do whatever we could to save our wounded Marines—and that the standard medical procedure of staying at the rear would put us too far away from the battle to save every man we could. All told, at least 70 Americans lost their lives in the streets of Fallujah, and more than 600 were wounded. The 1/8 fought right through the middle of the city, taking on what was probably the hardest duty of the battle. We lost 21 men killed in action (KIA) and another 200 wounded (WIA), too seriously injured to carry on the fight. As devastating as those lessons were, they fell well below the 30 to 40 percent casualty rate that had been predicted for the battle.

Americans tend to be fascinated with their Marines. But for the most part, the corpsmen who serve with them have been overlooked in the popular imagination. And that's a real shame. Hospital Corpsman is actually the most decorated rating in the U.S. Navy, with twenty-two Medals of Honor, for example, and Fleet Marine Force (FMF) corpsmen, those who are assigned to Marine battalions, go literally everywhere that Marines do. (It's a little-appreciated fact that U.S. Navy corpsman John Bradley is one of the four "Marines" in the famous photograph of the flag raising on Iwo Jima—he's second from the right when you're looking at the picture.) FMF corpsmen patrol with Marine platoons, they organize and run aid stations, and time after time in Fallujah, they lived up to the motto "Through the gates of hell for a wounded Marine." Whether on the battlefield or at an aid station, their job requires the physical strength and stamina of a Marine, the knowledge and skill of a medical professional, and the heart and nerves to answer the call to duty—"*Corpsman Up!*"—no matter what the conditions may be. For my money, the FMF corpsmen who serve alongside the Marines are among the most extraordinary members of America's military.

For the eight months I was with the 1/8, these were my guys—assistant battalion surgeon Lieutenant Carlos Kennedy and fifty-four U.S. Navy hospital corpsmen, including my senior enlisted man, Chief Hospital Corpsman (HMC) Russ Folley, Hospital Corpsmen First Class (HM1) Rick Lees and Bryan Zimmerman, and Hospital Corpsmen Second Class (HM2) Shawn Johns and Steve Meszaros. They came from every corner of the country, and they included everyone from straight-out-of-high-school HAs (Hospitalman Apprentice) to the several dozen HNs (Hospitalman) and HM3s (Hospital Corpsman Third Class), all the way up to the most seasoned veterans, like Lees, with nearly twenty years of service in the hospital corps, and Zimmerman, an IDC (Independent Duty Corpsman), meaning that he's the military equivalent of a civilian physician's assistant. If the battalion surgeon is a combination of primary-care physician and emergency doctor, then these Navy Sailors—known as corpsmen (pronounced "core"-men), or often to their Marines simply as "Doc"—fill just about every other role in a frontline medical operation, from first aid provider to orderly to emergency nurse and physician's assistant. The Army has its medics, but the Marine Corps has no medical wing of its own, and so it relies on the Navy to supply both doctors and corpsmen. The fifty-four corpsmen assigned to the 1/8 all volunteered for the hospital corps, and they all volunteered to serve with the Marines, rather than in the relative safety of "big Navy" service at the rear. I happen to think the FMF corpsmen I served with in Iraq are the very best there are, but like I say, they were my guys—I helped train them, I relied on them, and I did my best to lead them—so maybe I'm a little biased.

But you don't have to take my word for it. Sergeant Major Anthony Hope is what we call a "Marine's Marine"—a guy who pretty much embodies everything a Marine is supposed to be. As the senior staff Non-Commissioned Officer (SNCO) with the 1/8 in Fallujah, he was ultimately responsible for the performance, morale, and welfare of every enlisted man on the field of battle. And like a lot of Marines, says Sergeant Major Hope, he didn't think much of the fact that FMF Navy corpsmen wear the same uniform as the Marines they work with—right down to the eagle, globe, and anchor USMC emblem. There is a lot of pride in the military, and nowhere more so than in the Marine Corps. That patch is something that you have to earn, and to a "lifer" like Sergeant Major Hope—he enlisted a week out of high school in 1978 and is going to kick up an ornery fuss when they finally make him retire after thirty years—it didn't seem right that the corpsmen would wear it without going through Marine boot camp. Seeing my guys at work in Fallujah changed his attitude, though; when he says, "Those fifty-four corpsmen in Fallujah proved their mettle and earned the right to wear the eagle, globe, and anchor with pride," there is simply no higher praise any man could give.

It is for those fifty-four corpsmen, for the Marines of the 1/8, and for all who serve America in her military that I am writing this book. I was worried about it at first—worried that I would somehow be putting myself ahead of all the brave Marines and corpsmen who served their country with tremendous valor and bravery in the Battle of Fallujah. Or worse, that it would be blood money, that I might end up profiting from other people's misfortune, from tragedies that I just happened to be part of. But in talking about the project since, with my corpsmen, with Marines of the 1/8 and with our Gold Star families—the relatives of our fallen Marines—no one has taken that attitude. Command Master Chief Langholtz is one of those guys who have a real knack for cutting through to the heart of things, and I think he put it best. Describing the corpsmen, he said, "They don't jump out of planes or blow shit up or even kill people. All they do is hump a pack with the Marines and save people's lives. And that's a story that deserves to be told." I couldn't agree with him more. All of the stories in this book—stories of honor, courage, brotherhood, and service, stories of horror and of humanity—are stories that should be told. They are stories that we want to share with the American people, the people who we serve and the people who, ultimately, decide when and where it's time to call out the Marines—and the medical teams that help keep them fighting.

Commander Richard Jadick, D.O.
United States Navy
Medical College of Georgia
Augusta, Georgia
January 2007

CHAPTER 1
Battle Begins

November 8, 2004

T he sky had been trying to rain all day as we waited for the attack to begin that evening. We had been in Iraq for almost five months already, and finally we were on the very edge of battle. On the outskirts of Fallujah that day, it drizzled just a little, and the cloud cover was so low that it became almost like fog. There was no loudness to any of the sounds around us, not even the prep fires we were sending into the city—artillery shots to help smooth our entry into Fallujah—and the mortars coming back our way. Everything sounded flat and damped somehow. When you spoke, there was no echo. Words were just . . . there. Like they came out and just fell down, didn't go anywhere far. Only the calls to prayer from the mosques in Fallujah had any resonance to them, adding an eerie otherworldliness to the entire scene.

Was I ready? I didn't know. As the battalion surgeon for the First Battalion, Eighth Marine Regiment (1/8), I had pushed myself especially hard for the last two days: cross-training with the Army National Guard ambulance teams, running through our procedures over and over again, racking our brains trying to find and plug the holes in our plans. After that, there isn't much more you can do. You eat, you drink water, you dig heads (latrines) and use them. You get a little sleep if you can, you say your prayers and try to make your peace, every one of us in his or her own way. The breach was set for eight p.m. Everyone knew it. Everyone was as ready as they were going to be. There was nothing left to do but wait.

It was the line charges that brought our waiting to an end. They went off right on schedule, and even when you know it's coming, the intense force of the shock wave, followed immediately by the sound wave, shakes you from the inside out, rattling through your body. The rush of the rockets launching, the whip-lash hiss of the lines uncoiling behind them, the rolling thunder of the ultimate explosions: these sounds were the unofficial starter's pistol for the Battle of Fallujah. Consisting of a couple thousand pounds of plastic explosive strung out along hundreds of feet of nylon line like baited hooks on a deep-sea fishing rig, the rocket-propelled line charges were deployed to clear our routes of advance, taking out barricades, IEDs (Improvised Explosive Devices), and booby traps. Fired out in front of each attacking battalion, the line charges did that job admirably, and they took on the added effect of serving notice, like the cavalry charge played on a bugle—Ka-*boom*! Here we come, motherfucker. Good to go.

The first steps into the city were the easiest the Marines of the

1/8 would have for almost a month. They followed in on foot, behind the M1 Abrams tanks of the USMC's Second Tank Battalion, Company A, passing through the breach blown in a railway embankment and across a rail yard cleared and leveled by a pair of up-armored D9 Cats—huge Caterpillar bulldozers that would prove invaluable in the weeks to come, removing obstacles and demolishing buildings that housed entrenched nests of insurgent fighters. The 1/8 Marines moved into the city in leapfrog fashion, one company establishing a position and the next one moving on past. And my corpsmen went with them—Navy medical personnel embedded in every Marine platoon and company. Together, they pushed into the city through the night, coming up against moderate resistance—machine-gun fire from a black SUV here, harassing AK-47 fire sprayed around corners there, a handful of heavier engagements. By dawn, Bravo and Charlie companies were in position and ready to take their first major objectives in central Fallujah—the large, green-domed al-Hydra Mosque and a nearby building that housed a cultural center.

The rest of us continued to wait. I had set my two armored ambulances at the ready—one stationed at the breach point and ready to roll, the other five hundred meters behind the breach, with 1/8's executive officer (XO), Major Mark Winn, and his Jump Command Post unit at the battalion Attack Position. That first night, as the line companies established themselves inside the city, was slow for those of us who remained at the rear—and slow is what you want for a medical company. I was concerned, though. In urban combat we all knew it was just a matter of time; the official estimate was that we should expect 30 to 40 percent of our Marines to be wounded or killed during the battle. I remember sitting there and looking around, wondering who they would be. These were guys I had known for months now, as well as guys I had just linked up with in the last couple of days—guys like Second Lieutenant Todd Wilson, the officer in charge of the National Guard ambulance platoon. We had trained together for just a day or two, and now I was sending them into battle. *This must be what the colonel feels like about everybody,* I remember thinking. I had positioned their vehicles in pretty dangerous spots—the best tactics for the battalion, but maybe not what these folks would have preferred. I couldn't help but feel a little guilty and overwhelmed. I had become close with some of these people and I had to remind myself that I was a doctor and an officer—I had to keep the personal out of it and do what was best for the battalion.

I needn't have worried; the ambulance crews were magnificent, proving themselves as fearless and effective that night and throughout the battle. The plan was for them to take turns driving their tracked and lightly armored vehicles into the city that night, and by very early morning the first "track" was back out with casualties. We replaced the other vehicle forward and went to work. So far, so good; there was a flurry of activity at the Battalion Aid Station (BAS) we had set up near a spot the planners had designated Checkpoint 84, but none of the casualties were very serious, just enough to give our system a run-through.

The early rays of winter sun were still pushing at the morning mist when the first major call came, crackling through the radio. The battle in the city was heating up with the day, and there was a Force Reconnaissance corpsman down near the city's cultural center. Force Recon operators are Special Operations–type Marines, responsible for evaluating and reporting on the battle space forward of the assaulting units—the Navy SEALs of the

Marine Corps, essentially. Even the Navy corpsmen in their units take on active roles in their highly dangerous jobs, like identifying targets for artillery and close air support. This Force Recon corpsman was shot in the chest, the radio said, and the wound was sucking—air was pulling in and out of the bullet hole as he breathed. He was still conscious, but that status could change quickly.

Both of my ambulances were already in the city, and this guy wasn't at one of our preestablished casualty collection points. He wouldn't be able to get there on his own, and with a punctured lung he probably wasn't stable enough for his unit to carry him. I turned to Lieutenant Matthew Kutilek, a super Marine, clean-cut, whip-smart, and aggressive as they come. His Weapons Company third platoon—eight Humvees mounted with major weaponry, including MK19 40-millimeter grenade launchers ("Mark 19s"), M2 .50-caliber machine guns ("Ma Deuces"), and a TOW antitank missile launcher—was standing by in case we needed assistance. "We've got a man down and I can't go in on my own," was all I needed to tell Kutilek—I don't think I was even done saying it by the time he responded "Roger that!" and got his guys ready to roll.

Typically, a battalion surgeon will wait for the wounded to be extracted and brought back to the relative safety of the BAS. But a sucking chest wound is serious business, and I didn't want this man spending any more time without medical care than he had to. I hopped into Kutilek's Humvee—I couldn't go in alone, but I didn't want to send the Marines in alone either—and although he looked bewildered at first, he shrugged and accepted that I was going along for the ride. I could have sent in a senior corpsman, but I didn't want to do that either. For one thing, a leader has to be willing to take the same risks he's asking his men to take. And although I had trained my corpsmen well, I had seen sucking chest wounds before and they hadn't. I figured I would be in and out in about fifteen minutes.

We drove up to the edge of the city and dismounted warily. The northern rim of Fallujah was already a wreck of rubble and debris—the result of the previous night's battle and several days of our targeted artillery and aircraft prep fires—and I was more than a little alarmed by the sounds of rocket blasts and small-arms fire echoing all around us. The sounds were deadened by the moist, hot air that hung throughout the city. Each building was nothing more than a facade to us, each window dark and quiet inside—we had cut the city's electricity before the attack began. The debris made it difficult to walk and sent clouds of talcumlike dust into the air with every step. The city looked dull, like the weather and smoke had depleted it of any color. I don't know what everyone else was thinking, but I know what was in my head: *What the hell am I doing?* I had spent seven years as a Marine before going to medical school, but this was my first real battle, my first real casualty call, and I hadn't expected to be in the thick of it quite so soon. I began to realize that I hadn't really thought through my trip into the city too carefully. *But guess what, jackass? It's a little too late now!*

Kutilek's plan was for us to move on foot as a platoon through the city's narrow alleyways, with the vehicles following behind to provide support. Again, good tactics, but walking around was not exactly what I wanted to be doing. Every corner was a potential source of sniper attack. I was surrounded by Kutilek and his heavily armed Weapons Company Marines, and we all wore Kevlar helmets and protective body armor on our torsos and groins. But I still felt exposed and a little silly with nothing but my officer's 9-millimeter pistol to contribute to the fight. The M9 semiautomatic Beretta is a fairly impressive weapon as handguns go—less potent than a .45, but more accurate. It weighs a solid two pounds with fifteen rounds in the clip, but surrounded by the raging Battle of Fallujah, I felt like the guy who brought a knife to a gunfight. *Anyone actually gets close to me, I'm going to have to throw this thing at him.*

We started out along Ethan, the main road into town, alleyways on either side of us. Every explosion, every blast of gunfire made me jump, no matter how distant. Our necks twisted in every direction, looking for signs of movement, light, anything. My heart was racing—alleyways are a definite danger zone, a line of fire for the enemy. A tall, rail-thin lance corporal addressed me with polite anxiety. "Sir, cover the corner," he said. Well, there's no room for a shitbird in a battle zone, doctor or not. I got out my 9 millimeter and held down the corner as the platoon passed by.

My job was to be there for the wounded, not to shoot people. But right then, my job as I saw it was to get to my patient—that was the only way I could keep him alive. Kutilek and his guys didn't quibble with my being there, even though you could see the questions in their eyes. "Damn, we've got a doctor walking around with us—does he know how to maneuver, how to take cover?" A scene from an old episode of *M*A*S*H* flashed into my head: Alan Alda's doctor character, Hawkeye, is under attack, but he doesn't want to fire his pistol because he's worried that the bullet may fall down and accidentally hurt someone. I know a doctor's job is to save people, not to kill them. But the reality of a combat zone is very different. I was clear in my own mind that if someone was shooting at me, I would shoot back. I hoped it wouldn't come to that, but Kutilek's guys were already risking their lives to save my ass. I was going to pull my weight as best I could.

The early-morning sun started heating the city as we leap-frogged our way through increasingly narrow streets. Even though it was just after sunup, the temperature was already ninety degrees and the humid air made the dust stick to my skin. I was sweating through my cammies beneath my body armor and heavy gear. I'd see a potential source of enemy fire and couldn't help thinking: *Before I see the muzzle flash, I'm gonna have a round in my chest.* My brain was still struggling to accept the reality of the situation: this wasn't some training exercise, this was for real. Rounds were going off around us, and the Marines were returning fire, but it was mostly harassment, insurgents popping around a corner, squeezing off a couple of shots, and disappearing.

We kept moving. But we had a problem—we didn't know exactly where our wounded Sailor was. Our battalion had developed a detailed grid system for maneuvering around the city and locating wounded troops, but the Force Recon corpsman wasn't one of our guys and his unit didn't know our system. The radio call had given us nothing but a point on a map, not a specific pickup location. As we pushed farther into the city, the tension among us was rising. This was taking much longer than any of us had figured, and every extra minute we spent out there was an extra chance for the insurgents to add us to the casualty list. Anxiety and fear were creeping into my head, but I pushed them back and continued on. Where the hell was this guy?

As we snaked our way around one corner, we ran into a platoon from Charlie Company, and I saw one of my corpsmen, HN Barry Womack, pressed up against a wall with insurgents shooting at him from the other side. I thought his unit might know where the wounded Force Recon corpsman was, so I darted over. Womack, a funny, happy-go-lucky kid, cracked a huge grin when he saw me. "Sir, what the hell are you doing? This isn't a place for you—they're shootin' at us!"

I tried to explain and showed him the map.

"Aw, Sir, shit. I don't know! I just follow these guys around."

"Thanks a lot, Womack—hey, how you doin' anyway?"

"I'm all right, Sir. I'm just followin' 'em around. It's no big deal."

"All right, Womack, carry on."

"All right, Sir. See ya!"

Middle of a war zone and we're stopping for a chat—might as well have asked about the wife and kids.

Finally, after what seemed like hours but was probably close to forty-five minutes, we found our way to what appeared to be the right spot. Kutilek got on the radio and confirmed the building description. I scrambled over a fence into the yard with the Weapons Company Marines securing the approach. The building was pretty bombed out. The wounded corpsman was hunkered down upstairs, on the second deck. A tough kid with a solemn, still face, he was a corpsman himself, assigned to the Second Marine Recon Battalion. Like all Special Operations types, he prefers to keep his identity a secret. His buddy was standing there beside him, and had already done a pretty good job of patching him up. The corpsman had been hit in the left lateral chest with a small-arms round. He had a punctured lung, and he was "taching" pretty good—tachycardia, which means his pulse was racing but still regular. Could have been from the blood loss, could have been from pain, anxiety, fear. I couldn't find an exit wound, so the bullet was still inside. I found out later it had lodged in his T-10 vertebra, in the middle of his back. His partner had applied an occlusive dressing, a playing-card-sized sheet of plastic taped over the wound with the top side loose, so it would seal the sucking wound when he breathed in and act as an escape valve if he started building up air pockets inside his chest cavity. The corpsman had been hit on his left side, which is always a concern, because he could easily develop a tear in an artery and start to bleed so fast that it would kill him—what we call bleeding out.

"Get me out of here," he said, and I agreed. Kutilek radioed for an ambulance, and within minutes one of our crews arrived—vehicle commander Staff Sergeant Thomas Brennan, vehicle driver Specialist Byron Ferrell, and crew medic Specialist Robert A. Cook, all members of the 230th Support Battalion of the North Carolina Army National Guard. This time our casualty collection point system worked; we knew where we were on the grid by then and we could direct the ambulance crew right in. I grabbed an end of the stretcher and Specialist Cook grabbed the other and we carried the wounded man down the steps and loaded him into the back of the ambulance. The Vietnam-era vehicles are armored personnel carriers (APC) called M113s. They run on tracks like a tank and are specially configured for ambulance duty, with room for four stretchers or litters to be hung in the rear compartment.

Dust was everywhere as we hit the street, settling and swirling around the ambulance. The air was heavy with cordite, the smell of explosives going off. On a rifle range, the distinctive odor comes at you in drifts. But in Fallujah, the smell was constant, overwhelming everything else, hanging in the air like a thick, musty curtain. You breathe it in, and you can't help thinking: *the smell of war.* The ambulance's rear hatch, a huge metal tailgate, was dropped down to the ground by hydraulics; I climbed in last, and it slowly closed behind me. It was even hotter inside, almost claustrophobic, and dark. The only light inside is a dim red lamp; anything more would threaten what we call light security. The last thing you want is to have that tailgate open up and have white light pour out like a beacon in the night to tell everybody where your soft spot is.

We started pumping IV fluids into the wounded Force Recon man and settled in for a bumpy trip back to the BAS, escorted by Kutilek and his gun trucks. My patient was doing all right; even though he was tachycardic, his pulse was active at his wrist. That meant his blood pressure was at least 100 over 60, and so long as we didn't get a bullet fragment or a bone shard migrating around and causing more damage, he was going to make it out okay. I allowed myself a quick moment of relief—*Okay, I got in the game. I'm sweating, I'm pumped, but now let's get out of here.*

I'd barely exhaled when the radio came alive again. It was an urgent call: Bravo Company had gotten caught in an ambush near the cultural center. "We got two wounded, two casualties that are bad. We need an urgent evac." I got on the radio and said, "Listen, roger that; but we have a serious casualty, urgent evac, gunshot wound to the chest." They came back on again and gave me a choice. Weapons Company's commanding officer (CO), Captain Steve Kahn, an even-keeled Marine from Pennsylvania, was doing all he could to stay calm, but his urgency came through loud and clear. "Bravo's got two down, bleeding. You're there. It's your call."

I paused. My wounded Sailor was pretty stable, but he could easily turn south. It was tempting to just get him out of there as soon as possible. But how could I leave these other guys behind? They could be in even worse shape than the guy we had, and there was no way to know when other help might get to them. I made the call. "Let ops know, I got Kutilek; we're headin' down to the cultural center." Outside, the Weapons Company Marines were pumped and ready to go with us—zero hesitation. We turned around and headed back into the city.

CHAPTER 2
A Second Chance

There were plenty of people who thought I was crazy for going with the 1/8 to Fallujah. Especially since I didn't have to go. I volunteered. But somehow, at the time, it seemed like a good idea.

It was April 2004, and I was working as the brigade surgeon for the Fourth Marine Expeditionary Brigade, based at Marine Corps Base Camp Lejeune, North Carolina. It had looked like a great job when I took it on a few months earlier, and a big step up for me—the Fourth MEB was the Marine Corp's anti-terrorism brigade and I was just one position short of division surgeon. The brigade was full of cool elements, like the Chemical/Biological Incident Response Force, or CBIRF, and the Marine Security Guard, otherwise known as MSG. They also had the Marine Corps security force battalion, which included the FAST companies—Fleet Antiterrorism Security Teams—the guys who go out and augment embassies and other spots that need more security. A deployment to Greece to help out with security at the Olympics was coming up that August, so I thought at first that it was going to be an interesting posting for me. But no—it turned out to be almost all administration. I had reached the level where I didn't have to do real work anymore, it was just shuffling papers and going to meetings. Boring as hell, in other words.

I thought I had an escape plan in place, but it didn't seem to be working out too smoothly. I had spent seven years as a Marine officer before I went to medical school on a Navy scholarship, and I followed that with a series of overseas deployments with the Marines. As a result, I was a thirty-eight-year-old doctor who still hadn't finished a residency; I had started one a few years earlier, but things hadn't quite worked out. My wife, Melissa, and I had gone to medical school together and she had finished her pediatric residency years before. She thought it was well past time for me to stop fooling around with the Marines and finish the darned thing already. When I found out how boring things were going to be with the Fourth MEB, I agreed—doing a residency would mean qualifying for full-time out-service status with the Navy, which would get me out of the drudgery of paperwork. I had already settled on the surgical specialty I wanted to pursue, urology. My plan was to become a "gentleman surgeon."

All I needed was a urology residency that would take me, and the Medical College of Georgia said I had been accepted to start in their program in July—my escape plan. But I hadn't seen any paperwork from them yet, and every day that went by without it made me more nervous. I couldn't stand the thought of being stuck pushing paper at the Fourth MEB job for another year, but I didn't have another way of getting out of it. That's when I started seeing the e-mails.

The situation in Iraq was getting pretty shaky at that point and there was talk about having to do some serious fighting there again before long. Our division was going to be augmenting the First Marine Expeditionary Force, the California-based Marines who were leading the fight over there at the time, and one of our battalions, the 1/8, that was initially scheduled to ship out in May still didn't have a battalion surgeon. We were over a year into an increasingly dangerous war and doctors throughout the division were bailing out, finding ways to escape the approaching deployment. It was the division surgeon's responsibility to fulfill combat slots, but he hadn't held anyone's feet to the fire over it and now he was in trouble. There were just a few weeks until the scheduled deployment and he didn't have anyone who would go with the 1/8. His increasingly desperate e-mails weren't doing any good, and the subject came up one day while we were talking in his office. I just kind of said the fateful words: "Well, I could go."

I'm sure he figured I was joking. After all, I wasn't your typical candidate. I'd already been a battalion surgeon; I had also been a regimental surgeon, a Marine Expeditionary Unit (MEU) surgeon, and a brigade surgeon. Going back to battalion would be a little like asking a major to do a lieutenant's job. In other words, there was no way he would ask a guy as old, as experienced, and as senior as I was to go back to battalion. (It's strange in a way: battalion surgeon is the entry-level job, even though it can be the most intense, challenging medical position there is during wartime. And because medical officers don't need combat experience to get moved up the ranks, plenty of very senior Navy doctors might not actually have a very good appreciation for what that "lowly" job can be like when there's a war on.) Not to mention, the timing was horrible. My wife, Melissa—Missy—was a good seven months pregnant with our first baby, and when the 1/8's deployment was pushed back to a three-day period at the end of June, it actually overlapped with Missy's June 27 due date. She would have killed me if she had known that I volunteered to deploy to a war zone at that time. And besides all that, I already had one foot out the door with the urology program at MCG.

But still. It bothered me to see so many other doctors putting their own priorities ahead of the needs of the Marine Corps—and of the Marines. And there was also a matter of some unfinished business. My previous deployment with the Marines had ended in a freaky way: a bunch of my guys came down with malaria. It wasn't my fault, but I still felt bad about it, and I didn't like the idea that my deploying days might come to an end on a sour note.

What the division surgeon didn't know was that I thought being a battalion surgeon was one of the greatest jobs in the world. I never thought I'd get another shot at it. I would enjoy training the corpsmen and passing on some of what I'd learned over the years, and if we really got into it, I had trauma medicine experience, and I had some ideas for improving combat medicine. I thought I could make a contribution. And it occurred to me that this was quite possibly my last opportunity to see combat. It wasn't that I wanted to kill anyone; I didn't. But I did want to be part of the war, part of history. I had spent years and years training hard so that I would be ready if I ever ended up in a war zone. I didn't just feel like a football player who had spent his whole career on the bench; I felt like a football player who was going to spend his whole career in the locker room, and I wanted one last chance to get into the game.

Or maybe it really just came down to the fact that I have been a military person for longer than I've been a doctor. I wasn't from a military family, strictly speaking, but we came pretty close. I was born in Abington, Pennsylvania, the first child of Barbara and Richard Jadick. My father did attend the Citadel in Charleston, South Carolina—the first in his family to go to college—but he didn't take a commission after he graduated in 1961, even though he had gone through Air Force ROTC.

Instead, he went into retail. My parents met during the summer between Dad's sophomore and junior years at the Citadel, while they were both working at the John Wanamaker department store in Abington. Dad cleaned drain traps and changed lightbulbs and Mom was a salesgirl in the stationery department, but she gave in to his charm, anyway. Mom moved to the Wanamaker's in Philadelphia and was still working there, as a fashion buyer, when my parents got married. Then I came along, followed by my brother, Chris, and my sister, Denise. Dad moved over to Sears, Roebuck, and ended up staying with the company for thirty-five years, working his way up the executive ranks. Pennsylvania, Connecticut, Massachusetts, New York . . . every couple of years or so Dad would get a new promotion, and we'd have a new address. He was a real go-getter, and he never let a challenge get him down. I think he was actually in charge of ordering the bras and lingerie for a while—and my father is a big, tough, blue-collar kind of guy. But he just got to it and learned everything he could.

Somewhere along the way I became fascinated with the military. I was always one of those kids who just thought it was *cool*—playing Army, reading history books, watching war movies. The attraction for me was all surface—the adventure, the drama, the challenge. There was nothing deep about it, no wanting to honor the country or someone's death or anything. I just thought, *Yeah, that would be kind of fun to do for a little while.*

That "little while" turned into twenty years and counting. All that time invested, and I'd never really been to war. I couldn't resist, and I couldn't just let those Marines go off without proper medical care. I felt like I had to go, but I felt like I wanted to go, too. So I started to rationalize: I'm the doctor, who's going to kill the doctor? And even with all the deaths in Iraq, the chances of one guy getting killed aren't that huge, statistically speaking. Besides, division was expecting more doctors to arrive in July, and I figured that they'd probably relieve me and I could come back after just a couple of months—hit the training phases and be home by fall. Well, that's what I told Melissa anyway, and it could have been true. It could have been true that I was ordered to go as well, but it wasn't. That's something Melissa didn't find out until long after I was back. I just called her up from work and said, "Looks like I'm going to wind up deploying. They need someone to go and I'm it." It was hard for her to take—how could it not be?—and I knew she was angry at first, then sad and frustrated. She said it made her really torn about the upcoming birth. Of course she wanted our daughter to be born, but she also didn't, because she knew that as soon as MacKenzie, our daughter, came, I would be gone. But Missy was a military wife in a military community, and a lot of our friends had missed seeing their babies born because of deployments. She made the best of a hard situation, did her best to be happy and supportive, and ultimately gave me less of a hard time about deploying than my general at the Fourth MEB did. I'll never know what I did to deserve a wife like her.

It's a little hard for me to explain, but in my mind Melissa is just perfect—perfect for me. She's a beautiful woman with a beautiful smile and beautiful eyes, and that's why I fell for her at first. But there's so much more. Melissa can be quite a serious person, and that's good for me; I'm more of a free spirit and I need to get a reality check from time to time, maybe a little adult supervision. She can send a little chill my way when she needs to, but then her whole face lights up when she's happy, and whenever she's with MacKenzie, or when we're together as a family. Missy has brown eyes and brown hair, and in a strange way her whole being tends to remind me of the color brown—a soft, warm, cozy brown, the brown of autumn, my favorite season. Football games, jeans and flannel, cold nights and warm days; Melissa reminds me of them all, and I love it. And I love how she is with MacKenzie, a perfect balance of discipline and fun. Granted, we don't *always* get along, and we don't always see eye to eye on everything. But that's okay. We're best friends. We're good companions, good business partners, and good opposites. Life partners in love.

I took two weeks off after leaving the Fourth MEB before I checked in with the 1/8. I spent the time with Melissa, helping to get ready for the baby. The 1/8's medical team knew the sorts of things I would be needing for our deployment. I told them to get ready as best they could and I'd be over at the end of May.

When I showed up, ready to go to work, one of my top priorities was to get to know all of the corpsmen better. Most of them I knew already by sight, and we would all get to know each other well in the months to come. But two of my most senior corpsmen were new to the battalion, and I would be relying on them heavily, no matter what we ran into over in Iraq. My senior enlisted man, Chief Hospital Corpsman Russ Folley would be my right-hand man; together with his leading petty officer, HM1 Rick Lees, who had already been with the battalion for over two years, Chief Folley would be looking after all of our administrative, logistical, and supply concerns as well as taking primary responsibility for training and supervising the corpsmen. And HM1 Bryan Zimmerman would be our IDC, or independent duty corpsman. An IDC is kind of like a physician's assistant in the civilian world, and Zimmerman would take on responsibility for sick call, attending to all the day-to-day medical needs of our Marines, as well as helping with the training and motivation of our junior corpsmen. I looked over the crew in those first days and thought that they seemed like they had potential. I had no idea how right I would turn out to be.

I started connecting with some of the Marine officers as well. Some I knew from a Marine Expeditionary Unit (MEU) deployment we had done together the year before—I always made a point of getting to know the lieutenants especially, because they're the guys you need to be able to count on if you get yourself into trouble on the ground. Security is one of the three key elements of battlefield medicine—along with communications and the medical care itself—and in the Marine Corps, it's going to be platoon commanders who are providing it. Security is something that can easily be overlooked in medical planning, but it's absolutely essential. Without security you can't do your job, and if you get yourself into a tough spot you're putting yourself, your patients, and a lot more Marines at risk—somebody is going to have to come in and drag you, or your body, back to safety, and that puts them all in harm's way.

The thing is, as a medical team we can't provide our own security. Yes, FMF corpsmen—Fleet Marine Force, the guys who go out with the Marines, as opposed to corpsmen who work with Navy outfits—are weapons-trained, and armed with M16 assault rifles. And the medical officers carry their pistols, of course, for all the good that would do in most circumstances. But we're medical personnel. By international law, American policy, and just plain common sense—to say nothing of the Hippocratic oath—we only fire if fired upon, to preserve our lives and the lives of our patients against enemy attack. More practically, we're busy working, we've got our heads down, and we might as well have targets painted all over ourselves. We need Marines; we're all part of the same team, and we couldn't do our job without them. Fortunately, the lieutenants in the battalion, the platoon commanders, were all outstanding Marines—reliable, gung-ho, and ready to go to work. Marines like Lieutenant Kutilek, Lieutenant David Lee, and Lieutenant Sunny-James Risler, these were the guys who would end up escorting us through the heart of Fallujah once the battle was on. They performed brilliantly the whole time and would have whether I was a jerk to them or not, but getting to know them beforehand made the process go much more smoothly for all of us.

It's actually very easy as a Navy guy on a ship or in the field to never even come into contact or conversation with the younger Marine officers, especially the lieutenants. It's a strange dynamic: you outrank them, and in the Navy that kills most conversations. At the same time they're Marines, which makes them kind of scary even if you do outrank them. And so you get a little arrogance and a little intimidation mixed in with some institutional distrust—not a great recipe for communication.

Fortunately, I had been them. I had been a Marine lieutenant, so I wasn't afraid of them, and I think that my history made it easier for us to relate to each other. I made it my business on the MEU deployment and again when I linked up with the 1/8 to get to know all the Marines, and especially anybody I thought was potentially going to be security. The moment something happened in the field, I wanted to be able to say, "I need support, I need a crew of gun trucks because we're going in." And I never had a problem with that, not on the MEU and never in Fallujah. I worked with very good lieutenants all the time.

Before we knew it, it was June 23, the day I was to report to Camp Lejeune for deployment. I had to work hard to maintain my Marine composure as I left. Melissa wanted to come see me off. But she was still post-op; it was just four days since MacKenzie's birth. Melissa had been induced. She went through thirteen hours of labor and then had to have a Cesarean section. Between contractions, I had been signing for equipment and giving orders to my new medical staff. But I was with Melissa when our daughter—MacKenzie Marlena Jadick, a perfect, beautiful little girl—was born on June 19, 2004, at 4:03 in the afternoon. It was the highlight of my life. If I could have backed out of deploying at that point I might just have done it, but it was too late. *If I don't go soon,* I remember thinking, *I'll probably die of heartbreak.*

My mother and father wanted to see me off, too, but Mom would have lost it completely and I wasn't 100 percent sure my dad wouldn't have, too. I thought it would be best for everyone if my younger brother, Chris, who lived nearby, drove me. We pulled away from my house, my wife crying in our driveway, our infant daughter in her arms. I'll never forget what she said as she hugged me for the last time: "I love you so much, I don't want anything ever to happen to you because you have to come home." The night before, I had woken up to find Melissa shuddering in bed beside me, crying. Melissa is a strong woman—tougher and stronger than she believes herself to be, actually—and she's done a lot of hard things on her own in her life. I just held her and didn't say anything, and she didn't say anything to me. But I knew she was hurting, really, really hurting.

When we got to the base, I think my brother understood why I wanted him to drive me. He looked around at all the Marines packing up their gear, going about their duties in a very calm, businesslike way. That's what I wanted—calm, under control, and unemotional. I was ready to be on the road—the sooner you leave, the sooner you're coming back. I had my bags packed, my gear stowed, and my airplane to catch; in my mind, I was already gone.

I had done everything I possibly could to be sure that if I didn't make it back, Melissa and MacKenzie would be all right. My will was in order, the power of attorney was in place, and the life insurance was purchased. It wouldn't have been enough to set Melissa and MacKenzie up for life or anything, but she's a pediatrician, and the insurance would pay off our loans and the house, and if you get killed over there, the college tuition for your kids is covered. More rationalization: MacKenzie doesn't even really know me, so she'll be okay. Melissa's young. She'll be sad for a while, but she'll get over it and move on, her prospects are good. And my parents would always be there to help her out. I knew I was putting her through a hard time, but I think she also knew that I was doing what I had to do. But still, there was a moment, a catch in my throat as I climbed out of Chris's pickup to go. It was fear—for my little girl and my lovely wife, for myself, for whatever the future could have in store for all of us.

There's a photo of me from that day, wearing my tan desert digital cammies—the Marine utility uniform—and holding MacKenzie in my arms. My mother kept it tucked into the frame of her mirror the whole time I was in Iraq. Dad tells me he saw a single tear rolling down from under my sunglasses as I said good-bye. I don't know about that; I'm not a big tearful kind of guy, but maybe he's right. I really didn't want to have a big scene there at the house, though, so when we got to Lejeune I had Chris shoot a video of me. He works in the film industry, and he's my brother, so I knew we could get through it without breaking down. It's not much. I just said, "Listen, everything's fine; I'm going to be back. I love you all; I love you, MacKenzie." I wanted to say good-bye, and I wanted MacKenzie to have, if anything did happen to me, a last shot of her dad forever. But it wasn't a death letter—a lot of deploying personnel will write one, or make a death video before they go. It's something you do and leave with a friend to deliver only if you are killed in action. The video I shot with Chris was not that kind of message; he delivered it right away, as my fare-well. No way was I writing a death letter, because I wasn't dying, I was coming back and that was it. We shot the video, Chris gave me a big bear hug and told me he was proud of me for doing this, and I got on a bus to the airport at Cherry Point, North Carolina. Once there, we piled on for a pretty miserable chartered flight over, making stops in Ireland and Hungary before we finally arrived in Kuwait.

Everything military takes forever and is generally a pain—you expect that—but the commercial airline didn't seem to be worrying too much more about customer service or comfort than the United States Marine Corps did. We finally got settled on board, though, and I hunkered down in my seat for the long flight over. I had a pile of stuff with me, including a deck of cards and some other things to help pass the time, but I also had some trauma books out. I knew the material already, but I wanted to have some references ready just in case, and I figured it couldn't hurt to give myself a quick refresher course on the way over.

There was a massive gunnery sergeant, Ryan Shane of Bravo Company, sitting in front of me. The poor guy, he barely fit in his seat. Then he turned around and saw what I was reading. "Sir, so you're our new battalion surgeon," he said, giving me a slow once-over in that way Marine gunnies have—a sort of automatic assessment that almost always comes out looking like "you don't rate shit." He waited a beat before adding, "God, that's one job I wouldn't want to have with the place we're going."

Well, that set me back a little. The usual take is that the doctor's job is the cushy job. I'd been in plenty of places where I had reached that conclusion myself. But here was this hulking big gunny, tough as nails, who knew he was going to be in the middle of whatever shit we managed to get ourselves into over there, and he was thinking that I was the one who was in trouble. I would find out later that Gunny Shane is a very friendly guy, and he was just trying to start a conversation. But still, his words hit me hard. *What had I gotten myself into?*

CHAPTER 3
Corpsman Up!

November 9, 2004

As our armored ambulance ground toward Fallujah's cultural center on its tracks, we could hear the gunfire outside intensifying. *Ting! Ting!* AK-47 rounds were bouncing off the ambulance's metal skin; the deeper, more serious growl of our escort's Humvee-mounted .50 cals answered back. *How safe is this thing—could something actually punch through?* The vehicle was feeling old, vulnerable under direct fire. Cook, the crew medic, said it wouldn't stop much more than a 7.62-millimeter round, and I doubted it would even stop that. But Bravo Company's third platoon was pinned down from three sides, trying to make the cultural center, and they were getting hammered. There was no choice—we pulled up right in the kill zone.

The hatch opened onto madness. I could see Marines down in the street, caught in the insurgent cross fire. Bravo Company was hunkered against the building and partially protected by a low wall running along one side; two tanks were in the intersection, blasting away.

Kutilek's Weapons Company gun trucks roared in, posting security for each other as they went, suppressing each potential line of approach, ensuring they always had a safe way out. *Be aggressive, take the initiative*—they sound like great ideas, but they take on a new meaning when you're storming into the heart of a ferocious hail of enemy fire to protect your fellow Marines. The return fire was intense: RPK machine guns, AK-47s, rocket-propelled grenades (RPGs) were coming in from every direction. An RPG ripped through the air two feet from the head of one of Kutilek's machine gunners, Corporal Danny Myers.

The first night of the battle had been a tough one for Bravo Company. They'd come under fire just inside the city until almost four a.m., but as the night wore on, they'd started making better progress. They'd finally arrived at this position near the cultural center just two hours before daylight. The building was one of two major battalion objectives at that intersection. It sat across the street from the other, al-Hydra Mosque, where a street code-named Phase Line Cathy crossed Phase Line Ethan, the main north-south thoroughfare. The plan was for Bravo Company to take up positions in the cultural center and provide cover so that Captain Theodore Bethea II and his Charlie Company Marines could cordon off the mosque while the Iraqi forces with them went in and cleared it of enemy personnel. Al-Hydra Mosque would prove to be a major staging and resupply center for the insurgents, and the source of deadly sniper and machine-gun fire.

First platoon Bravo Company set up covering the Ethan-Cathy intersection toward the south and east, second platoon moved in covering to the west, and third platoon was getting ready to move into the cultural center, across the four lanes of PL Cathy. A Force Recon unit radioed in—they had already made entry to the cultural center, with no resistance. Bravo settled in to wait for the "all clear." The sun was just coming up when they started taking intense fire from all directions. The Marines returned it with a wall of suppressing fire. "We're all shootin'," Bravo Company's commanding officer, Captain Read Omohundro, recalled. "First Sergeant's firing, hell, even I'm firing." He had brought an M16 along, not even expecting to use it, he said. "My job is to be on the radio and kind of run things. So if it gets to the point where I'm using my rifle, you know we're in kind of a shit sandwich."

The insurgent fire died down, and Omohundro got his Marines ready to push across the road to the cultural center building. As soon as Bravo Company entered the road, though, the enemy fire returned full force. Sergeant Lonny Wells got his squad across the road safely, only to be taken down hard himself, caught up in cross fire. Gunnery Sergeant Ryan Shane, the same massive gunny who didn't want to trade jobs with me back on the flight over, didn't hesitate. "I didn't know who it was," he remembered later, "I just knew it was a Marine." Shane ran out into the line of fire to attempt a rescue. "There were sparks kicking up all around me and rounds snapping past my head," Shane recalls. He grabbed the wounded man's outstretched hand; Wells, a popular third platoon sergeant famous for putting his men before himself, was hit in the groin and bleeding badly.

Doc Lambotte ran out to help, too. One of Bravo Company's line corpsmen, HN Joel Lambotte from Topeka, Kansas, heeded the universal Marine Corps call of distress, *Corpsman Up!* Gunny

Shane was trying to pull Wells out of harm's way. Doc was pulling too, and the other Marines were doing everything they could to lay down covering fire. But the bullets were still flying in, and Lambotte took a round in the heel. Gunny Shane was next, hit hard just above the tailbone and knocked down the road by the impact. He froze where he fell—show movement and you let the sniper know you're not done yet. "I could still see the bullets and sparks and chips of asphalt flying up," Shane says. "The first thing I thought was, *Ah, geez, I don't know if I'm paralyzed*." He wiggled his toes in his boots—movement, a good sign. Hunker down and hang on for help.

It wasn't long in coming. No Marine is going to stand by and watch his buddies get shot up without doing something, and Bravo Company was certainly no exception. First and second platoon fired with everything they had, and Omohundro managed to get some men into the cultural center and onto the roof, where they laid down suppressing fire to the south, and toward al-Hydra Mosque. (American forces avoid firing on religious establishments, but when the enemy is using one as an attack base, all bets are off. As the battle wore on, there would be few mosques from which the Marines didn't receive fire.) Omohundro called in more support. Artillery fire was directed at insurgent strongholds. The tanks moved into position in the intersection and started firing on the enemy while providing some shelter for the Bravo Marines with their armored hulls.

Back in the street, a group of Marines—including Corporal Nathan Anderson; Sergeants Jacob Knospler, Kenneth Hudson, and Michael Ramirez; and Private First Class Samuel Crist—ran out to retrieve the fallen men. Hudson and Crist were hit as well, but the Marines got everyone out of the middle of the road, if not to perfect cover. Lambotte was shot but he ignored his own wound, scrambling to get the others patched and stabilized.

"*RPG!*" someone screamed—a rocket-propelled grenade was whistling in for a direct hit. Lambotte had just told Shane he was going to have to wait for morphine, but that didn't mean he had forgotten about the gunny. "That corpsman threw his body on top of mine," Shane recalls. "I'll never forget that. The RPG never went off, but that's not the point. That corpsman tried to cover me with his body. All those guys were great young heroes. These were everyday Americans, and they were extraordinary."

As we pulled onto the scene, Kutilek and his men swarmed into the intersection and laid down a barrage of suppressing fire while Staff Sergeant Brennan and Specialist Ferrell pulled our ambulance in right in front of the ambushed Marines, providing cover from another angle. Good tactics all around, and damned fearless; Marine gunners are exposed in their gun turrets, and Specialist Ferrell operated the track with his head sticking up through a hatch. Inside we were safer; we could hear the firefight raging, and hear rounds bouncing off of the track's thin metal walls that stood between us and the chaos outside. The rear hatch dropped down to the ground, and it was time to go.

The ambulance crew, Kutilek's Marines, Bravo Company, they may all have been fearless. Me? I don't remember anything except for tremendous, gripping fear. I was on the knife's edge— I fully understood at that moment why some guys just cower in their holes and refuse to get up and fight. I had never wanted anything so badly as I wanted to stay inside that vehicle and lie under something and cry. Every neuron in my brain, every cell in my body screamed it—*Stay inside, stay inside, stay inside.* I felt like a coward. There were rounds going off everywhere. Smoke, hot fresh cordite, and unbelievable noise. I have no memory of this—too much fear—but a round ricocheted off of the inside of our track. Cook had his M16 at the ready and fired one round at an insurgent he saw running into position to fire on us. The Marines fired, too, and the man went down.

I remember feeling like it took me forever to move. Kutilek says no, that I hopped right off and rolled into action, running like I was trying to dodge bullets. Well, why not? But somehow that point in time seemed to go on forever, like the entire mass of my existence had been compressed down into a black hole, this tiny pinhead of a moment when I could have gone either way.

This is it, I was thinking. *I'm on the edge of where I've wanted to be my whole life, and what comes next?* It wasn't my life up until that moment that flashed before my eyes—it was the life I was going to have to live if I failed to act. Was I going to be sitting safe at home someday telling my kids the story of how Daddy hid in the track and wouldn't come out? *Aw hell, no. That's not going to be me.* I didn't want to fail my guys. I didn't want to fail myself. I didn't want to fail my family. I remember Bravo's First Sergeant Ronald Whittington yelling, "Get these fucking guys off the street. Get Wells in here, get him over the wall—you fucking can't let him die!" That snapped me into action—I went.

I stepped off the track and noticed that everything was heavy. *Holy fuck, am I even going to make it?* Fear is like deep water, slowing every step, but training takes over and we were moving, getting the job done. *Pop! Pop! Snap!* Two wild shots from an AK, one straight on. The books were right: everything changes when they're shooting at you. I was waiting for a shot to find me, but I just kept moving.

Physical fatigue, peaks and dips of adrenaline, sweat and fire, straps, gear, armor were all getting in the way. But I put my head down and sprinted for the wall. Specialist Cook started helping Lambotte with the others, and I grabbed Lonny Wells and got us both over the low wall. He came over heavy, faceup, his helmet stuck to his chin and covered in blood. Our eyes met, and then I saw the groin wound, a gaping hole through some of the largest blood vessels in the body, and some of the hardest to block off with bandages. He was bleeding out fast. *Fuck, he's not breathing. Pulse?* No, and there was so much blood down his leg and down the street, I didn't know if I could bring him back. *Gotta get him into the ambulance where I can work on him, gotta get to the other guys.*

I worked faster, packing Wells's wound in his groin with rolls of sterile gauze bandages. *Gotta stop the bleeding, gotta stop the bleeding.* But nothing I did seemed to make a difference. The blood just kept coming. I took a quick look around—three, maybe more guys were down now in a firefight that was far from over. *Leave those beyond saving. Focus on the guys you can save*—that's what the books say. Battlefield triage makes perfect sense to the mind, but deciding who gets your help first can be brutal on the heart. "Hold this wound—pressure!" I told the man next to me, and moved on.

There were so many wounded, and there was only so much we could do. Everyone was hunkered down, firing back, with rounds going off all around us. I had been scared earlier, but training and adrenaline had taken over. Cook and I quickly triaged the rest of the wounded, working on the most urgent cases first. We managed to stabilize them and stop all the bleeds we could find. We started to load the wounded onto litters and into the back of the ambulance when an RPG glanced off the top of the vehicle without exploding; we later saw that it had shattered an external water tank. We loaded faster. Lonny Wells went in first, on the top right, the Force Recon corpsman was on the top left, and we slid two more wounded Marines in below them. A second RPG skimmed over the top of the ambulance and slammed into the wall behind us—another dud, but that kind of luck doesn't hold. The ambulance crew was getting itchy and they desperately wanted to get us out of there. But they held fast as we continued to secure our casualties. We still had Gunny Shane to load, but he was too big and we couldn't lift him. It would turn out that he had serious internal damage; his tailbone was practically shot off, and his pancreas, bladder, and intestines were a mess. I made room for him underneath the stretchers. Shot through as he was, Shane mustered the strength to drag himself to the ambulance and haul himself up that ramp on his belly, before he collapsed onto a spine board on the floor of the track. He lay there on his stomach, still hoping for a shot of morphine. He finally got it.

One more Marine came limping up as we were piling in— he'd just been shot through the calf. I dressed the wound, but there was no more room. "Hunker down," I had to tell him. "We'll be back, or see if you can hook up with Kutilek over there." I can't imagine how much he must have hated me at that moment, but I couldn't take him out on the top of the track and there was no more room inside. Maybe I should have just stayed out, sent him in. *If he dies,* I remember thinking, *it will be my fault.* But I also knew that if we lost any of the guys already on the track, that would be my fault, too. Fortunately, he got a ride with Kutilek.

It was a rough ride back to the BAS, and the track was cramped. It would have been cramped with just five in the back, and we were eight: the six wounded, including Lambotte with his wounded heel, crammed in between Cook and me in the narrow aisle. There was pain, fear, and adrenaline, and precious little room to move. In our hurry to load up, we had positioned our patients backward, with their heads toward the front by the engine compartment—it made for a worse ride for them, and put Cook at the heads. As the doctor, that should have been my position, but I might not even have been able to move up there; Cook is only five feet seven and about 145 pounds, and his shoulders were wedged tight between the litters. We got IVs going on the guys, feeding them Hespan (a clear blood expander) to keep their pressure up. As we worked, the question kept coming: "How's Wells, Doc? How's Wells?" I knew the answer but there was no way I was going to tell them the truth right then. I changed the subject and kept working.

"Everybody take a man, find the bleeds and pack them," I ordered. We stripped our patients down in the dim red light, and searched for wounds using the white light headlamps on our helmets. Lambotte and Cook found and patched a serious hole in the shoulder of one of the injured Marines, dropping three pairs of scissors in the shaking ambulance and finally resorting to a knife to cut back his cammies. Shane, tough as he was, was hollering for more morphine, but he'd already had all we could give him. Cook leaned in and gave him a hell of a jab in the ass with his pen. A dirty trick maybe, but it worked for a little while—long enough to get the gunnery sergeant back anyway, and still in condition to go into surgery as soon as he got to the Bravo Surgical Center at Camp Fallujah, our base outside the city. We would bypass my Battalion Aid Station on this run, I decided—we'd have the wounded men stabilized already by the time we got there and there was nothing more to be done at the aid station. The sooner we could get them to surgery, the better.

I was vaguely aware that Cook was working on Wells on the way out, trying to insert a combi-tube airway into his throat to try to get him breathing again. But I had to signal Cook to move on to the next man. I had been working on the man below Wells when I started feeling fluid running down my neck and my back and down the front of me; that's when I realized that Wells had released, a kind of whole body relaxation that occurs after someone dies. It's like the body, having fought so hard to live, finally just gives up entirely and lets all of its fluids—blood, lymph, whatever else is in there—go. Sergeant Wells had fought hard to live, but his war had come to an end. The loving father of five—two sons, two daughters, and a stepdaughter—Wells had decided on a career in the Marines at age five, and started preparing with martial arts classes at seven. He remained a true Marine until the very end—his last words to his squad, I would learn later, were "Keep going. Keep going and get the job done." That was advice we all needed that day, and I knew that we had to focus on the others. I know that it was the right call, the only call I could have made, but the questions still stab at me: Could I have done more for Wells? Did I do enough? I don't know that I'll ever have the answers.

After we reached the regimental ambulance exchange point at Checkpoint 84, just outside of Fallujah, Cook stayed with his vehicle and saw to the unloading—it was his vehicle, his command—and he got Shane, the Force Recon corpsman, and the other wounded Marines handed off to the convoy that would take them up to the surgical unit. He had plenty of work left to do; just clearing the blood out of the back of the track would end up taking a half dozen five-gallon jugs, and his team would be called out on another brutal ambulance run almost immediately after he finished. But Cook took a moment first. Using a poncho liner, he covered Lonny Wells inside the ambulance. He took the head of the litter, and a corpsman who was stationed at the exchange point took the foot. They carried Wells's body around to the far side of the ambulance and Cook knelt down beside him, made the sign of the cross, and said a prayer for this brave Marine whom he had not known but had risked his life trying to save. He might as well have been saying it for us all.

I walked the short distance back to the BAS. HM1 Rick Lees came out to meet me, and I noticed that everyone was staring. I looked down and saw that I was covered with blood. I can't imagine what that must have looked like to the corpsmen—the doctor, literally soaked through. I reached down and grabbed sand by the handful, rubbing it into my uniform. I didn't want everyone thinking, *Look at the Doc. He's covered in blood—shit's really going down.* I don't know—it's a line commander's job to keep his men brave by never showing his own fear, and I guess I wanted to keep my corpsmen as confident as I could by covering the signs of my failure. Iraq is a country of dust and sand, and you spend a lot of time cursing the stuff. But I discovered that day that it has at least one use: it turned the blood on my uniform dark. I would do the same thing time and again over the next month.

An incoming mortar round had landed just thirty minutes before in the dirt about ten feet away from the BAS tent. Luckily it was a dud shell—it didn't go off, just stuck in the dirt with its tail fins up. But it was clear that my guys were definitely not out of the danger zone. Everyone was playing it cool, but HM2 Shawn Johns seemed to take it personally. "That fuckin' thing landed like fifteen feet away from where I was sitting," he told me, sounding genuinely pissed at the shell. He had been in front of the BAS with HN Collin Stedman and HA Ernesto Argueta when they heard the muffled *foompf* of the shot, followed by the *tssss* of its stabilizer fans cutting air. "That was the day that I learned that if you actually hear incoming, you're probably fine," my assistant battalion surgeon, Lieutenant Carlos Kennedy, deadpanned later. "Because as soon as I heard that hissing I had about as much time as it takes to startle before I actually heard it strike the ground." The shell didn't detonate. If it had, we would have lost a good portion of the BAS, and as HM3 Jason "Smitty" Smith noted in his North Carolina drawl, that would have left him and maybe two others to treat all the wounded.

The guys at the BAS didn't seem real glad to see me—not too happy that I had gone forward myself, I think, and not too happy that I had bypassed the BAS with all those casualties. Why were they stationed that far forward if I wasn't even going to use them? This wasn't working as well as I'd hoped. We had saved more than we had lost, yet all I could feel was a profound sense of frustration and failure.

CHAPTER 4
Becoming a Marine

Frustration. I'm no stranger to the emotion. My first vivid memory of it came on my ninth birthday. We were living in Longmeadow, Massachusetts, at the time and we had a new baby in the house. Gregory had been born just a month before. I was in the fourth grade, a happy kid, playing sports and doing well enough in school so that it wasn't a big worry for me—I really didn't have any big worries at all. And then all of a sudden it was October 2, 1974, my ninth birthday, and my youngest brother was dead. Gregory died of Sudden Infant Death Syndrome, SIDS.

We had had a big birthday party earlier in the day. I was watching *Little House on the Prairie* on TV when I heard my mother in the back room screaming. I ran to find her with little Gregory, who was just as still as he could be, with blood running down from his nose. I would think back to that awful image decades later, when Sergeant Wells released his fluids in the back of the ambulance. Mom was trying to resuscitate him, and calling out to me to dial "0"—there was no 911 back then, you just had to call the operator. I tried to dial that one number, and I don't know why, but I just couldn't. I couldn't do it. Someone else must have, because I remember the paramedics rushing in and doing CPR, and then taking him and my mother to the hospital, but it was too late. Gregory was already gone.

I remember my mother coming home without her little baby, and just crying, crying, crying. She was absolutely heartbroken. She has always been the glue in our family, the strong one, but this was just too much. Losing Gregory was incredibly hard on all of us, but my father? I think it just about killed him. Dad is a big man, a large, broad-shouldered guy. He used to lie on the couch while we were watching TV, with my baby brother on his chest, and it was just such a sweet thing—this big, steadfast man with this great big happy baby perched up there on his chest. Years later, he would tell me that all through that time, his chest would hurt, almost like he was having a heart attack. And it turns out that very stressful events can cause exactly the same type of pain as a heart attack. They call it Broken Heart Syndrome. I think I may have experienced that myself the day I left MacKenzie and Melissa for Fallujah.

I wrote a report for school a couple of years afterward on SIDS—I actually became quite a bookworm on the subject for a while, always studying up on it—and I learned that a large proportion of families who lost a child to the syndrome ended up falling apart. That didn't happen with us. Instead, my father decided then and there that he wasn't going to spend so much time working. He was a regional executive with Sears at that time and was on a pretty fast track for high-level executive positions. He was on the road several nights a week. But when Gregory passed, that all stopped. He dialed way back at work. We moved to Albany, New York, in 1976, but my parents didn't move again until Chris, Denise, and I all finished high school. From that time forward, I don't think my mother or father ever missed a football game, or a wrestling match, or any of my sister's events ever again.

A week or so after Gregory's death, we had a presentation at school from one of the local physicians. His daughter happened to be in our class, and I had a crush on her. She, of course, had no idea who I was, but when her dad came to the class, it was kind of a big deal to me. I was a shy kid then, but I sat up in the front row. The doctor brought in a model and talked about the human body. And I remember asking him this question: Why, when people die, even if they haven't been hurt or in an accident, why does blood come out of their nose or mouth or wherever. That's what I had seen with Gregory, and it was an image I couldn't get out of my mind.

Well, the doctor laughed and said that only happens in the movies, not in real life. Now, if you can imagine a fourth-grader sitting there and being told by some adult that that's not how it happens, that you're wrong and kind of a joke, even though you've just seen it with your own eyes—I was miserable. Of course, he didn't know about my brother's death. But I can remember thinking that it wasn't fair, and almost in tears, I just mumbled, "Oh, okay," and didn't say anything else. And then I got very, very mad. And I guess that was the beginning of a theme that has been replayed over and over in my life—someone doesn't take me seriously, or tells me I'm not smart enough or strong enough or good enough, and I take it as a challenge.

People were always telling me I didn't have what it takes when I was a kid. In football, they said I was too small to be an offensive or defensive lineman. I played on the line in high school, and I was team captain, too. Or my buddies told me that a certain girl was too good-looking, or too popular to go out with me. I'm not saying I was a Romeo, but there were a few surprises for people along the way. I figured out pretty early on that you just had to be a little quicker on the football field, or you just had to be a little braver about asking the girl out.

My dad says that I've always been "a guy who is really five foot ten inches trying to be six foot four," and I guess that maybe he has a point. My brother, Chris, was the natural athlete, the guy who could trot out to the outfield and catch a fly ball over his shoulder without even thinking about it. And even my sister, Denise, who used to say she was going to be a football player when she was a kid, could catch a down-and-out as well as anybody. For me, it always took a little more work, but then, I didn't really mind doing the work. My parents started me in football when I was about nine, and a couple of years after that my dad made this rig for me down in the basement. It was pretty crude, I guess, just a couple of weights tied to a rope and slung over a pulley, with a lawn mower handle at the other end. And I used to just go nuts on that thing—I'd get up early in the morning to work out before school, early enough so that I woke up my parents with it sometimes—because you know what? If you really want to do something, then you put your head down and you work at it, and you keep doing it until you get the job done.

Given my get-it-done attitude and my fascination with the military—and the fact that we were living in New York State by then—it probably wasn't surprising that by the end of high school

I had set my sights on the United States Military Academy at West Point for college. It's a very long application process, but I went through it all, right down to the required nomination from our Congressman, Sam Stratton. It was a huge series of this evaluation, that evaluation, go spend a few days at West Point, which I did. The school is on a bleak outcropping over the Hudson River, and I remember the sun never did come out while I was there. It was just this long, low gray line of clouds. And honestly, it crossed my mind that it was actually kind of hellish, but I decided it was an intriguing hell and part of me craved that challenge. I got accepted. And then they went and disqualified me. They said I had a physical disqualification.

I was born with strabismus. My right eye occasionally wanders off on its own. It's not a big deal, it just means that my eyes don't always track together when they're scanning, so I look a little cross-eyed sometimes and my depth perception isn't all that great. I had surgery on it when I was eighteen months old, and since then it hasn't been a problem for me. I think the only time I really noticed it was when everyone had those 3-D baseball cards. I could never figure out what the big deal was—for years on end I was thinking, *So they shimmer, big deal.*

But that was my physical disqualification from West Point. That was my defect. At most, it should have disqualified me from flying fighter jets. I was capable of doing anything else they could have thrown at me. But West Point didn't want to hear about it from me, and they didn't want to hear about it from Representative Stratton either, even though he put in a waiver request for me.

Okay, so then I had to scramble. My mother had put in some applications to state schools, but if I wasn't going to end up at

West Point, my next thought was to enlist. So I went to a Marine recruiter. I must have been a recruiter's dream—not that I was such hot stuff, but my application package was as complete as only West Point could make it and I wanted in. "Hey, we got full ROTC scholarships," the officer recruiter said, "you interested in that?" I had actually been thinking that I might just have to enlist now and then find a way to go to college later, so those two words—"officer" and "scholarship"—were really all I needed to hear. I could become a Marine officer and I wouldn't have to take out loans or stick my parents with a big bill for college tuition. I'd always liked the idea of paying for stuff myself. So two weeks later, about the beginning of April 1983, I got the call—I was going to be a Marine. *Cool.*

One problem left to solve: I had the scholarship, but I still didn't have a college. My best friend, Scott Ryan, had an idea. He was going to Ithaca College in upstate New York, which had a Marine ROTC option at nearby Cornell University. Okay, one more problem—they'd already finished admitting for the fall. Scott and my dad actually pulled it off for me; I was out of town, and they put an application together with my high school wrestling tapes in it and sent it to the wrestling coach. Amazingly, the coach got me in. If I have one regret, it's that I didn't actually spend one minute on the wrestling mats at Ithaca. My scholarship was coming from the Marines, and because ROTC was on the Cornell campus, I had to go over there three or four times a week. That didn't dovetail very well with wrestling practice twice a day and being a biology major on top of it, so I had to let the wrestling go. But I kept up the weight lifting I'd started in high school; by the time I finished college I was 210 pounds and bench pressing 405, which on a five-feet-ten frame is not half bad.

I spent that last summer before college preparing as much as I could, and if nothing else, I definitely got into the Marine spirit—or as close to it as possible without really knowing much about it. My workout routine was a little crude; it involved long runs along the railroad tracks, scrambling over a plywood climbing wall I had nailed up against a tree and painted with a huge "USMC," and beating on an old tree stump in the backyard with a sixteen-pound sledgehammer. Like I say, pretty crude stuff, but the Marines would smooth out my rough spots soon enough.

It was hard leaving home for college—I imagine it is for any seventeen-year-old—but Ithaca was only three hours away from Albany, and my best friend was going with me. The world looked pretty wide-open and exciting.

Ithaca College was a decent little place, about five or six thousand undergraduate students on a small campus tucked away more or less in the middle of New York State, which is more or less in the middle of nowhere. And that suited me just fine. There were enough new people for it to be exciting, it was small enough so that you didn't get lost in the crowd, and it was the sort of place where you could get into trouble without really serious consequences. My ROTC program was based just across town at Cornell, which was nice, too—close enough that it wasn't too much of a hassle to get back and forth, but far enough away that most of the trouble I ended up getting into at Ithaca didn't follow me to ROTC.

That was good, because the military isn't always as understanding about the dopey shit that a teenage boy does as, say, a small, private liberal arts school would be. My father learned that lesson the hard way. He never talked much about his time at the Citadel when we were growing up, and when I hear some of the stories now, I can understand why. I take after my parents and I've learned an awful lot from them, and for the most part that's a very good thing. But when I hear about some of the things they got up to when they were kids, well, maybe I take after them even more than I thought.

Dad evidently always had a mind for business, and he knew an opportunity when he saw it. In his senior year, his roommate was dating a girl whose father was a wine merchant, and the guys somehow convinced him to let them buy stuff wholesale. So before you know it, these guys were selling champagne on Friday afternoons after parade—they were running a speakeasy out of their dorm room. Dad says they got the idea from watching *The Untouchables* on TV. And evidently their bootlegging business was going great, until they expanded their sales to other brigades and word got out in the form of a drunken freshman hollering for a drink at parade one week.

Mom came to the rescue—yes, they were already dating— and she and another girl pulled up in the getaway car, loaded up the booze, and headed off campus. And just like that, the evidence was gone. But the Citadel being what it is, several of Dad's friends were going to be facing an honor violation if he didn't come forward to take the blame. Dad and his two partners in crime turned themselves in and got busted down to private, and this was just a month before graduation, too. It wasn't quite the end of my father's military career—he served active duty with the Army Reserve at Fort Knox, Kentucky, shortly after my parents were married in October of 1963—but it does kind of help explain where I got my troublemaker gene from.

My college life was riddled through with stupidity. I'll spare you most of the gory details—the commandeered bulldozers, the drunken skinny-dipping, the midnight cat burglary and pilfered office equipment—and point out that I did actually graduate, if not exactly *cum laude*. We lost a friend or two along the way, expelled and kicked off campus, but amazingly, Scott and I both managed to get out of there not just alive, but with degrees in hand. I actually remember the point at which I started to realize that lifting weights, getting drunk, and carrying on weren't going to be enough to get me where I wanted to go.

It was junior year, and I was walking across campus one night, coming back from a party. Some students had made a whole series of signs out of bedsheets and hung them from the side of their dormitory tower, advertising some event or other. In my inebriated state, I decided it was my job to go up there and tear them down. I think I was actually surprised when the campus police pulled up and asked me what I was doing, hanging off the side of the building like King Kong two and a half stories up and tearing the sheets down, for no reason at all. "Uh, I needed a bedsheet," is the best answer I could come up with, and that went over about as well as you'd think. They got me down and asked for my ID. After glancing at my name, one of them said, "Oh, you're that guy." Apparently I had earned a reputation, and not a particularly good one.

I had been getting decent grades as a biology major, and I was actually thinking about medical school somewhere down the road. It became pretty obvious that "that guy" was not going to end up anywhere near a medical school unless it was on a gurney in the emergency room, so I made up my mind to buckle down. It would be an exaggeration to say that I actually straightened out, but I definitely started putting more effort into my classes and a little less into staying one step ahead of the cops.

ROTC was almost a parallel experience for me; other than the occasional threat that my scholarship would evaporate if I got in trouble one more time, the college and the Corps really didn't overlap that much. That's at least partly because during the academic year, ROTC didn't amount to a whole lot more than putting on a uniform and marching around once in a while. The summers, however, were an entirely different situation.

Quantico, Virginia, is known as "the crossroads of the Corps" because pretty much everybody goes through there at some point for training of one kind or another. My introduction to USMC Base Quantico came during the summer between my junior and senior years, with the grueling six weeks of Officer Candidate School (OCS). My first summers in college, I had spent time in training at the Marine Corps Recruit Depot in Parris Island, South Carolina. But it's OCS that really marks the transition into getting serious about becoming a Marine officer. It's what they call a push camp—six weeks of a physically and mentally demanding, four-hours-of-sleep-a-night existence designed to weed out those who can't make it. OCS, called "Bulldog" for ROTC, is a little like the "boot camp" basic training that enlisted Marines have to go through, but there's an important difference.

There were a lot of prior-enlisted guys in my class that year, so they had been through boot camp at Parris Island. That had been physically demanding, they all said, but OCS was a bigger mental shock for one simple reason—you're on your own. At boot camp, your drill instructor is responsible for everything you do or fail to do, so they push you and get you back into the groove of things if you fall out. But in OCS, you're supposed to be able to take responsibility for yourself—if you can't hang, you're out. You're also expected to handle a lot more stress and strain than your average recruit. Your body takes plenty of physical abuse at OCS, all day long, every day, but then at the end of the day, you've got a list of things you have to do before it all starts again at four a.m. the next morning. And of course it's way more than you can get done in a night, so you need to prioritize, because you're evaluated not just on how much you get done but also on how well you figure out what's most important.

From reveille at 0400 on the first morning, OCS is a sink-or-swim proposition. The first day, they take you on a five-mile run. You're expected to show up in good shape, but already on that first run we had heat casualties going down, and within a week our class of fifty-eight was down to thirty-eight, based on the physical conditioning and examination failures. After the first week we didn't lose anybody and remained at thirty-eight. There was no nonsense about it. Someone falls out of an exercise, can't keep up with a run, and they were just done—they waddled off to sick call and you never saw them again. There are no second chances, and the stakes are high. If you're weeded out, then you either have to pay back your ROTC scholarship or you report to boot camp at Parris Island.

It's a brutal process, but if you make it through, OCS is a nice confidence builder. And I made it through okay. But none of what they put you through comes naturally to people. It's not natural to get up at four in the morning and suffer all day, every day. It's not natural to stand at attention and let people shout at you. And it sure wasn't natural for me to stand there while my drill instructor ranted nonstop about my lazy eye. Hey, I know I'm supposed to be looking straight ahead, but sometimes the eye just doesn't cooperate. *What are you eyeballin', Jadick? I'm gonna pluck that thing right out of your head!"* So, you do a lot of push-ups, you get punched in the chest once in a while, and you take it. You just grind it out—and you learn that really, you can grind through pretty much anything if you have to.

I didn't enjoy OCS exactly, but I did discover that I was pretty well suited to the selection process. I didn't have the natural talent of an athlete, I didn't have the raw brain power of a rocket scientist, but perseverance? Yeah, I can do that. It's about heart—how badly you want to make it through—and I guess it's about stubbornness, too. Tell me there's no way I'm going to make it through? Are you kidding? So, you learn that you can suffer and come through it okay, and that just leaves you in a better position for whatever challenge comes next.

So, that was it. I made it through OCS and became an officer candidate, and made it through senior year and became a college graduate, class of 1987. And then that's when it finally happens—you get commissioned as a second lieutenant in the United States Marine Corps. Finally, you get to call yourself a Marine. And then it's back to Quantico for six months of TBS—The Basic School—so you can finally figure out exactly what that means.

TBS is essentially six months of studying everything the Marine Corps has to offer, from USMC history to combat, aircraft and infantry tactics, to processing Marine Corps paperwork. And you drill and train hard every day—not quite as harshly as at OCS, but it's still pretty intense. There are also a lot of dinners and other events, including Mess Night, which is a very formal dinner about four months in. Everyone is in dress whites and on their best behavior, but it also involves drinking. The Marine Corps is full of traditions, but getting loaded at Mess

Night is definitely not one of them. That night, however, we tried to make it a tradition.

I had been doing relatively well with TBS up until that point. I had taken it seriously, worked hard, and stayed out of trouble. But I wound up, along with every other lieutenant there, flat-out loaded. One thing led to another, and before you know it we'd sprayed down and soaped up a hallway and guys were being propelled—I mean just physically thrown—the whole length of the hallway on their bellies. We call it tailhooking, which is what happens to an aircraft when it lands on a carrier deck, but it's not actually that different from the Slip 'n Slides my mother used to create in our backyard out of a roll of plastic garbage bags, except that everyone was older, drunker, stupider, and stripped down to their underwear. There was an impressive madness to the whole scene—I remember one guy in the corner eating someone's vomit off the floor on a dare—and what can I say? I'd been suppressing my hooligan instincts for a long time. It felt good to let loose.

Allowing women into TBS was still a relatively recent innovation when I was there, and by pure rotten luck, we just happened to be sloshing our way up and down a female hallway. We didn't know that at first, and probably would never have figured it out if someone hadn't ended up getting swung headfirst through one of the women's doors. And I wouldn't have been in nearly as much trouble the next morning if that head hadn't been mine. It was a light, paneled wooden door, so it didn't really hurt when my head went through it. The effect on my military career was another matter.

Your performance is scrutinized all the way through TBS, and the class is split into groups of thirty and ranked accordingly—one through thirty in each group. When the school ends and the jobs are handed out, those rankings are what determine where you're going to end up for probably the next twenty years. It's a little like a sports draft in reverse, actually, where the players get to pick their team, instead of the other way around. As lieutenants, you request the job of your choice, but the most popular assignments go quickly. The higher your ranking in your column of thirty, the better your chances are of drafting yourself onto the team you want. Well, I was sitting pretty comfortably in the middle of my column until Mess Night came along.

The next morning, I had to face the commanding officer of TBS. The CO is someone you usually don't meet. He's just sort of a mysterious power you don't ever really see. Colonel T. J. Ebbert was a true war hero—he was awarded the Silver Star for his service in Vietnam—and to stand there and hear him talking about how disappointed he was in us was literally and figuratively very, very sobering. I received a letter of caution a couple of weeks later, and I've kept it all these years—it still makes me shake when I read the words now: "It is apparent that your conduct . . . included . . . acts of immaturity substantially inconsistent with the self-discipline, judgment, and ideals requisite of every Marine officer. Regardless of rank or length of service, you personally tarnished what was an otherwise festive and meaningful evening." It was a "non-punitive" letter, meaning that if I kept my nose clean it wouldn't become part of my official record, but I still took it very seriously. I spent weekends for the last two months of TBS in my cammies, cleaning, gardening, painting— and putting up with the laughter of my buddies. My TBS ranking dropped all the way down to the bottom of my column, putting most of the jobs I had wanted out of my reach. The punishment was tough, and it was entirely appropriate. This was not college anymore, and I wasn't going to get through on charm and good luck.

I took Colonel Ebbert's lecture to heart, and applied it to my conduct going forward. I won't say that I've been an angel ever since, but I did start to understand that if I was going to be a Marine officer, it was a full-time responsibility—on duty or off, in uniform or not, I was duty-bound to uphold the reputation of the Corps. I also learned an important lesson about leadership, something I would apply time and time again as an officer. Real problems need to have real consequences. When they do, even a troublemaker like me can be turned around.

And that's how I ended up being a communications officer. Honestly, my first choice would have been a navigational flight officer, the guy who rides in the back of a fighter jet, like Goose in *Top Gun*. No chance there. Tanks were also gone by the time I got my pick, and artillery too. Combat arms had been my fall-back but I really didn't want infantry. So when all the combat-arms jobs were gone and communications came up, I jumped at it, thinking that everyone needs communications, so I could still wind up getting some pretty cool assignments. And it ended up being a terrific experience for me, and something that would prove highly valuable as a medical officer generally, and in Fallujah in particular.

When you're a communications officer, it's a leadership position—you become the leader of a communications platoon or a communications company, so all of the radio operators in an infantry battalion work for you. You set them up, you train them, and you put them out in the units. It's quite similar to being a battalion surgeon, because you've got your own guys, but they're also farmed out to the line companies, so that each line company has a radioman or a corpsman, as the case may be. And it's always an interaction between you and your guys, and between you and the company commanders, the guys you're sending them out to. You have to learn how to negotiate those relationships, and you discover very quickly that if you're sending out guys who are not well-trained or disciplined or reliable, then you're going to be very unpopular with the line commanders. Plus, you end up actually understanding the equipment and logistics of the various communications systems in the Marine Corps, and that was something I was always grateful for.

So that was it—another three months of communications school, and I was off to the fleet. By April of 1988 I was finally ready to put training behind me and start life as an active-duty Marine. I was a platoon commander for a field message center, I was a detachment commander for a communications squadron, and I spent time with a long lines platoon, providing long-distance, multi-channel radio linkups. And finally I was assigned to MASS 1, Marine Air Support Squadron 1, a close air support squadron, to provide their communications requirements. Through it all, I was learning about leadership, I was learning about how to get things done in the Marine Corps, and I was learning how to be a Marine. It was a good life, and I enjoyed it, but once or twice along the way, I got a peek at another way of life that looked pretty good to me too.

I did a short stint with Third Battalion, Second Marines, in 1989, including three weeks suffering with them on a mountain in the Sierra Nevadas in California, at the Bridgeport Mountain Warfare School. One of my Marines sprained his ankle up in the snow—the first night we were there, we got three and a half feet in a twenty-four-hour period—and so I had to medevac him about a half mile down the mountain to the Battalion Aid Station. We had been living in tents, and then we lived in snow caves, and finally they had us in what they called "Norwegian tent sheets," which are basically nothing—just a piece of canvas that you put on top of the snow to sleep under. So, cold, tired, and annoyed, I arrived at the Battalion Aid Station with my injured Marine. And the first thing I noticed was, hey, the doctor's got heat: I'm sleeping under a crappy sheet of canvas up on the mountaintop, and he's sitting down here all warm and cozy. He still gets to be up on the mountain, but then he comes home to this sweet tent with a big old heater going full blast. I started to think that battalion surgeon might be a neat job to have.

For as long as I could remember I'd had this dichotomy in my life—the military side was obvious, but there had always been a medical side under the surface. I had been interested in becoming a doctor ever since Gregory had died, and that's why I majored in biology at college. Still, my life had been all military up until that point, but as I sat and talked with the doctor that night, it kind of came together in my mind. I started to see that maybe there was a way to combine my two big interests.

Not long afterward, while I was with MASS 1, the First Gulf War started. I was the communications electronics officer for the close air support squadron, which was a great job to have and is usually filled by someone who's been in communications for a decade. I had only three years in the Marine Corps at that time, but I guess the group CO was desperate to fill the position, and he must have thought I had a pretty good head on my shoulders because I took over a very large account—a lot of Marines. Part of our duties was to install and maintain a communications van: a large container crammed with electronics that can be installed into a C-130 cargo plane or onto the back of a truck, and used as a mobile air traffic control center. They're used a lot in combat situations, for calling in air support, and also for coordination of medevac flights.

I was still a young, gung-ho communications officer at that point, and I wasn't thinking about medicine—I was thinking how the hell was I going to get over to Iraq and get into this war. Being on the East Coast, I was assigned to the II Marine Expeditionary Force, or II MEF. But Operation Desert Storm was a I MEF fight, the California boys from Camp Pendleton. II MEF basically stayed home, and that disappointed an awful lot of Marines, me included. It was much more than just knowing that nobody gets promoted sitting stateside during wartime. Marines think of combat the way football players think of the Super Bowl. Combat is what we train for. We learn how to engage the enemy. You don't put your heart and soul into that kind of training for years just to be left at home when the big game comes. Everybody was convinced that this was going to be the only Marine Corps war in our lifetimes, so if you didn't get to go to this one, you would never get your chance.

The First Gulf War may have been a I MEF fight, but that didn't mean there was zero chance for a II MEF outfit to go. Marine units are all set up to be interoperable with each other, so it's a common thing for elements from one MEF to augment the others, and quite a few II MEF units were getting into the fight. But I never got that chance. The last straw came for me in the form of a group of I MEF communications Marines who showed up needing to know how to install one of our communications vans into a C-130. We knew it cold. But instead of sending us, the

Corps had us show the I MEF Marines how to do the job, and then watch them go off to the glorious war while we sat at home like a bunch of Cinderellas. That's when I realized I was not going to get my chance.

I was twenty-five years old by the time the Gulf War was over in 1991, and I felt I'd been stood up for the big dance. I was seriously frustrated—and I started thinking hard about my future. I still loved the Corps, but I was bitter. I decided that it was time for something new.

CHAPTER 5

Becoming a Doctor

I may have decided after the First Gulf War ended that it was time to leave the Marine Corps, but you know what they say: once a Marine, always a Marine. So of course when I started thinking about medical school, I approached it with a Marine-like attitude.

The Marine Corps really is a unique military organization, and it's built on a lot of principles and philosophies—being interoperable, being expeditionary, taking the lost causes and turning them around, taking the tough fights and winning them. But the whole thing basically boils down to this: Identify the problem, do what you have to do in order to neutralize that problem, and move on. A lot of times that means scrounging around to find the gear or the people or whatever it is you're going to need, and a lot of times that means finding another member of the team to get the job done, if they're going to do a better job than you are; in other words, delegation.

So, my problem: I want to be a doctor. Solution: Go to medical school. Execution: (a) get into medical school, and (b) get out again. It really didn't matter to me very much where I went, or how I got there, and I figured that if I could find a way to get in, I could get myself through. I was doing what I could for myself. I took a recruiting job in Baltimore and enrolled in some courses at a local community college in an attempt to bump up my grade-point average. But I figured I could use some help in other departments. So I did what any good Marine would: I marshaled my assets, and I delegated. I called my old friend Scott Ryan and told him that each of my med school applications required a "personal" statement. My request was simple: "Pretend you're me and write something that sounds good about me." Scott had earned a master's degree in English and I knew he would do a better job of it than I would have. I also got my then-girlfriend to help me pull together all the details I needed to complete the applications.

But then I realized I had kind of blown it. I was applying to traditional medical schools—allopathic or M.D. schools—and in very Marine-like fashion, I took everything very literally. So when the date on the application said September 30, I followed all of the instructions to the letter, and put the application in the mail on September 30. In the meantime, the people who actually knew what they were doing had put in their applications early, taking advantage of rolling admissions. By the time my applications arrived, the classes were all full.

The prospect of waiting another year to go to medical school was pretty unappealing. I didn't want to spend the time getting more and more frustrated with life in the Marines. Then I heard from some friends about something called a D.O.—doctor of osteopathy. I looked into it a little, and it seemed that D.O.'s did pretty much the same work as M.D.'s—they could write prescriptions, do surgeries, the whole deal. So what the heck, I put in some applications to osteopathic schools, too, and wouldn't you know it, I got in.

I read up some more on what a D.O. was the night I was flying in for my interview. Osteopathy got its start in the 1800s as a reaction against the prevailing medical wisdom of the time, which was more or less that you put a bunch of chemicals into people or cut something out of them, and then hoped they got better. Osteopathy, on the other hand, focused on a patient's health by promoting prevention and the body's innate ability to heal itself. And you know what? This was back in the 1870s and 1880s, when none of them really knew what was going on with health, illness, and the human body.

Times have changed. M.D.'s are now talking about innate healing, D.O.'s are writing prescriptions, and everyone is getting into preventive and alternative medicine. Some M.D.'s still look down on osteopaths, and some D.O.'s still have what I'd call an inferiority complex, but as far as I'm concerned, the only real difference these days is that we go to different schools for four years at the beginning of our medical careers. That's the time when we collect the information, knowledge, and skills—the intellectual and practical "tools"—that we'll need to practice our trade. Then, as doctors, we use them to the best of our abilities to help our patients. In your heart you have to know that what you do for a patient is the right thing, whether you're a D.O. or an M.D. It is osteopathy that provided me with the tools to interact with, diagnose, and treat my patients, and I owe my allegiance to that profession. Perhaps some physicians would have a very different view from mine on the differences between D.O.'s and M.D.'s. But that's okay—I didn't think about it much at the time and I haven't thought about it a whole lot since.

When I got to the interview, I asked all the pertinent questions to assure myself that I would have a good chance at surgical residencies and fellowships. And I confirmed that they would let me in that fall, so I wouldn't have to defer for a year to get into an M.D. school. Sounded like a good deal to me—I didn't care what it was called, I was in.

So, at age twenty-seven, I was ready and eager to take on my new mission. I still loved the Corps, but it was time to start the next chapter in my life. I packed my bags, loaded the car, and headed north to the New York College of Osteopathic Medicine, in Old Westbury, New York, on Long Island, just outside of New York City.

But now that I was in, I had to deal with the little matter of paying the tuition. I had taken out federal loans to cover my first year but I hadn't spent much time doing the math. I was making something like $40,000 a year as a Marine captain when I resigned my commission, and my annual tuition for medical school was right around $26,000. Ouch—not a good ratio.

It was 1993 and I had made it to that point in life without accumulating a whole lot of debt, and I really didn't like the idea of changing that situation. So I reassessed my options and found that while I may have been a little bitter about my military experience because I didn't get to go to the Gulf War, I wasn't *so* bitter that I couldn't see the appeal of not having over $100,000 worth of loans to pay off after four years of medical school. A Navy medical scholarship just made too much sense to pass up. And I wasn't going to half-ass it, either: I decided then and there that if

I was going back in, I was going back in all the way. I wanted to be a battalion surgeon, and if at all possible, I wanted to deploy overseas. I wanted the adventure, I wanted the challenge. Once that decision was made, getting the Navy scholarship was simple—it really didn't take much more than a phone call. I was already into my first year of medical school, so it was too late to get that covered, but I got a three-year scholarship, and in return, I would owe the Navy three years when I was done. Hey, I'd already done almost seven years in the Marines—three years in the Navy was going to be a breeze.

And so I settled into four more years of school. With so many TV shows built around medical students and interns these days, you'd think I would have more to say about my experiences in medical school. But honestly, it wasn't such a big a deal for me. I enjoyed the learning and loved everything that took me closer to surgery. The cadaver lab, observing surgeries—working anywhere was better than sitting in class.

I didn't skate through medical school, but I did figure out pretty quickly that I could get a lot more done by studying on my own, or with my friend Andy Cohen, than I could by going to class. It just struck us as inefficient—why listen to a guy talking for an hour when you could read the textbook for twenty minutes and have a good working knowledge of the same material? And so Andy and I studied together, and we spent a lot of time playing flag football and drinking beers and doing a lot of other things you're not really supposed to have time to do in medical school. I also got myself involved in the student government and ended up being president of the class for three and a half years.

In the end, we both made it. Andy was the smart one, so he

ended up as a pediatric neurosurgeon at Cornell. And I got re-commissioned in the Navy, which is right where I wanted to be. Mission accomplished.

But I got much more than that out of my time in medical school. I also met a smart, beautiful brunette who would become my wife. We were in the same class, and I met her on my first night there. But sometimes it takes me a couple of tries to get things right. I actually started out dating Melissa's friend, another of our classmates at NYCOM. But that eventually got straightened out, and by about January of our first year, I was with Melissa, where I was obviously meant to be.

Melissa and I stood by each other through a lot of tough times at medical school as well, everything from stressful exams to the death of her mother, who was her best friend. But it was during our internship year, when she stopped calling me for four days, that I first realized I couldn't live without her. So, long before we even talked about marriage, I knew it would happen. But that was a mission that would take me a little longer to accomplish; we both had our medical educations to finish first.

When I started out in medical school, I wanted to be the guy who could come into a situation that was going the wrong way and change the course of events for the better, the way a fireman does, or a cop, or for that matter a Marine. Four years later, I was a doctor, but I still had a lot more to learn. Medical school was a start, but it was the years that came afterward that would really teach me what I needed to know, and prepare me for what we would face in Fallujah.

That preparation started in earnest with my first surgical internship, which I did at the National Naval Medical Center in Bethesda, Maryland. Otherwise known as the Bethesda Naval

Hospital, the center is located just outside of Washington, D.C., and it's pretty much the heart of Navy medicine. It's a full-service research and treatment institution, and famously provides medical care to government leaders in Washington, including the president and his family. It would also become an important treatment stop for many of the wounded Marines coming home from Iraq, including more than a few of the 1/8 Marines we treated in Fallujah.

I did my surgical internship during peacetime, though, from June 1997 to May 1998, so I was seeing a different sort of patient population. It was an unbelievable time for me—my entire life was at that hospital, literally 100 or 120 hours a week on a regular basis. But I loved it: out of the textbooks and into the OR, this was the kind of medical education I could relate to. And within the first two weeks I had put my name in to go on to a Marine Corps battalion as soon as I was done with the internship. It turned out I didn't have to be in such a rush—signing on with deploying battalions was not exactly the most popular option for interns—but I was excited. This was something I had wanted to do for a long time, and I sure wasn't going to miss any application deadlines this time around.

On May 30, 1998, I packed my bags for Camp Lejeune to become the battalion surgeon for Third Battalion, Sixth Marines. As if to underscore the point that I had come full circle, the commanding officer of 3/6 was Lieutenant Colonel Ron Johnson, a large, tall, gruff Marine who had been the operations officer—the guy responsible for the battalion's training and mission planning—with the 3/2 Marines when I spent those three frigid weeks with them on a California mountaintop as a communications officer, almost nine years earlier.

Almost immediately upon joining with the 3/6 battalion at Camp Lejeune, I would make a new acquaintance, and this one would turn out to be one of the most important of my career. Will Dutton, my assistant battalion surgeon, had done a surgery internship as well, and even though he had no military background, he was one of the few other doctors who actually wanted to come out to a battalion. So we had plenty in common—and we hated each other right from the first moment we met. Dutton is an absolutely huge, six-foot-something crazy Texan. He wanted to be in charge, but I had seniority because of my military experience. So I was the boss, and that drove him nuts.

But it didn't take much head-butting for us to work that out—we became good friends and are to this day—and to realize that we shared a lot of the same ideas. We both loved being battalion surgeons, we both took the job seriously, and we both realized that our responsibilities went beyond simply looking after the day-to-day health of the battalion Marines. That's all that a lot of battalion surgeons do, and when you consider that active-duty Marines are probably the healthiest patient population imaginable, that means that a lot of peacetime surgeons don't do much more than ice sprained ankles and hand out aspirins for hangovers. In fact, during peacetime most battalions would rather have their battalion surgeon just sit in his office while the chief and the other enlisted men run the day-to-day operations of the BAS. The logistics of deployment, the training of corpsmen, all of that is usually left to the chief with the surgeon really playing the role of a technician.

But Will and I both wanted to be involved in every aspect of the battalion's medical operation. We took our role as officers seriously, and realized that a crucial part of our job was to prepare the corpsmen for the eventuality of war. This was peacetime, of course, and we didn't know if war would come or not, any more than a battalion commander or a company commander or a platoon commander could know if war was coming. But just as any Marine must, we thought it was our job to prepare our troops, our corpsmen, as if war was an imminent certainty.

It was at that time that Will Dutton really hit upon the concept of the Forward Aid Station, and over the next two years we worked together to turn the theory into practice. It's not a complicated idea—far from it. But it was a departure from Navy medical doctrine. To understand how radical the idea was, you need to know a little bit about how battalion medicine usually works.

Battalion medicine is built around the Battalion Aid Station, a medical clinic essentially. The BAS is designed to provide what's known as level-one care, which includes everything up to but not including surgical interventions. Minor procedures, like excision of abscesses or removal of skin moles, sure, the BAS can handle those, but anything more serious has to be evacuated to a level-two care facility, such as a battalion surgical unit or a military or civilian hospital. (MASH units, for example, were the Army's level-two surgical companies; the Army calls them CSHs now, for Combat Surgical Hospital.) At base, when you're in garrison and not actually operational, the BAS is just a single unit running a medical clinic for the battalion. Once you deploy, the BAS generally consists of a large tent, filled with all of the medical equipment, instruments, and supplies that the battalion can be expected to need during a lengthy deployment, which may or may not include combat. And because the battalion may split into a maneuver element and a headquarters element, which can be separated by miles or more, the BAS actually has to be able to set up and support two distinct aid stations.

During a time of war, each battalion is supposed to have two doctors and sixty-five corpsmen who provide medical treatment for the battalion's nine hundred to a thousand Marines. (When the 1/8 deployed to Iraq in 2004, we had only one doctor at first—me—and just fifty-four corpsmen, including my chief, HMC Folley.) One or more of the corpsmen might be an IDC, or Independent Duty Corpsman, who acts as an additional medical provider for the Marines and can do things like write prescriptions and perform minor surgical procedures in the military context.

Each battalion has a headquarters and service company, and four line companies—three rifle companies, given letter names like Alpha (A), Bravo (B), and Charlie (C), and a weapons company, which carries heavier armaments. Each of these companies in turn is made up of three numbered platoons, and each of those twelve platoons is assigned between six and nine corpsmen. These "line" corpsmen are embedded into their assigned units, going everywhere and doing everything with their Marines; the remainder of the original fifty-three support the aid stations, with the chief and the battalion surgeon deciding who goes where.

Okay, so that's your basic setup—those are your challenges and those are your assets. But the standard system starts to break down very quickly on deployment. The BAS is a very large tent with a lot of equipment, so maneuvering with it becomes a major pain. In any maneuver, there's always a rear area, the main command post logistical support center, and that is where the BAS is traditionally set up—at the rear with the HQ, communications, and service platoons. It's safe, it's stable, and for my money, it's potentially too far away from the line companies to do them any good. Battalion leadership deals with the distance issue by establishing what's called a Jump Command Post, a mobile headquarters element that follows with the line companies who are out on maneuver. And this was Will's big breakthrough—why not have a jump aid station? You could tailor it as you needed, take whatever the specific maneuver might require, stuff it into a vehicle or two, and off you go, following the guys who might actually need your help. Simple. Logical. Brilliant. And completely controversial.

You may be wondering why this didn't become standard practice a hundred years ago. Well, it goes back to the fact that Marine medicine is provided by the Navy, and the two branches of the service have a substantially different outlook on the world. The Navy, like the Army, is focused on major installations and permanent fixtures—bases in the Army, ships in the Navy. The Marine Corps is the only branch that is explicitly designed to be expeditionary, to not spend very much time in any one place. So from a Navy perspective, it makes perfect sense to have all of your medical assets in one place—on the ship, so to speak—but from a Marine perspective, you can see pretty easily how you're going to end up with your casualties in one place and the guys who can help them in another. You would think these issues would get worked out over time, but they don't.

Will and I came to think about the concept as "far forward" medicine, and settled on the term Forward Aid Station, or FAS, for our jump aid station. It made too much sense not to pursue, and we soon had our chance to start putting the idea into practice. The 3/6 was getting ready to go on a MEU—a Marine Expeditionary Unit, or what we call "a float"—to the Mediterranean that would have us at sea through the millennium, from October of 1999 until March 2000. In preparation, we participated in a CAX, a Combined Arms Exercise, at the Marine Corps Air-Ground Combat Center (MCAGCC) near Twentynine Palms, in the California desert. CAX is a pretty intense live-fire training exercise, and the Marines really push themselves physically during the proceedings. We ended up with a couple of fairly significant injuries—guys falling off of trucks and breaking bones, that sort of thing—and Will and I got pretty expedient at calling in air support for medevac.

But what we noticed was that our BAS wasn't really taking care of any of the injured. It was just so far to the rear that we were doing medevacs straight to the hospital from the field. These may not have been combat casualties but they were real injuries, and it was obvious to us that the best treatment was to get them to a surgical ward, not to get them to the BAS. So projecting forward, what happens if this is a real combat situation? How are we going to get a medevac helicopter in to airlift them out, or at least get them back to a secure area where a bird can get in safely? It could be a matter of an hour or more in a vehicle, over bumpy roads or no roads, before the casualties got to the appropriate level of care, or even basic stabilization. Far better to set up Forward Aid Stations, we reasoned, smaller aid stations that would have everything needed to stabilize casualties for medevac, and positioned so that they're within easy reach of any vehicle on the ground, not more than four or five minutes of travel time. You avoid a force reduction for the Marines, because they don't have to send men and a vehicle all the way out to the BAS with the casualty, and your wounded Marines get better care faster. With a major fracture, an hour over bumpy roads could mean extreme discomfort and unnecessary tissue damage; with serious penetrating trauma—shrapnel or a bullet wound—it could easily mean death. Saving a life, a lot of the time, doesn't mean performing a miracle; it just means knowing what to do, and doing it at the right time. "The right time" almost always means "as soon as possible."

And so we set out on the MEU—from Spain to Egypt, Israel and Jordan, then on to Italy and Malta—with the idea of far-forward medicine in mind. And we had a good start on working out the details of how to make it work—everything from stripped-down lists of the gear and supplies needed to make an FAS effective and secure to the realization that having a detailed evacuation plan for every place we went was an essential part of the approach. We set up far-forward aid stations in Egypt, Jordan, and the Israeli desert, among other places. Being forward allowed me to make an appendicitis diagnosis after a Marine came in with belly pain that worsened over a three-hour period. We medevaced him out for surgery. Later, in the Israeli desert, Will was forward in a vehicle moving with the maneuver element when someone fell off a truck and fractured a femur. If Will hadn't been there to stabilize the Marine and get his leg into traction, the injury could have resulted in amputation. But for the most part our deployment was uneventful. Oh, except for one very important stop in Italy.

Melissa was a pediatrics resident at East Carolina University at that time, and she was getting a little antsy. We had been dating for almost six years, and the subject of marriage hadn't come up a whole lot. But it certainly came up when I first checked into Camp Lejeune and again before I deployed with the 3/6. In fact, Melissa's friends were telling her that if we didn't get engaged before the deployment, it was time for her to move on. Fortunately, she held on just a little longer. Melissa planned to fly out to meet me in Italy in December, in time for New Year's Eve and the changing of the millennium. We would be ported in Naples and I was going to take a four-day leave so we could have a little vacation, and that's when I planned to ask her.

I had already talked to Melissa's father, Theodore (Ted) Hemlock. I asked for his daughter's hand in marriage, and I also asked if I could buy her mother's engagement ring. Melissa's mother had passed away in 1994, while we were in medical school, and her ring had been sitting in her jewelry box ever since. Ted happily sent me the ring, and of course refused to let me pay for it. It was a beautiful, emerald-cut, one-carat, VS2 stone, and I took it to a jeweler to have it put in a new setting. The problem was, it wasn't ready to be picked up before I deployed. Will Dutton and his wife, Shannon, saved me on that one—Shannon picked up the ring and brought it with her to Italy. She even left her husband in Florence a day early so that she could deliver it to me in Rome, where Melissa and I were staying. So on New Year's Eve, I was ready. Exactly six years after our first date, and our first kiss, I proposed on the Spanish Steps in Rome. Lucky man that I am, she said yes.

That was a wonderful time in my life. Melissa and I were great, and I had all the adventure, camaraderie, and just enough suffering and excitement with the Marines to make life interesting. After completing the MEU with the 3/6, I moved up to the regimental level, taking on duties as regimental surgeon for the Sixth Marine Regiment, at Camp Lejeune. It was peacetime, so we did a lot of training, but there were no deployments as a regiment, which in the Marine Corps are made up of three infantry battalions plus a smaller headquarters battalion, about thirty-five hundred Marines in all. In fact, it probably would have been an entirely uneventful year at regiment except for one thing: that's where I met Joe Langholtz.

It was May 2000, and I was just arriving at the Sixth Regiment headquarters, getting settled into my office at the regimental aid station, when there was a blast of banging on the hatch. I had my back turned, hanging a plaque or something on the office wall, when in comes this short, scrappy-looking little guy, a little older than me and a lot more grizzled. He rolls across the deck like we're in fifteen-foot seas, gives me a "Hey, Sir, I'm gonna have a seat," and bam, he throws his feet up on my desk. Now this guy's an E-8—a senior chief and the highest-ranking Navy enlisted man in the regiment. Practically speaking, he reports to the commanding officer and no one else. I was just a lieutenant commander, but he's enlisted and I'm an officer—my O-4 beat his E-8 hands down, so this was a pretty ballsy move. Not as ballsy as what he said, though: "Okay, the first thing we're going to need to do is we're gonna have to get straight how shit's gonna run around here." Inside, I was smiling. But outside, I stared him down and told him that if he didn't get his feet off of my desk, I was gonna jump over the top and kick his ass. And that was that. We both kind of laughed, shook hands, and said, "I'm going to enjoy working with you." And we've been great friends ever since.

I found out later that Langholtz had seen an article about me in one of the base papers—something about the Marine-turned-doctor thing—and I guess he was expecting this know-it-all Marine type who was going to show up and try to tell him how to run the show at regiment. It's usually the chiefs, the senior enlisted guys who have been around for a long time, who actually run the show, and Joe didn't want someone who knew less than he did about how to run a regimental medical operation coming in and messing things up. Langholtz has been around like no one: he enlisted straight out of high school at seventeen, was in the Navy as a corpsman for twenty years, and intends to stay on for another ten years. Joe definitely had some opinions on how to run the aid station, and he didn't want some punk coming in and telling him what to do.

But fortunately, Joe and I saw most things the same way, and I learned a lot from watching him work. He's a guy who puts an incredible amount of concern into his mission, and his Sailors. I've seen him put his own career on the line for guys who were in trouble, and then help them turn it around and get themselves together. At the same time, I've seen him send real troublemakers packing because he was afraid they would compromise the mission. He's a genius at what you could call creative requisitioning—if you can imagine it, Joe can get it for you—and no one understands how to negotiate the differences between Navy and Marine procedure and culture better than he does. When it comes to getting work done, he's almost a Tom Sawyer–type character. That scene where Tom convinces the other kids that he's doing them a favor by letting them whitewash the fence for him? That's Joe all over, and a lasting inspiration for me, too.

Joe got the FAS concept right away. He helped me hone the leadership and requisitioning skills I would need to put it into action in Iraq, and we worked together on figuring out how to really make it a part of battalion combat medicine. He helped me find the gear and equipment to make far-forward combat medicine practical, and we did a lot of very Marine-like training with our corpsmen, running drills in the field in full camouflage. Joe also happened to be responsible for the bar-none worst hangover of my life—it involved Greece, ouzo, and a disappearing tent in the middle of a goat pasture—but that is another story altogether.

CHAPTER 6

From Baltimore to Liberia

Being a battalion surgeon and regimental surgeon with the Sixth Marines had been challenging and fun, just like I hoped it would be. But it was time for me to take stock of my future. I didn't want to be in the military forever and I had always planned to pursue a residency in a surgical subspecialty. I decided it was time to get going on that. Melissa and I got married in May 2001, and I wasn't planning on deploying again with the Marines. I was determined to enter a medical field where I could be close to home, with Melissa, and have children. I chose urology, which I felt would have the right balance of interesting, challenging work and a reasonably manageable schedule. So I returned to the Bethesda Naval Hospital for a residency in urology in the summer of 2001. And that, unfortunately, is where my good luck finally ran out.

Melissa had just signed a two-year contract as a pediatrician in Hagerstown, Maryland, and we had just closed on our first house together. But we had barely unpacked when word came down that the urology residency program had failed its Residency Review Committee accreditation. This committee credentials all residency programs across the country, and it ensures all residencies are in compliance in terms of teaching and patient care. When Bethesda's urology residency program failed the committee's review, the hospital considered eliminating the whole thing. I was not happy with the situation. My entire program was under the very watchful eye of the higher-ups throughout the hospital in a last-ditch effort to save the residency. It was becoming clear to all of us in the program that at some point enough was going to be enough and it would be time to move on.

My rotations continued in the meantime, and one of them was to go to the University of Maryland's R. Adams Cowley Shock Trauma Center in central Baltimore to do a three-month rotation with their general surgery trauma teams. My initial reaction was anger. I didn't see the point now that my urology program was going to close, and I wasn't sure why a future urologist needed to spend three months in shock trauma. When would I ever need this? But I went just to get away from the tension at Bethesda. As it turned out, those three months in Baltimore gave me the most-needed training of my life.

Life at the shock trauma center was intense, even by residency standards. There were often sixty to a hundred patients in the center at any given time, and residents were on duty for thirty-six hours straight, followed by eight to twelve hours off. It was a brutal schedule—just like OCS or boot camp in the Marines. The only silver lining was that going through that kind of extreme experience makes you more able to get through it again the next time, because you know you can handle it. Maybe civilian doctors don't necessarily need that kind of practice, but for a battalion surgeon in wartime, thirty-six hours straight is expected, and having the experience of working like that should probably be an essential part of battalion surgeon training. It was a painful, exhausting three months, and I would never volunteer to do it again, but I loved it.

It wasn't just an endurance test, of course. It was at the Cowley Center that I learned many of the surgical and trauma techniques that would help save lives in Fallujah. It may be surprising to people how busy we were, but the level of trauma in a major American city can be quite sobering, and Baltimore is no exception. Traffic accidents account for a large number of the casualties, but there is a lot of street and domestic violence as well. Fistfights, beatings, knife wounds, gunshots—it doesn't take three months to see all of that and more. You learn the techniques that work, and you learn what interventions have a very low chance of success, even under the best possible conditions. I cracked three chests while I was at the Cowley Center, opening patients along their left lateral rib cage to gain direct access to hearts that had stopped beating. It's a dramatic procedure, and a favorite of the medical movies and TV shows. I did manage to get one of those three patients back, but then he died soon afterward. Those experiences helped me realize that the chances that a patient would survive a procedure like that were only about 2 percent, and that was under ideal conditions.

In a trauma center, you can afford to try everything. You've got the personnel, the life-support facilities, the sterile conditions, and the luxury, usually, of only having a patient or two at a time. Not so on the battlefield, where mass casualties were an all-too-common occurrence. Knowing in advance what's likely to work and what's a long shot helps make the hard decision of moving on a little easier.

Cardiac tamponade, in which the protective sac surrounding the heart becomes filled with blood or other fluids, is a common complication of battlefield wounds, either penetrating trauma to the chest or just massive blunt trauma, like you might receive from an explosion or a vehicle accident. The fluid buildup puts pressure on the heart, keeping it from beating properly, which, if left untreated, can easily be fatal. I had learned about pericardiocentesis—inserting a large needle into the sac, or pericardium, to drain off the excess fluid—before, but I had never actually done it. At Cowley, I got the opportunity to do that procedure as well as other lifesaving techniques, such as inserting a chest tube to drain off fluid or air from around the lungs, under sterile, controlled conditions. I got very good at putting in chest tubes, in emergent and nonemergent situations. So when I left my rotation I had the ability to perform advanced lifesaving procedures very quickly and effectively.

I found that I had the stomach for the work; not everyone does. I also discovered that I, too, had my limits. The most difficult cases for me to handle were the ones where I was able to save the patient's life, but the damage would be so severe that I had to wonder if I was really doing them any favors. I performed my share of amputations, and I lost my share of patients, too. You want to be able to take people in crisis and get them out of it. But trauma rehabilitation can be an extremely arduous process—lots of wounded Marines will tell you that boot camp is nothing compared to trying to live a normal life coming out of trauma surgery, maybe missing a couple of limbs or a large piece of lung, or living with a lot of pain that never goes away. Did you really get someone out of crisis, or did you just put them into a new, longer-lasting hell? It's a hard question to answer and one that still troubles me today.

Brain trauma has always been the worst for me. I'm not sure if it's because I know there's very little rehabilitation that makes a real difference after brain damage or if it's just a purely visceral reaction. But the smell of gray matter—of brain tissue—has always given me a very particular feeling, something between nausea and fear. I remember the first time I had to deal with severe cranial trauma. It involved a suicide attempt. I was working at the Washington Hospital Center in Washington, D.C., as part of my surgical internship. Because I hadn't been there long, my job was to stabilize the cervical spine of the patient, to get down low behind the patient's head and immobilize his neck and head with my hands and forearms. With a gunshot wound to the head, that's a very difficult place to be. There's a distinctive chemical smell to brain tissue; there's a tangible sense of skull plates moving around. I'll never forget the feel of warm brain matter and cerebrospinal fluid leaking out of this patient's left ear and onto my gloved hands.

Our patient that night was skinny and unkempt, with a strong smell of alcohol and filth about him. Mercifully, he was unconscious when he came in, and he never revived. That was my first gunshot wound to the head and it was difficult to deal with; I've since seen many more, and they never get easier. We did everything we could in that Washington hospital, with the best facilities available. Our patient actually survived in a coma for a day or two before dying. We couldn't have done nearly that much in a combat situation, but that is not something I regret. If you save a guy's life like that, in all probability you've done him no favors at all.

Maybe that's one of the reasons I'm not a trauma surgeon today. It was an invaluable experience, though, especially seeing that some injuries are beyond the touch of even the most advanced treatment and care. That would help take some of the pain out of decisions we would have to make in Fallujah; if you know a man cannot possibly survive his wounds, even under ideal conditions, you feel slightly less miserable about losing him in the field. Slightly.

After three months in Baltimore, I returned to my so-called urology residency at Bethesda. There was talk that they might keep the program open after all, and I did do some urological work, as well as a brief rotation in plastic surgery. But when the Residency Review Committee returned in the spring, their assessment wasn't any more positive. I had a couple of options: I could shift over to general surgery, or I could stick around for a couple of months, hoping to transfer into a urology residency at another institution. Just then, Joe Langholtz called and offered option number three: Come on back to the fleet.

It was nine months after the terrorist attacks of 9/11, and things were heating up at Camp Lejeune. Joe was a command master chief and was getting ready to accept orders to become the command master chief of the USS *Cole*, the ship that had been bombed in the Yemeni port of Aden on October 12, 2000. He was also getting ready to assist II MEF in sending out the Twenty-sixth MEU and said he could get me orders to go along as MEU surgeon. It would be a nice step up for me, and a chance to make a contribution to the war on terror. Plus, if I left the residency I would qualify for a $15,000 bonus. That was appealing, because

I was more than a little worried about the financial situation we'd gotten into with the house. Melissa and I discussed it, and we agreed; she managed to terminate her pediatrics contract early and I presented my orders in Bethesda.

It had been a rough, frustrating year, and I was glad to have it behind me. I'd never work in urology again, they told me, but I couldn't let that bother me. *If it's not meant to be, it's not meant to be,* I thought. I returned to Camp Lejeune in July of 2002 and things just started falling into place again. We were preparing for what's called a MEU (SOC), a Special Operations–Capable Marine Expeditionary Unit. That meant we'd be going out with the training and capabilities required for missions such as embassy evacuations, covert raids, mass casualty treatment, humanitarian assistance operations, and so on—pretty cool stuff. And as MEU surgeon, I was responsible for ensuring that medical and health supplies and regulations were in place for the twenty-two hundred Marines, and to coordinate with the battalion surgeons and Marine Logistics Group surgeons to get our procedures set and our corpsmen trained.

As I've said before, there are three key elements to every effective battlefield medevac or mass casualty situation: you have to get the right medical personnel to the scene; you need to have the proper security so that you don't become a casualty yourself; and you need to have effective lines of communication, so that you can call in air support or medevac if you need it. And that's it. If you've got those three things covered, you'll be all right. I'd already worked through these systems with Will Dutton and Joe Langholtz, so now my job was to train every doctor and corpsman in the MEU. That's the fourth element, really—everyone needs to be on the same page, working from the same play book, or the whole system will fall apart.

We were really gearing up for this MEU, and it was going well; we were pumped, actually, ready to go out there and do some good in the world. Then all of a sudden it was 2003 and talk of war was everywhere. We slipped from the top of the priority list to the bottom. A MEU is an independent fighting unit—the smallest MAGTF, or Marine Air Ground Task Force, in the USMC—and it's designed to stay afloat and be self-sufficient for six months at a time. A MEU can be called in to help out with an ongoing war, but its main mission is to be at the ready to handle unexpected contingencies anywhere in its region of operation. In our case, that was going to mean the Mediterranean and most of Africa and the Middle East. So there was some chance we'd see Iraq, but it was pretty slim. We went from pumped to feeling left out, a too-familiar feeling for me.

Still, preparations continued, if somewhat less eagerly and with a little less ease. The units that were prepping for Iraq got first dibs on most everything supply-wise. You've got three primary ships, what we call "gator freighters." Our ships included the USS *Iwo Jima*, or LHD7, as the command ship, the USS *Carter Hall*, and the USS *Nashville*. The LHD is a large ship that looks like a smaller version of an aircraft carrier because it has a very large flight deck. The other two ships have smaller flight decks for helicopters, but they also carry open-well decks in the stern that can receive and deploy amphibious vehicles. The sole purpose of these Navy ships is to transport Marines around and drop them off at trouble spots. (Sailors call these embarked troops "diners and defecators," and that's not far off the mark, although the Marines get a lot of weight lifting and movie watching done, too.) A MEU carries not just an infantry battalion, a MEU service support group (MSSG), and a composite aircraft group or air combat element (ACE), but also tanks, artillery, amphibious assault vehicles, five-ton trucks, light armored reconnaissance vehicles, transport helicopters, and harrier jets. Once a MEU is set up, you never know where you might be sent, so you have to be sure that you have a six-month supply of just about anything you could possibly need under any circumstances. That's hard enough to do under the best of conditions, but when the rest of the division is getting ready for what's looking more and more like major warfare, well, you can't always get what you want.

We deployed on March 4, 2003, as prepared as we could be. We headed for the Mediterranean, not knowing where we would go next—could be Italy, could be Kenya, could be Djibouti, you just don't know. We spun around in the Mediterranean for a while, and then, lo and behold, our presence was requested in Iraq. Our ground combat element—our Marine battalion—was the 1/8, and they were needed to help establish the coalition presence in the city of Mosul. So we got a thousand Marines and Sailors, plus some light armor, all the way from the Mediterranean to Mosul, Iraq, way inland and in the north. Baghdad was pretty stable at that point, in April 2003, and Delta Force had already been into Mosul. It's a largely Kurdish area, and since the Kurds had opposed fallen dictator Saddam Hussein, the Marines were able to establish order with minimal fighting and no casualties.

I was MEU surgeon, which meant that I oversaw the 1/8's two battalion surgeons. They had everything under control at the Mosul airport where the battalion set up, so I took on duties with an Army Civil Affairs unit in downtown Mosul. It involved a lot of linking up with people—the local hospitals, the French humanitarian group *Médecins Sans Frontières*, or Doctors Without Borders, some of the U.S. governmental agencies that were in the city—to see if we could assist with providing health care for the local population. In some cases, like with the aid group, we could get Marines to provide security—once we convinced the French doctors that we weren't the embodiment of evil. For the local hospitals, we could offer supplies. And we provided medical care directly on occasion, too.

The 1/8 Marines set up what's called a CMOC, a civil-military operations center, in Mosul, to start coordinating reconstruction. It was a good idea and the right thing to do. There hadn't been heavy fighting here, and there was no reason for us not to get along well with the population. But things couldn't have gone worse. The Marines were nervous: this was their first time in a war zone and they had trained for war and Special Ops, not for handing out job applications and dealing with upset civilians who wanted someone to shout at.

The situation turned south very quickly. A crowd had gathered outside of the CMOC, and they started chanting, wanting jobs, wanting money, wanting the Marines and the United States to provide them these things. The situation intensified as more and more demonstrators grew angry before the Marines even really managed to get set up. Then, from the rear of the crowd, there was a flurry of gunfire. The Marines reacted the way they had been trained—they opened fire.

I wasn't there when it happened, but I did see the results. These young Marines were trained as warriors; they were pumped up and *Oorah*-ed to the hilt, ready to get into the shit and kick some ass. Then they were asked to work a job fair and handle an angry mob. If you egg on a dog until it's in a frenzy, that's not a good time to ask him to go play with children. Somebody's going to get bit. But if you sit that dog down and calm him, you can put him on a leash and he'll be okay around kids—so long as you keep that leash good and tight. I don't blame these young Marines; they were scared and wanted to stay alive. They hadn't made the mental transition into civil affairs work, and the battalion did not have a lot of experience with that type of situation. Unfortunately, that is the chaos and horror of war.

Any hope of goodwill evaporated; the crowd scattered and the Marines returned to our base at the airfield. The next day, Colonel Andrew Frick, the commander of the MEU, a great man and leader, sent me to the trauma hospital in town, and I have to say, I was a little concerned when I got that assignment. To go out into the city in uniform after that fiasco, to have to see these wounded people, was very difficult. I went with the Civil Affairs team—three Humvees, an orthopedic surgeon from a reserve unit, and me. We went to see what damage we had done and what we could do to help. Sure, there was provocation before we fired, and we were still operating under the rules of war, but that didn't make what I saw at the hospital any easier to take.

The trauma hospital was just a raggedy little place in a very industrial section of town. When I walked in, I looked for the senior surgeon there. He grabbed me and brought me to see a little girl, twelve years old, who he said had been wounded in the incident and was now paralyzed from the waist down, no movement in her legs at all. She had a raw wound and in the X-ray we could see a large round lodged in her spine, larger than an M16 or AK-47 round, maybe a fragment from a .50 caliber. I don't know.

Was it one of our rounds? Was it one of their rounds? There was no way to tell. But looking at those X-rays made me feel awful; I couldn't fix it, I couldn't justify it, and I hated the fact that I was standing there representing it. Her family was there, and a small crowd. Some of them were crying, some were shouting. There were worried looks on their faces, and anger. There were a few other patients, men who had been shot too. I don't know who they were and I don't know how they were shot. Most of their wounds seemed to be old, though, so they couldn't have been from the incident. But a little kid, a little girl? That's not supposed to happen. We're supposed to be better than that.

All of this took place during the first week we were in Mosul. We worked hard for the next two weeks we were stationed there to do better. I went in and met with the faculty from the Mosul medical school, which had been looted. There wasn't much I could do as MEU surgeon but I tried to get the ball rolling with the Civil Affairs people to see if we could give them some help. One of the doctors there told me that his daughter was in a pharmacology program in Michigan, and he hadn't been able to contact her, could I reach her? I sent an e-mail that night to my parents, and they called this man's daughter to let her know he was okay. Not a big deal, but kind of nice—making some human contact, trying to be the good guys. That's the way you want these things to work.

The Marines weren't really getting into gunfights anymore after the first week in Mosul, and we carefully started to circulate a little, eating at street vendor stands and that sort of thing. There were a lot of people who needed medical care, and I wish we could have done more to help them, but if we had opened up the aid station on base, there would have been a flood, and we were very fearful of another mob developing. We set up another CMOC just outside the airport, so we could have some control and not have to go into town and put ourselves at risk. We did what we could medically from there, and if we couldn't help directly, we at least got them to an Iraqi hospital. Intel warned us to stay away from the trauma hospital because they had received human intelligence about targeting it for a terror attack; not everyone wanted us there, whether we were helping the local population or not.

On base, we were actually getting shot at by kids. There would be a group of kids playing soccer behind a wall, and every once in a while one of them would pull out an AK-47, point it over the top, and pop off a couple of rounds, and then return to the game. One of our snipers actually saw a kid do it—the sniper was sighting the area and had the kid in his crosshairs. Under the rules of engagement, the Marine could have legally taken the shot, but he didn't. And I believe that sniper showed very mature judgment and did the right thing. We went and found the kid and his father, and it turned out they were being paid to harass us. Who pays a kid to do that? So you've got your rapport and goodwill, and then you've got some serious issues to contend with as well. It's not an easy balance to strike.

By our third week in Mosul, though, it was really starting to come together. We had managed to free up a truckload or two of supplies and equipment for the hospitals, and the Civil Affairs guys had things going now, trying to get some items repaired, trying to get people some jobs and some money. I had been going around to the hospitals, helping out where I could. A few days before we were scheduled to leave, I was doing my last social rounds, visiting with the administrator at one of the nicer hospitals after supplying the other hospitals with needed equipment. This hospital was the tallest building in town. I had become friendly with the administrator, and he called me over. "Hey, Dr. Jadick, I want to show you something." He took me all the way to the top of the building, where we had never been before, and I couldn't believe what I saw. The whole floor was stuffed with listening equipment; this had been an Iraqi Republican Guard surveillance post, which had been used to spy on the whole city. Then he took me downstairs and showed me two ambulances. Same thing—packed with surveillance equipment. The hospital administrator had found out about it because he investigated after the Republican Guard and the local police had left his hospital, leaving the ambulances behind.

Defense Secretary Donald Rumsfeld ended up presenting the ambulances on TV, as evidence of Saddam Hussein's war crimes; ambulances are off-limits for military use. Honestly, I'm not sure it was such a great find, but the signals intel people from the National Security Agency were in love with it. It wasn't a bioweapons lab, but by that point, I guess Washington would take what they could get. To me, the fact that we had built up enough rapport and goodwill that they brought me in to see this stuff outweighed the significance of the discovery itself.

It did give me a sense of what life under Saddam must have been like, though. But there was another discovery, out at the airfield where we were set up, that made the point much more directly. It had been a military airfield, and there were several large earthwork aircraft bunkers, basically huge piles of dirt with a cave hollowed out of the middle to provide overhead cover. I was on the last flight out of Mosul, back to the MEU, and we had a few days toward the end of our time there with very little to do, other than poke around and see if we could get into trouble. Well, we stumbled onto a series of little rooms dug into the sides of these earth bunkers—prison and torture rooms, complete with eyehooks set into the ceilings. Pretty grisly. These were Saddam's "fun rooms," people told us. But they were nothing compared to the insurgent torture and execution rooms that the Marines would find in Fallujah later on.

The Army came in to take over from us, and as soldiers tend to do, they brought in a mountain of gear and supplies. They actually set up a large hospital, and it looked like they were settling in for a good long stay, so that was it for us. I spent my last couple of days in Mosul bored out of my skull. They actually had me stand watch, literally surrounded by the Army, with my 9-millimeter pistol. There's a tank down there, and I've got a pea shooter. Oh well—Iraq ends on an anticlimax. I figured that at least I managed to get in-country for a few weeks this time around. Little did I know that I'd be back again before this war was over.

We got back on ship and headed south through the Suez Canal, to the Red Sea and the Horn of Africa. We did an operation in Djibouti, where we landed on the shoreline and set up camp for some shooting and maneuvering exercises. It was so hot that the wind felt like a jet engine blowing on you even at night. We were taking heat casualties all over the place, and this was just for a training exercise. So I was relieved when Colonel Frick came and asked me to join Dave Graves, who was a Marine Corps captain and the supply officer for the MEU, on a side trip to Kenya, for more civil affairs work. We linked up with embassy personnel and the deputy to the American ambassador, and we headed out in a bush plane to a village called Lamu, on an island just off the coast. The area had been part of the major Arab trading routes for hundreds of years, and the concern now was that it was being used by terrorists for gunrunning through the Horn countries—Djibouti, Eritrea, Ethiopia, and Somalia.

We were given a budget to provide aid to the village and try to build some goodwill in the region. We toured sites all through the area and figured out ways we could help—get the combat engineers in here to level out a soccer field, set up a clinic there, bring in the surgeons to do a bunch of operations. Be the good guys and maybe make some friends, so they're not going to be as quick to make friends with the terrorists. I thought it was a pretty great deal, a friendly exchange of cultures and a bit of "I scratch your back and you scratch mine." But we were just getting it all written up when we got an urgent message: return to the embassy immediately, the MEU is under way for Liberia, which is on the far side of Africa. We handed the Kenya projects off to an Army unit—I read about their completion later on, which felt good—and took off for Italy, where we would rendezvous with the MEU before steaming toward Liberia.

Djibouti had been an inferno, but Liberia in August was even worse, hot and soupy all day and night. The country had been fighting civil wars for most of the previous twenty years, and the capital, Monrovia, was under attack by rebel militia groups that included child soldiers and drugged-up, cross-dressing lunatics. It was a seriously messed-up situation and the civilians were really suffering. The U.S. embassy was taking some mortar fire, too, so we parked ourselves in the Atlantic, just offshore, in case we had to go in to evacuate. A few Marine teams went in to help bolster security.

My job was to go forward again, to see if I could help out with the hospitals and health care. The United Nations had been reporting a medical crisis in the refugee camps—massive dysentery, starvation, the whole thing. I went into the camps, and I just didn't see it. Granted, these people were not in a good position, but the kids were getting vaccinated, and the ones with diarrhea were getting treated with antibiotics and doing fine. I did run into a lot of stillbirths in the camps, but there weren't large numbers of malnourished kids and people weren't dying in large numbers. There were a few dying of cholera and a few dying from poor medical care, but nowhere near what I expected.

The crazy thing was, while I was out there looking after civilians, my Marines were getting into serious medical trouble themselves. Malaria is endemic pretty much throughout the tropics. A MEU never goes out without taking measures to protect the troops from this disease. Malaria is caused by a nasty little blood parasite called *Plasmodium falciparum*, which gets injected into humans when infected mosquitoes bite them. It can be an awful disease—you suffer from alternating fevers and chills, and it can easily be lethal if you get a virulent strain. Standard preparations include Marine Corps cots with mosquito nets, prophylactic drugs that are supposed to be taken every week to ward off infection, and uniforms sprayed down with the contact insecticide permethrin. The spray treatment remains active for several months, but it was in short supply as we were prepping for deployment. Did every man spray every uniform he brought along? Did every man take his pills regularly or haul his cot into the jungle? You can guess the answers.

We had put 157 MEU Marines ashore near the Monrovia airport, as part of a joint task force (JTF) sent in for stabilization operations. They didn't engage any rebels, but they sure found a virulent strain of plasmodium. The Marines had set up in a bushy area near the airfield; it was on the edge of a hot, steamy, thick jungle filled with the humidity and standing water that mosquitoes love. In that kind of wet heat, the Marines slept without their shirts on and without their mosquito nets. As a result, they got bitten all night, and being tough guys, they pretended it didn't bother them.

By the time I returned to my ship, there were reports filtering in from the battalion surgeons that a lot of our guys had cyclical fevers. I started bringing all of the sick Marines onto my ship, and they were in rough shape. I told the medical officer on board, the Navy Amphibious Readiness Group surgeon, Commander William Archer, of the situation, and he gathered the medical staff together. Green side and blue side, Marine and Navy, we tried to figure out what it could be. We all should have known more about this just by being doctors, but this was not an area of expertise for any of us. We came up with three options—Lassa fever, leptospirosis, or malaria. We talked to Bethesda particularly and they didn't think it was malaria—too many people, too sick, too fast. And the Marines were supposed to be taking mefloquine, the preventive malaria drug, once a week.

We didn't take any chances. We were particularly concerned about Lassa fever, which has a high human-to-human transmission rate, so the Navy quarantined our ships until we came up with the diagnosis of certain malaria. Each disease has its own treatment regimen, and we started hitting them all even before determining for sure what they had. The standard way to get a diagnosis for malaria is a blood smear sample; you can see the parasites in the red blood cells under the microscope. None of us had much experience with that, but the ship's surgeon, Lieutenant Commander John Newman, set the smears up, and it was blindingly obvious even to a bunch of surgeons—these guys were packed with malaria parasites.

We went into crisis mode; everyone with a fever went on Malarone, the oral treatment for malaria, right away. Anyone still ashore had visual confirmation that they took their doxycycline every day, and we checked everyone for fever, all the time. I flew onshore myself every day or two since there were still Force Recon Marines out there without a medical officer. Some of the Marines with malaria admitted that they hadn't been taking their preventive medicine, some because they considered it a hassle, others because the drug can cause strange side effects, like nightmares. But I know I was taking mine, and I tested positive for malaria too—one round of fevers and I put myself on Malarone. All told, 69 of our 157 shore-stationed Marines experienced symptoms of malaria—44 percent—and another 11 Army and Air Force personnel, who were members of the stabilization JTF, came down with the disease as well. It's remarkable that we didn't lose any of them. Four guys went into a coma from cerebral malaria—a huge percentage of their blood was overrun with the plasmodium parasite—and we hit them hard with IV quinidine sulfate right away. They didn't regain consciousness on board, but they were medevaced to Bethesda, where they subsequently recovered.

We got lucky—we spotted the problem and jumped on it just in time to avert a real tragedy. But malaria is something that should never have been a problem, and it's a disease that plays an infamous role in American military history. In Burma in 1944, members of the provisional volunteer Army commando unit best known as Merrill's Marauders distinguished themselves to the point that every man in the unit was awarded the Bronze Star. But most of those medals were posthumous—only about 200 of the original force of 2,750 survived the campaign. And while many fell in battles with the Japanese, historians have concluded that their biggest foe was malaria, along with dysentery and typhus. At one point, the diseases were causing more than seventy deaths a day. Memories of that loss run deep in military medical circles, and no one wants to see it repeated.

An investigating team showed up to find out what was going on. We had everything under control by that point, so they were coming to assign blame. So they investigate—real gumshoe stuff. One of them thinks he'll just wander around the ship in civilian clothes and none of the Marines will suspect that he's an investigator. Well, he didn't have to bother; the investigators concluded easily enough that the Marines hadn't taken their cots and bed nets with them into the jungle. You can buy a fifteen-ounce mosquito net rig from any camping store for about thirty bucks, and that was something I tried to requisition before the MEU set out, but my request was denied by number crunchers higher up. The Marine setup, a cot with a bed net on it, easily weighs thirty pounds. None of these investigators had ever humped a pack, let alone tried to do it through jungle with a thirty-pound cot and bed net rig strapped on top. But that's okay—they figured out who to blame and headed off to Washington to have a big meeting and talk about how we screwed this all up.

No one from the ship was invited to the meeting; not even the investigators were invited. It was big Navy medicine only, a collection of officers in Washington who had not served with Marines and probably didn't understand the difference between policy and operations. We weren't invited, but I showed up at the

October 9, 2003, meeting anyway, along with Commander Archer. The MEU was winding down and had moved on to Spain by then. Colonel Frick bought me a commercial airline ticket over to Washington, God bless him. The senior blue-side medical officer and I went over and attended their meeting. We had an interesting time together. I probably didn't behave myself very well, and I probably wasn't their favorite person for a while. But they got input on the operational side of the situation, and the BUMED (Navy Bureau of Medicine and Surgery) "consensus conference report" puts the blame pretty squarely with leadership, discipline, and equipment, not with the medical staff or our conduct and oversight.

The investigation came out okay—tragedy avoided, no one died, the Marine Corps needs to make some changes. Colonel Frick came out as the bad guy, though, and since I was the senior medical advisor on board, I came out as the surgeon who let everybody get malaria. Or at least that was my feeling and impression, and not a feeling I relished. Because we showed up at the meeting, I think the brass was persuaded to make real changes that will save lives down the road. I take some comfort in that. But I hated the fact that I was now stigmatized—Malaria Guy. Not long afterward, I was in California to teach something called the combined landing for surgeons course, which is a rundown of what new surgeons need to think about from the operational side. And one of the participants piped up with, "Hey, aren't you the malaria doctor?" I almost hit the guy. It was February of 2004, and I was feeling pretty bitter, which meant that it was time for something new once again.

CHAPTER 7

Life at Haditha Dam

There were a lot of reasons why I volunteered to go with the 1/8 to Iraq in the spring of 2004, and the malaria incident was definitely one of them. I hated the idea that the MEU crisis in Liberia would be the last entry in my deployment history, and I hated feeling like I was stigmatized. Even the rumors that the Marines might end up in Fallujah weren't enough to change my mind. The 1/8 needed a battalion surgeon and I needed a chance to redeem my reputation. Maybe we could do something for each other.

By late June, as our charter from Camp Lejeune arrived in the Mideast, it seemed even more likely that American forces would have to enter Fallujah to clear it of the terrorists, insurgents, and criminals who were running wild there. There were several reasons for this, not least that the longer we waited, the stronger and more entrenched the insurgents would become. By going into Fallujah with full strength, we would have a chance to beat the insurgency on two levels. First, we would be able to capture and kill a large number of very hardened terrorists, the kind of people whose hearts and minds we were never going to win, and the kind of people who just might have information we would need to really unravel Iraq's interwoven networks of terror, insurgency, and crime. Just as important, a win in Fallujah would show the terrorists and the world that America meant business—just as a loss, or avoiding the showdown, would confirm the insurgents' claims that America was weak and soft, and would quickly shrink from any real confrontation.

Nothing less than the future of Iraq was at stake; national elections had been scheduled for January 2005, the first free and fair elections the country would have. But they would only be considered a success if Iraqis from all of the country's three major ethnic/religious groups showed up at the polling stations. Kurdish and Shiite Arab Iraqis had been eager voters in earlier balloting for Iraq's provisional government, but most Sunni Arab Iraqis boycotted those elections. The success of the liberated country depended on drawing the Sunnis into the democratic process. And that meant getting rid of the thugs who were making Fallujah their home—men like Abu Musab al-Zarqawi, the leader of the notorious terrorist organization al-Qaeda in Iraq—who were doing everything they could to convince the Sunnis to fight the Americans, fight the provisional government, and fight their fellow Iraqis. Success in Fallujah would rob the terrorists of their stronghold and their bragging rights. Failure—unthinkable—or failure to engage would amount to ceding control of the entire region to the terrorists, and quite likely lead to the collapse of the new and struggling Iraqi democracy.

But there were democratic concerns back home, as well.

America's presidential elections were scheduled for November 2, 2004, and the prospect of a bloody urban battle being telecast into American homes just before the voting started didn't sit well with anyone hoping to hold on to the American public's already-wavering support for the war in Iraq. The timing of our eventual push into Fallujah would have to be delicately balanced, probably after the American elections in early November 2004, but certainly before the Iraqi elections in late January 2005; avoiding, if at all possible, the Muslim holy month, Ramadan, as well as major American holidays like Christmas and New Year's. There was no perfect time for the battle, and no one knew when the order would be given. But we did know, or strongly suspect, that when the order came, we would be going in.

In the meantime, the 1/8 would establish itself to the west of Fallujah, near the small desert city of Haditha, a farming community of something under 100,000 inhabitants on the banks of the Euphrates, about a hundred miles upriver from Fallujah. We were in the same province—al-Anbar, the large, Western-most province of Iraq—and it had a well-deserved reputation as a major stronghold of the Iraqi insurgency and a very dangerous place for Americans. Al-Anbar stretches from the more-populated western edges of Baghdad—and the town of Abu Ghraib, home of the notorious prison—all the way out into huge, sparsely inhabited stretches of desert along Iraq's borders with Syria, Jordan, and Saudi Arabia. The population in al-Anbar is primarily Sunni Arab, but they tend to have much stronger tribal connections than any allegiance with the former, Sunni-dominated government in Baghdad. Saddam Hussein himself evidently feared the region's unruly nature, and he put a fair amount of effort into alternately trying to subdue the al-Anbar Sunnis and to buy their loyalty.

The two major cities in al-Anbar—Fallujah and the capital, Ramadi—were hotbeds of insurgent activity. Fallujah in particular had become a no-go zone for Americans. Earlier that year, in March 2004, a team of four American contractors—all of them seasoned veterans of elite American military units working for the North Carolina–based company Blackwater Security Consulting—had been ambushed in central Fallujah by insurgents, who sprayed their SUVs with bullets. The shooters took off as soon as the murderous attack was over, but a crowd of Iraqi men and boys swarmed around the disabled vehicles and fell on the Americans, attacking survivors and deceased alike in a frenzy of desecration. The four security contractors were hacked to pieces, and their bodies doused in fuel and set on fire. The mob ran wild for hours, dragging smoldering body parts through the streets of their city and finally hanging two corpses from the iron superstructure of an old green bridge spanning a bend in the Euphrates River from Fallujah's oldest neighborhoods on the right bank to the Fallujah General Hospital on the left.

Photographs and video of that abomination went out around the world, along with the mob's chants—*Fallujah is the graveyard of Americans!* The incident signaled to the world that no matter what anyone thought of the war to begin with, Fallujah had become a haven for the most barbaric and cowardly elements of the growing anticoalition insurgency. Four Marine battalions—the 2/1, 2/2, 3/4, and 1/5—were ordered into the city in April of 2004, seeking to capture the perpetrators and to drive the growing number of foreign and native-born terrorists from their safe haven. Politics intervened, though, and the Marines were pulled back before they could complete the mission. The negative PR hit from television images of civilian casualties robbed Washington of its resolve, and handed the insurgency its first major victory. A shaky truce left Fallujah under the control of the self-styled Fallujah Brigade, a collection of insurgent fighters organized by former Iraqi military officers from the city. Fallujah would govern itself, the theory went, and the violence and mayhem would disappear. The plan failed miserably as the city became a self-governing city-state of cruelty and terror. Many of the insurgency's leaders, including al-Zarqawi and his group, al-Qaeda in Iraq, set up their headquarters in Fallujah and the local population suffered greatly under the same kind of brutal repression that the Taliban had practiced in Afghanistan.

Our initial destination when we first arrived in Iraq was al-Asad Airfield, home of the largest U.S. base in western Iraq, a secure area not unlike the famous Green Zone in Baghdad. We stopped there for several days of orientation. It soon became clear that an invasion of Fallujah was not imminent. Waiting would only make things harder, everyone knew, but we weren't the ones making the decisions. So instead we did our best to get used to Iraq at al-Asad. The biggest challenge was acclimating to the Iraqi summer; temperatures were regularly over 120 degrees. Keeping our men hydrated and avoiding heat casualties while training for whatever was coming next would be a major challenge.

Our ultimate destination turned out to be a large dam built across the Euphrates near Haditha. It was a major hydroelectric installation, the largest in Iraq, and provided something like 60 percent of the electricity to Baghdad at that time. The Marines of the 1/8 would relieve the Third Battalion, Fourth Marines, who were protecting this important part of the strained Iraqi power grid and conducting stabilization and security operations through-out the surrounding area. We would be the primary American presence in the region, and our mission was to maintain order and do what we could to protect and befriend the inhabitants.

And so we set up. The dam itself would be our home, and it was massive. The concrete structure stretched at least half a mile across the river, with another mile or so of embankments on either side. The large, shallow Lake Qadisiyah on the upstream side was a major source of water for irrigation as well as for driving the six hydroelectric turbines in the dam. I wouldn't let our Marines swim in it, though, no matter how much they wanted to or how high the temperatures climbed. The water was absolutely filthy and the last thing we needed was a battalion-wide case of schistosomiasis, a bladder infection caused by a nasty little microbe that lives in fouled water. The dam facility itself wasn't much better. The thing had been built in the mid-1980s, and it didn't really look like anyone had spent much time or effort taking care of it since.

Haditha Dam was built with a pair of "wings" stretching out along the downstream side. They were basically twin outbuildings that tapered down from the dam itself alongside the Euphrates, ten stories above ground and eleven stories below at the dam itself. I suppose they must have been filled with dam workers and administrators at one time, but those rooms would now serve as our headquarters. My first priority was to get the Battalion Aid Station set up because the 1/8 Marines were starting to go out on combat patrols right away and I wanted to be ready in case anything happened. Plus, even though Marines are awfully hardy guys and it takes a lot to get them to complain, there is still always a trickle of daily sick-call issues, the basic lumps and bumps that go along with military life. Bryan Zimmerman, my IDC, and the corpsmen took primary control of sick call, and I focused on ensuring that we had everything we would need in case we took casualties. That included making sure that the corpsmen were all fully trained in combat lifesaving and trauma skills and familiarized with the procedures we would be using.

We were in a good situation at the dam. Security was taken care of by the Marines and by a unit of a coalition partner's military that was also stationed at the dam and took primary responsibility for protecting it from attacks and sabotage. Communications were in good order as well. We had telephone contact at the dam itself, and good radio links and air evac to al-Asad, which would serve as our main evacuation point for serious illness and combat casualties. And we had everything we needed to run a full, effective Battalion Aid Station, which we established on the top floor of the dam. I turned my attention to training and drilling the corpsmen in everything I thought they would need to know, no matter what the months ahead would bring.

The first requirement was that the corpsmen know their first aid and basic life support cold. They would be worse than useless if they couldn't dress a wound, treat for shock, start an IV, or initiate CPR. Just as important, they had to know how to handle a mass casualty, a situation where there are more men down than you can help all at once. The word "triage" comes from the French "to sort," and that's what it is—the thought process you use to sort through all of the victims of a mass casualty event to decide who gets your help first. There are a bunch of different triaging systems, but it comes down to knowing who needs help right away, who will be okay if they have to wait for a while, and who is already beyond your help. Then for every wounded man, there's a standard protocol based on what you check and treat first, before moving on if you find a problem. The mnemonic is ABCDE: airway, breathing, circulation, disability, exposure. Does the casualty have an open passage from his mouth to his lungs; if not, clear it. Is he breathing? If not, start artificial respiration. Is his heart beating, and does he have any serious bleeds? CPR and bandaging if so. Any gross fractures? Stabilize them. And finally, make sure the casualty stays warm and doesn't go into shock. Most of this is not terribly complex stuff, but you have to be able to make a lot of decisions very quickly, and under very stressful conditions. The only way to really learn that is by doing it, but we drilled the corpsmen on detailed simulations of realistic situations, scrutinizing their decision making and their lifesaving techniques, and always pushing them to be better and faster.

The next step was to do something about our living quarters. The dam was filthy. The office buildings had been looted, there was graffiti everywhere, and as far as I could tell the 3/4 Marines had been happy to live in squalor. Mark Winn, 1/8's executive officer, wasn't going to put up with that, and neither was I. No matter what the situation, I'm a big believer in constantly trying to improve your position, and that's something I tried to emphasize to my corpsmen all the time. Complaining is fine, but it gets old fast if you don't actually try to do something about whatever it is that's bothering you. If you're standing in shit, I always say, why not move your foot? That's definitely something I learned from my time in the Marines. Especially for an expeditionary force, there has to be a lot of emphasis on constantly improving your position, and that can mean everything from sandbagging an open window in a free-fire zone to pimping out your living quarters at the rear.

Chief Folley, HM1 Lees, HM1 Zimmerman, and I bunked together. We established ourselves at the top of the dam, near the aid station, and set out to make it the sweetest spot there. I pushed the corpsmen to improve their position as well. We set up a small gym with a dip bar and a sit-up bench. We set up a lounge area. I had the corpsmen build a wall around the squad bay they were sleeping in so that they could install an air-conditioning unit and have a little comfort. Chief and I had our biggest coup by finagling a satellite TV rig, complete with the converter box you need to descramble the Armed Forces Network. It wasn't a big deal, just a few backdoor deals with a Navy chaplain at al-Asad and a couple of Army Blackhawk helicopter pilots, and all of a sudden we had real-time access to football games or whatever else was on. Captain Jake Jenkins, the CO of Headquarters and Service Company, could never quite figure out how we managed it, but we were generous. We brought our box down to their setup on Sundays and the entire battalion could watch football together. Then I would sneak the box back up to our room, where I became addicted to the TV show *Charmed*, which ran for a couple of hours every afternoon. I took a lot of grief for that, but come on, three cute witches on TV or a bunch of sweaty corpsmen in real life—which would you rather watch?

The Marines had started going out on their combat patrols as soon as we arrived at the dam, and the line corpsmen who were assigned to their units were patrolling with them. (My team was split between the corpsmen that were embedded within each Marine platoon and the company command units, and another group that manned the Battalion Aid Station.) I wanted the Marines to know that they could rely on me and my corpsmen, so I made a point of going out on patrols as well. That surprised a lot of the Marines; doctors usually stay as far away from the dangerous stuff as they can. But I thought it was important to show them that medical was part of the team, that they could count on us all the way. There wasn't a lot of activity in our patrol region at first, though. The Marines ran into a few roadside bombs and improvised explosive devices, or IEDs, and found and destroyed several enemy weapons caches, but we avoided combat casualties at the beginning of our deployment.

The truth is, even in Iraq, finding ways to deal with downtime is a big part of military life, and we had a lot of downtime at Haditha Dam. It might just be because I don't like being bored myself, but I think it's an important part of any command to keep your men on their toes, too. There are a lot of ways to do that. We trained and practiced trauma procedures all the time, and worked out as a unit every day. We played a lot of cards and everyone took full advantage of his daily half hour in the battalion Internet café. But that still left a lot of time to get bored. So I was relieved when the chance came up in July to go down to Fallujah for a month with our battalion commander, Lieutenant Colonel Gareth Brandl, and a group of Marines. The U.S. military had set up a large firm base at a former Iraqi army post on the outskirts of town, and the detachment from the 1/8 was heading in to help with security and stabilization operations around the perimeter of the city. Truth be known, I was starting to feel left out of the war again, stuck up at our now-cushy quarters in the dam and far away from the action.

I almost didn't get to go, and I owe Mark Winn for fixing that.

He knew I was bored because I'd complain about that every time he came up to our room to complain about the colonel. Mark convinced Lieutenant Colonel Brandl that it would be useful to have a senior Navy guy along to talk with the Camp Fallujah medical staff in case we took casualties there—send an enlisted man in and the snooty Navy doctors would blow him off. I loved Mark for saying that, and it might even have been true. But Bryan Zimmerman was not happy. It meant he'd be staying back at the dam on sick-call duty. And there wasn't a man among us who didn't want to get down off that dam and into someplace a little more interesting. It wasn't the only time I would piss off Zimmerman, I'm afraid. He was qualified to take the lead, and he wanted that responsibility. But I assured him that we would all get our chance in the breach. Not knowing how true those words would end up being, I left Zimmerman in charge at the dam and packed up for the eight-hour motor march down to Fallujah.

To be honest, the best thing about the mission was the Camp Fallujah latrines, or "heads," which is the nautical term and definitely the most polite word for a toilet or its equivalent in the Marine Corps. They were a sort of deluxe port-a-potty setup, about eight of them mounted together on a trailer, with a flush system and air-conditioning. Standard port-a-potties can be a nightmare; all the blue sanitizing fluid in the world can't fight the effects of overuse, poor maintenance, and 120-degree heat. And there is always the risk of splash-back from the holding tank; catch a little blue juice on the backside in the morning and you don't feel right about yourself all day. Add in the chances that some wiseass would plop a few stones down the aerating vent just to screw with you, and there was no way you could come out of one of those plastic booths with a positive experience. At Camp Fallujah, the only worry was that the guy before you didn't get a satisfactory flush out of the low-volume water tank. All you had to do, though, was time the trip right and arrive just as the cleaning staff was leaving. It was a half-mile walk across sun-baked open terrain from our tents on the outskirts of Camp Fallujah to the cool, clean heaven of those heads, and it was worth every sweltering step of the hike.

Fallujah was hot in more ways than one, though. We were taking sporadic mortar fire most days, and even some shrapnel through the top of our tent. The insurgents scored a hit on one of our ammo dumps, too, and when it blew up, it blew up good. We all just kept going about our business—there's nothing you can do but let the thing burn itself out—but it must have been cooking off for twelve hours straight. Most of the mortar fire was relatively harmless, though, and the guys firing them at us didn't seem to have much of a clue what they were doing. I'll be forever grateful for that. I was about halfway into my half-mile hike to the heads one day when I heard the whistling noise of an incoming mortar shell. I looked around and saw it hit about two hundred yards to my right. *Bam!* A moment to reload, and another one comes down two hundred yards to my left. *Bam!*

Holy crap, I thought, *they're bracketing!*—adjusting their aim to zero in on a target, which I figured had to be me. I sprang into action, sprinting across the berm I was on and diving headlong into a ditch, where I realized that it was very unlikely that an insurgent was wasting rounds trying to kill me; I had just happened to be in the middle of two wild shots and got scared. Sure enough, the mortar fire stopped as soon as I hit the deck.

But the first sergeant and company gunny who saw my crazy dash? Those guys are probably still laughing.

One of my favorite things to do in Fallujah was to go out with Marines on patrol so I could get a sense of the place. On one of the last nights we were there, I went out with a group of combat engineers led by Sergeant Paul "PJ" Stephens. A very large weapons cache had been found in the middle of a field, buried in ten old septic tanks. Our job was to assemble the stuff from one loaded underground tank and blow it up. The problem was that the floor was piled waist deep with grenades and ammo, mortars, AKs, plastic explosives, all kinds of dangerous stuff. You did not want to step on anything or jump into the hole because there was nowhere to stand. So we came up with a plan: Sergeant Stephens and I took turns holding a flashlight in our teeth while we were held by the ankles and lowered headfirst into the tank, time and again, until we had cleared enough space on the floor for us to climb inside and stand. It took us more than seven hours to empty the thing. But we still couldn't blow it up until after the sun came up and we'd given the community time to say their morning prayers. I guess we were being polite. In the meantime, however, we were stuck in our vehicle, waiting. I was trying not to fall asleep, but there was a young corporal in the car named Marshall Davidson who was in the mood for some conversation. He asked me what I was going to do when I left the Navy, what kind of doctor I was I going to be. I told him I was planning to become a urologist. Well, that lit him up. He couldn't wait to tell me all about his big nuts. In fact, that was all he wanted to talk about for two hours straight: what makes nuts get so big and whether that was a problem or could it mean he had a tumor. I was at a loss—but it completely entertained everyone else in the truck. I guess I wasn't surprised to learn that everybody called him Nuts Davidson.

We were laughing that morning, but we were all well aware of how dangerous these patrols could be. And I guess it was appropriate somehow that our first real tragedy happened there on the outskirts of Fallujah. The Scout Sniper platoon was out on a covert mission around the edges of the city, when their position was given away by a passing goatherd. The goats startled when they passed the concealed Marines. So a combat patrol drove in to extract the snipers before insurgents could zero in. HM2 Johns was out with the combat patrol that morning, July 20, 2004, just about seven thirty a.m., because they could hear the dawn call to prayer coming from the nearby mosques. The call can sound ominous to American ears, especially if you're already on edge, but it was nowhere near as chilling as the taunts of a crowd of teenage boys the convoy soon passed. "American! American! Fuck you, American. Boom! Boom!" Three hundred yards up the road, an IED (three 155-millimeter artillery rounds and two rocket-propelled grenades) detonated in a massive fireball just after the lead Humvee passed by. The vehicles were spaced out—standard procedure to ensure that only one is hit at a time—and the Marines piled out of their Humvees to establish a security perimeter. Word came back: wounded Marines. Johns handed off his weapon, grabbed his med bag, and started sprinting the 150 meters to the lead truck. "I wasn't even thinking about it for the first hundred meters," Johns recalls now, "but then it hit me. This is how they initiate ambushes. We're going to get hit right now, and I'm running down the middle of the road by myself." That, at least, didn't happen, and Johns reached the

In front of the government center Forward Aid Station (FAS), with ambulance crews. Front row (left to right): HA Daniel Avila, HA Ernesto Argueta (behind), the author (seated, with cup), HM1 Bryan Zimmerman, HM3 David McArdle, HM3 Thomas Stahura, HN Collin Stedman. Back row (left to right): SFC Rick Cary, HM2 Shawn Johns (behind), SPC Robert Cook, 2LT Todd Wilson (with cap), SPC Byron Ferrell, SSG Thomas Brennan, SPC James Strock, SGT Jeremy Hurt.

Preparing the Check Point 84 Battalion Aid Station (BAS) as the battle approaches.

On the eve of Fallujah: With the M113 armored ambulances at the 1/8's battalion assembly position, we held a final briefing on casualty evacuation procedures. (The railway berm is visible in the distance.)

BAS security. HM2 Steve Meszaros and HM3 David Lester test out antimortar fortifications at the Battalion Aid Station.

Captain Gregory Starace, the 1/8's Intelligence Officer, explains the plan of battle to 1/8's company and platoon commanders and other battalion leaders. Battalion Commanding Officer is seated to Captain Starace's left, partially obscured.

A little recreation on top of Haditha Dam, in the helicopter landing zone. Kneeling (left to right): HA Avila, HN Roger Millhouse, HM3 Martin Graves. Standing (left to right): HM2 Johns, HM1 Zimmerman, HMC Russell Folley, HM3 McArdle, HM3 Lester, HN Stedman, HM3 Jobriath Burn, HM2 Meszaros, HA Argueta.

Sanitation duty: HA Argueta does his part for base morale. Marine "heads" (toilets) in the desert don't flush. They burn—with help from junior corpsmen.

HM3 Kevin Markley. As senior corpsman for Bravo Company, he brought more wounded Marines to our aid stations than any other corpsman.

The cultural center ambush: Bravo Company Sergeant Lonny Wells is down in the street; Gunnery Sergeant Ryan Shane, and HN Joel Lambotte (standing) rush in to help—both are wounded moments later.

Bravo Company takes cover by a low wall alongside the cultural center.

Protected by the wall, the author (middle) helps lift a severely wounded Bravo Company Marine onto a stretcher.

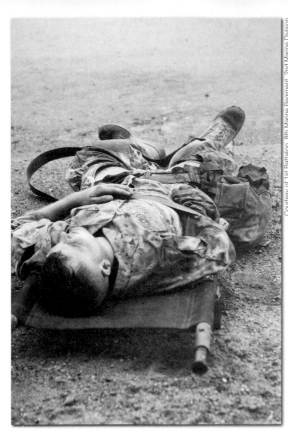

Bravo Company Private First Class Samuel Crist, wounded rescuing downed men at the cultural center ambush, ready to load onto the ambulance.

Loading a wounded Marine onto the ambulance.

Gunny Shane from the 1/8, wounded and waiting for transport.

HA Argueta and HM1 Zimmerman restocking supplies at the government center FAS, after a mass casualty event.

HM3 Burn (right) and HN John Paul Rosales (left) transport a wounded Iraqi to the Forward Aid Station.

West Virginia Army National Guard armored ambulance driver SPC Strock at the government center FAS returning from casualty evacuation (HA Argueta behind).

The author (center) with the 1/8's senior Petty Officers, HM1 Zimmerman (left) and HM1 Rick Lees (right), after the battle.

II MEF Command Master Chief Joe Langholtz visiting our corpsmen after the battle (HM3 Lucas Jushinski [left] and HM1 Zimmerman [right]). The men were "pinned"—awarded their Fleet Marine Force warfare device signaling competency in the Marine Corps.

The motto and motivator of the medical team at the 1/8. This was written wherever we set up shop.

lead vehicle just as a Humvee from another unit pulled up with another corpsman.

The two men climbed up to the top of the high-back Humvee, an open-topped version of the vehicle with seating for as many as eight Marines in a steel-sided rear compartment. It was the first real combat casualty in Johns's seven years as a corpsman, and it was bad. "I worked EMS at the fire department before," Johns says. "I'd seen car wrecks, and some of 'em were pretty bad. But nothing in my life prepared me to see this." Corporal Todd J. Godwin, a twenty-one-year-old scout sniper from Muskingum County, Ohio, was the first man from the 1/8 to be killed in action. Our first KIA. "He took one piece of shrapnel," Johns says. "Just one big freak piece of shrapnel." The spinning chunk of metal struck Corporal Godwin on the right jaw with such force that it punched clear through the back of his neck, killing the Marine instantly; the men sitting all around him were covered in blood, but entirely unharmed. Todd Godwin was known as a caring, loyal, and good-natured Marine, the kind of guy who just smoothed tense situations over and brightened the situation, no matter what. His parents later said that they were sure that if Todd had known that one man in that Humvee was going to be hit by the IED that day, he would have said, "Please let it be me, not my friend."

"We drove Corporal Godwin back to Bravo Surgical," Johns recalls, "and we didn't have to stop at a single gate on the way in. Everybody knew we were coming, and the guards all stood at attention as we passed by." Chief Folley, HM1 Lees, and I were waiting for the truck when they pulled into Bravo Surgical; we had been told that Corporal Godwin was still alive. Johns just put his head down, started to cry, and walked away. "I slept for two days after that," Johns says. "First time I woke up, I woke up scared to death, replaying the whole thing in my head. The chaplain was there, asking if I was all right. 'Yes, Sir, I'm fine,' I said, but he tried to talk to me about God and stuff, and I had to tell him, 'Sir, I don't care.'" Johns was shutting down, and it was hard to blame him. We all felt the loss of this young Marine, and I recognized my own frustration at not being able to do anything in Johns's eyes. But the stakes were getting higher and I needed Johns back. He was a crucial part of our team, the main interface between the staff and the junior corpsman. He had a tough first death, but Johns showed a lot of strength and came back full force.

We returned to Haditha on August 4, 2004—Johns's birthday, by coincidence—and found that the rest of the battalion had been having an even harder time. In fact, we would take over thirty casualties between July 14 and October 23, 2004. One of the worst incidents had happened while I was away in Fallujah. A detachment of about twenty Marines was stationed at the Haditha police station, working with the police and helping them to patrol the city. On July 15 a suicide bomber drove his vehicle into the station, and it exploded, wounding eight of our Marines. They were evacuated back to the dam, where HM1 Zimmerman did an outstanding job of handling the situation. Our battalion formed a lot of close ties with the Haditha police department, and it was horrifying to hear how quickly that area descended into chaos after we pulled out. Not long afterward, a band of insurgents rounded up dozens of police officers in Haditha and executed them publicly in a soccer stadium.

I was already starting to learn that boredom can be a blessing, but that lesson wouldn't truly be hammered home for months to come. What was good about being settled in at the Haditha Dam was the e-mail access and the fact that we could get time on the satellite phone fairly often as well. Probably for 80 percent of the time I was in Iraq with the 1/8, Melissa and I had daily contact. The time difference could be rough on her, though, because it was eight hours earlier in North Carolina than it was in Iraq. I'd try to call as late in my day as I could, but I didn't always have a lot of control over that. Melissa lived with her cell phone on, she said, and certainly never complained even if I called in the middle of her night. On earlier deployments, we'd used a coded e-mail system so that I could let her know my approximate whereabouts without giving our position away. I did the same in Iraq so she would have a rough idea of where we were, and then she would learn the rest of the story from the newspaper; sometimes she ended up knowing where I was going before I knew myself. And I always tried to tell her if I was going to be away from e-mail or sat-phone access for more than a day or two, so she wouldn't worry if she didn't hear from me.

Meanwhile, we continued to train and drill, and Chief Russ Folley and I did what we could to keep morale up and ourselves amused. Card games, especially spades, were a key element in that program, and Chief Folley and I always played together as a team. Spades is a simple game: two teams of two, you try to capture as many hands as you can. But this wasn't about complexity, it was about bragging rights. Chief and I had a system all worked out with hand signals. Yes, we cheated in almost every game we played, but it's okay. That was all part of our plan to build morale and team cohesion.

It's such a simple thing, but it's true—just sitting there and playing cards is a great equalizer between staff and enlisted, and when you have this game in front of you, it allows you to talk about everything else. That gave the guys a chance to vent some of their frustrations, too; you can call your medical officer or your chief an A-hole to his face over a deck of cards in a way that maybe you can't when you're on duty, and maybe getting it out helped them to calm down a bit and focus on their work. Don't get me wrong, we gave as good as we got, and we never let it get out of hand. But I knew that I needed these guys to be able to tell me when I was doing something stupid, and I think we established that kind of relationship pretty well, up there at the dam. The intense competition helps, too. Chief and I are older and a little slicker than the corpsmen, plus we were cheating, so we almost always won. That got the corpsmen incredibly worked up, which was fun to watch. But it also helped them pull together as a team. With every loss, they became more and more determined to find a way to win. And whenever they did beat us, it was huge: joyful smiles and high fives all around.

There's a lot of cursing and rough behavior in my line of work, the kind of stuff that would get any civilian manager sued or fired in a heartbeat. But when you're working with several dozen amped-up guys out in the middle of nowhere, having a relaxed attitude about busting on each other helps to keep good order and good morale. The Navy has strict rules about harassment and hazing, and Chief in particular kept a tight lid on anything that crossed the line. But there's an awful lot of stress that builds up on any kind of deployment, and a little rough humor can help relieve the tension, build some camaraderie, and pass the time. Navy rules against officers fraternizing with the enlisted Sailors can be pretty restrictive, too, but I was the senior Navy guy out there, so I didn't let that get in the way.

Rules are good, but sometimes you need to just do the right thing, because you know it's the right thing to do.

I really couldn't have asked for a better group of corpsmen, from Chief Folley on down, and that made everything easier for me. Russ Folley is a Cajun from St. Martinville, Louisiana, and he's still got a pretty good dose of that crazy bayou accent. He says no one could understand a word he said when he first joined the Navy about twenty years ago. Folley is a very savvy guy, and even though he had not done a lot of deployments at that time, he had a very good sense of how to do it, and of how to take care of Sailors on deployment. We got along very well, and in the end he probably did more than anyone to keep me sane out there. We had similar opinions on how to spend downtime as well. We did a lot of work fixing up our quarters, building shelves and whatnot, and we had a lot of fun razzing the corpsmen together. We actually made them move quarters twice while we were at the dam, for their own good and to their total discontent. We used to laugh a lot about how they would rather sit and bitch in bad accommodations than get busy and make the situation better. As time went on at the dam, we ran a cable from the TV in our quarters down to the corpsmen's area, so that they could watch what we were watching, but only what we were watching. *Fear Factor* was a popular show, mostly because of all the female contestants. That led to a favorite trick: we'd wait until one of the female contestants was about to climb out of a swimming pool, and flip channels to *Jeopardy!* That would get Chief cackling every time. Alex Trebek was no substitute for a wet T-shirt, and the corpsmen let us know it more than once. We both took our licks from the corpsmen, too. They mostly made fun of his cheesy little mustache (Chief Folley spent a little more time on his appearance than the rest of us) and my wandering eyeball. I guess Folley had the advantage on that one because he could've shaved his defect off if he wanted to.

Folley took care of those corpsmen like they were his children, but he could be a strict parent when he had to be. He kept a close watch on the corpsmen's attitudes and behavior, and would bend over backward to help one of them out. But if a corpsman ever screwed with Chief—especially if one promised to do something and then went back on his word—watch out. Chief's only real defect was the fact that he never liked anybody to sleep in. If he was up, everybody should be up, no matter what time it was. Even that wouldn't have been so bad if it hadn't been for his favorite wake-up call: "Wakey, wakey, time for eggs and bakey!" I have no idea what kind of ridiculous bayou crap that was, but it sure did annoy the hell out of all of us.

HM1 Rick Lees took on a lot of the hard work of daily operations for our aid station, "Freeing Chief up to be Chief" is how he said it. He's a serious guy, a seventeen-year veteran at the time, and you got the impression that he was born an old man. I've never seen such self-control. He loved these little candies called Runts, but he would ration himself to just one or two a day to make them last. And he was the only smoker in the battalion who never had to break down and buy Iraqi cigarettes, because he always made sure he had just enough American Camel Lights to last him until the next mail call, and that included getting up two or three times in the middle of every night to go out and have a smoke by himself. But Lees took a lot of care and patience mentoring the corpsmen, and he was very strict about discipline, which I thought was great because it let me goof off more. He was very good at logistics and administration, too. More than anyone else, he always knew where everything was and where it was going. His attention to detail saved us many times over during the chaos and turmoil of the Battle of Fallujah. But Lees's most impressive talent was for packing. I swear he could fold a month's worth of supplies into a day pack. The highlight for the corpsmen was that he managed to find space for the 1/8 battalion mascot—a beat-up ugly old rubber rat that has evidently been on every 1/8 deployment since Vietnam—in our shipping container back at Camp Lejeune. Johns and three other corpsmen had been trying for days to get all of our supplies into the crate, and couldn't do it. HM1 Lees came by and repacked it top to bottom, getting all the gear in and the rat, too. Lees pissed the corpsmen off to no end with his meticulous, by-the-book approach to everything, but he'll always be a hero for fitting that rat in the box.

My other hospital corpsman first class, Bryan Zimmerman, was essentially the opposite of HM1 Lees. Zimmerman was an excellent IDC, but he had a wild streak that earned him the nickname "Freak Show" and made even me uncomfortable sometimes. He knew his medicine very well, though, and handled sick call for us often. He could have been an IDC on a ship without a doctor's supervision, no problem. Zimmerman was hypercompetitive, and I think that's why he was good at medicine; he never wanted to lose. But I was concerned about his maturity level, and his lack of trauma experience. HM1 Zimmerman was eager for responsibility, and Chief and I rubbed him the wrong way plenty of times by not letting him be the boss. We became very good friends, though, because of all the things we went through together, and it would probably piss him off to hear me say it, but I think he matured quite a bit over the deployment.

HM1 Zimmerman was also a good motivator for the junior guys. We were helping them study for a qualification called the Fleet Marine Force pin, which involves getting boarded—passing an oral exam on just about every detail of the Marine Corps, from history to weapons to organization. Zimmerman spent several hours on his own initiative coming up with a quiz game to help everyone study, and without a doubt that helped them pass the time, and the test. He also ran, and won, a fantasy football league for us, and organized a lot of flag football games. But he never lost his freaky side either. Just before we left the dam for Fallujah, Zimmerman organized a group "streak the dam" run for all the Navy personnel there. There was no way I was going to participate, and not just because they planned to do it in the middle of the night. But the corpsmen were so excited, and they insisted that everyone *had* to do it. HM1 Lees sat it out and Chief Folley took the photos, and I did my best to keep up with the pack. Am I proud? I don't know. But how many people can say that they've run across an Iraqi dam at one o'clock in the morning, wearing nothing but combat boots and a goofy grin? The event may not have done much for our local political relationships, but it was the final bit of glue that would keep our team cemented together through the hard times ahead.

HM2 Shawn Johns was an E5, the middle rung of the Navy's pay grade scale, and that made him our equivalent of a sergeant. The junior corpsmen actually did call him Sarge, when they weren't calling him worse, and he rode those guys hard. If you didn't know him, you wouldn't have been able to tell that he was doing it for their own good and not just because he was pissed off at the world and looking for someone to take it out on—most of the time. His other nickname was Misery P.O., for Petty Officer, and it seemed that he was at his happiest being his most unhappy. Then again, Johns was twenty-eight and had to deal with a gang of chuckleheaded kids all day, every day. He ate, slept, showered, and fought with them nonstop. Johns and Chief hammered home the point to the corpsmen that it was their job to help the Marines no matter what. Chief emphasized the Second Marine Division corpsmen's motto: "Through the gates of hell for a wounded Marine." Johns focused on the less-high-minded reality that there is nothing a Marine hates more than a shitbird. The meaning of that term varies. It can include anything from not keeping your uniform in good condition and falling behind on a run to showing cowardice under fire. But the implication is clear: unreliable, a liability. "Shitbird" is probably the dirtiest word in the Marine vocabulary.

Johns is a big guy, and he served some time as an Army infantryman before he came over to the Navy. Together with HM3 Ryan Hirkala (Hirk, or "OCD," as we called him), Johns was the most immediate help for any of the corpsmen who were having trouble, even if in Johns's case it tended to be tough love. He had a very good head on his shoulders, and he would end up being the real mainstay of our Forward Aid Station in Fallujah. Right through the worst of the battle, if I had to put a number on it, I would say he was probably responsible for a full 50 percent of our success, Misery P.O. or not.

Hirkala, on the other hand, was just a very sweet kid: as blond as a Swedish bikini team member, a little on the shy side, and more in love with his wife than just about any man I've ever seen. He also happened to have all the classic symptoms of obsessive-compulsive disorder, thus the nickname. No quirk, unusual physical characteristic, or personal challenge goes untaunted in a military outfit, and Hirk took his licks like a champ. It was almost too easy, but watching him freak out after finding out that the Oreo he was eating had been on the floor could be enough to keep everyone entertained for hours. His neat-freak ways could be irritating up at the dam, but he was the most organized person you could imagine. Hirk's quirks were an asset around the aid station. He literally became a lifesaver on several occasions because he had everything so well organized and had obsessively checked the supplies over so many times that he could always find just what you needed at a moment's notice.

Like me, a lot of the Marines and corpsmen had wives or girlfriends and young children at home. Melissa and I had been through deployments before, so we had an advantage, but the big difference this time was that Melissa had MacKenzie to take care of as well. She says that was a help for her, because she had someone to look after and something to keep her busy all the time, but of course that was also a lot of work. I was supposed to find a babysitter before I left for Iraq, but I didn't get it done in time. Fortunately, Missy managed to find a good one, and she ended up going back to work after ten weeks. Melissa isn't the kind of person who asks for a lot of help, but she says taking care of MacKenzie on her own changed her in that regard. "You just ask for help and you take it," Melissa said later. "You don't fight it." My parents were there right from the get-go. They moved into our house when Missy went into the base hospital to get induced and they were great. They had our room all ready when we got back, dinner on the table, the whole thing. We had only two days together because we got home from the hospital on a Monday, and I left on Wednesday. I was worried that she would be lonely. But it worked out really quite well. "Friends from college, friends from all parts of my life would come and just be at my doorstep," is how Melissa described it. "I know no one talked to each other, but you couldn't have planned it any better." Every few weeks, a new friend would show up—usually without their husbands, maybe with a child or two of their own—and settle in for a week or two of "girl time."

I found out later that the first weeks were the hardest on Melissa, and I guess that's no surprise. She was working in a private pediatrics clinic at the time, but she says it was too hard emotionally to take MacKenzie to her colleagues for checkups. "I actually couldn't go back at first," she remembers. "I was just such a wreck. I was so emotional, and I guess it's something I didn't want them to see." Melissa took MacKenzie to a pediatrician on base at first, but after a couple of weeks, she took MacKenzie into her own clinic. They joked with her that they thought they were going to have to call social services because she hadn't been getting care for our new baby, but they were very supportive. And when Melissa did go back to work, it became an important source of information for her. It's one of the advantages of living in a military community; many of Melissa's patients were the children of the wives of Marines and Sailors who were also deployed to Iraq, and she says that all the mothers there became a support network for each other. The Marine Corps has a family support system called the Key Volunteer Network. Spouses of Marines and Sailors in the unit act as a link between the battalion and family members, and send e-mails or make phone calls to all the families to share information and check in on everyone to see how they're doing. "But I received the majority of my information from mothers who would bring their children into the office for a visit," Melissa says.

Most of the military moms were quite a bit younger than Melissa is and they hadn't been through as many deployments as we had, so I bet she was a lot of support for them. Sometimes, she says, the kids weren't even that sick, but that was okay. Missy would examine the children and then start talking with the mothers about how they were doing. One thing was tough on her, though: a lot of the younger mothers would tell her things like "Oh, your husband is fine, he's just one of the doctors over there. He's not where my husband is up at the front line." That was hard for Melissa to hear. She knew that no one was ever really safe in Iraq, doctor or not. And she knew me. She knew that I wouldn't be sitting at the rear if I could help it.

We took several more casualties during our final months at the dam, including one Marine who lost part of his foot to a mine, and another suicide-vehicle mass casualty in October. On August 18, 2004, we suffered our second combat loss. Weapons Company Sergeant Richard M. Lord was killed by shrapnel when the vehicle he was in was hit by an IED. Known as Ricky to his family and friends, Sergeant Lord, from Fanning Springs, Florida, was a well-respected Marine and a gifted leader who always made an extra effort to take care of the people in his life. He died two days before his twenty-fifth birthday and left behind two young sons; his fiancée, Rosanna Powers, had lost her brother, Marine Lance Corporal Caleb Powers of the 2/4, just the day before. Lance Corporal Powers was also killed in enemy action in al-Anbar province. HN Eric Matos was the first corpsman on the scene and he did all the right things; in fact, Sergeant Lord was relatively stable for a while. It might not have been a survivable wound, even with immediate surgical care, but I was concerned about how long the medevac flight down from al-Asad took. I talk all the time about how critical communications and evacuation routes are. It was one of the first things that Will Dutton and I had realized years earlier while I was on my first tour as a battalion surgeon. Losing Sergeant Lord emphasized the point, whether faster evacuation could have saved him or not.

We would go on to lose two more men before our deployment at the dam was over: Lance Corporals Michael J. Halal and Cesar F. Machado-Olmos, both members of Headquarters & Service Company, were killed in a nighttime vehicle rollover accident on September 13. They were returning from escorting a bulldozer out to Charlie Company so they could fortify their position along the main route from the Syrian border to Ramadi. The convoy was driving without lights to avoid attacks, with the drivers using night-vision goggles. But the road was steeply embanked and the vehicle ended up rolling into a ditch, and the two Marines were killed. Michael Halal was twenty-two, from Glendale, Arizona. He had actually gone AWOL from the Corps for a short time but came back after the terror attacks of 9/11. Lance Corporal Halal realized his mistake and had the courage to admit it and face the consequences. He paid his dues—taking a pay cut and spending time in the brig—and he refused the opportunity to leave the Corps once he had served his time. The Marine had come back to stand with his brothers no matter what, and that was what he was going to do. Lance Corporal Halal earned a reputation as a tough, determined Marine. And though he didn't know it, he also earned his promotion to corporal. It became official, his mother says, "the day that he entered the gates of heaven." Cesar Machado-Olmos, from Spanish Fork, Utah, died just one week before his twenty-first birthday. Machado-Olmos was a specialist who worked with water-purification systems and other hygiene equipment, and he was very gentle for a Marine. A permanent resident of the U.S., he loved America enough to serve it before he could become a citizen. Lance Corporal Machado-Olmos was granted American citizenship after his death, and he earned it with honor, dedication, and sacrifice.

My assistant battalion surgeon finally reported for duty toward the end of August. Carlos Kennedy was a tall, laid-back guy, just out of his surgical internship, who managed to be sort of nerdy and suave at the same time. Lieutenant Kennedy was one of the new doctors who I initially thought might relieve me partway into the deployment, but as it worked out I was lucky just to get an assistant. Chief Folley went down to al-Asad with a convoy to pick him up, and the three of us sat around the night they got back to try to get to know each other a little. Kennedy was a smart guy, we could tell that right away, and he had his eye on orthopedic surgery. He had spent some time in the Washington Hospital Center trauma center, and he was a little older than the corpsmen, in his late twenties. But he was still green. You could tell that he wanted to be the take-charge guy, but I think he saw that Chief and I already had that covered and he did his best to fit in to our system. It was good to have another medical officer on board, and another pair of surgeon's hands to rely on. There were going to be times ahead when we really needed them.

The Marines continued their patrol duty, and despite the nerve-wracking prospect of running into IEDs and sniper fire, the work was going well. I credit the discipline and seriousness of our battalion leadership, which is something that spreads down quickly through the ranks. I don't know if the people of Haditha were glad to have us there or not, but we maintained good relations with them. The Marines and the corpsmen made a big effort to be friendly wherever they went, and it was common now for children to run out to patrols when they passed by. The kids were attracted by the novelty and the candy that the Marines handed out, no doubt, but still, when the kids are running up to patrols, their parents aren't planting roadside bombs. I think we developed some real trust and friendship with the people of Haditha, and we all wanted our presence there to help make their lives better.

Our battalion was having a lot of interactions with Iraqi people at that point, and almost all of them were positive. I tend to like Iraqis—they're very friendly as a culture, and I almost always found some way to relate to all of the people I interacted with. There are definitely some cultural differences, and more than once I'm sure I was hoodwinked by a fast-talking street vendor. There's always a negotiation over everything, which is kind of fun, even if you know you're not coming out on top. But, like I say, most of my interactions were positive.

There was one significant exception to that rule, though. A unit of Iraqi support forces had joined us at Haditha, and they set up their base on the opposite side of the dam. I don't think anyone had ever seen such shitbirds, and they became a major headache for Mark Winn. He's a big neat fanatic, and kept on our guys about things like littering around the dam. Then the Iraqis show up and start dumping stuff all over the place and into the river: trash, garbage, old food. We would all have ended up with the plague if it had been up to those guys. But that was nothing compared to what happened when they started using our heads. Cultural differences are expected, and maybe I can't tell you to stop polluting your own river, but I can sure as hell speak up when you start smearing shit all over the inside of my port-a-potty.

The problem really came down to technology as much as culture. Iraqi toilets are usually just a ceramic hole in the floor that you're supposed to squat over. There's no throne, nowhere to sit down. Evidently it works fine when you're wearing a dishdasha, or man-skirt, as Johns liked to call the traditional dress; just lift your robes and down you go. But it's hell with utilities on, and you run a serious risk of messing up the color scheme of the official Marine Corps camouflage pattern. But try to take the Iraqi approach into an American head and the problem is a thousand times worse. These guys would squat down over the seat and let fly from a height. Then to finish it off, they wouldn't use toilet paper—never shake an Iraqi's left hand—and that's how the feces hit the wall; wipe with your hand, then wipe your hand on the wall to clean it off.

One day we had good, decent American port-a-potties. Twenty-four hours later, we had sun-baked boxes of shit: shit on the walls, shit on the seats, piles of shit everywhere. I can't tell you how much shit. And it's not like they didn't have their own facilities. They just fouled them so much that they started coming over to use ours. I lost my mind—and I thought the corpsmen were going to march across the dam with their M16s out. We just couldn't believe it. Okay. So I think, improve your position, affect your sphere of influence. (The concept of a "sphere of influence" is something I've come to believe in more and more strongly through the years; there are some things you can change, and there are some you just can't. Knowing the difference and sticking to the problems you can solve, the issues you can affect, is one of the best ways I know of to keep from going crazy in the military, or in life for that matter. If you can solve a problem, you have a responsibility to do it; if you can't, then you have to let it go.)

We took the doors off, figuring the Iraqis would be too modest to do their business in the open. No good; they brought pieces of wood over with them to block the door and they'd go in and shit on the floor. I went over and talked to their colonel. A little cross-cultural dialogue and we'd get some understanding, I figured. The conversation that followed taught me everything I ever needed to know about international diplomacy:

"It's a little unhygienic the way you guys are using the shitter," I said through an interpreter. "I mean, you go up and you stand on the seat. I don't get it."

"Well, we don't understand why you don't think it's unhygienic to put your ass on the same seat that someone else has put their ass on," he responded.

Hmm, okay, a small but possibly valid point, I conceded. "However, the wiping your hands on the wall with shit doesn't make any sense whatsoever."

"Well, you've got to get the shit off your hand."

"Why not use the paper?"

"We don't like to use the paper because that sticks to our hand."

I think that's what the State Department types call an impasse. We called it unacceptable, and I finally just put hasps on the doors and locked our heads down. It was a lot less convenient for us, but it got the Iraqi troops back to fouling the facilities on their own side of the dam. And the added hassle wouldn't matter for much longer. Word came down in October that we would all be moving out for Camp Fallujah at the beginning of November. You could feel the change in the air that last week; nighttime temperatures were starting to cool off, but there was something different in the men's faces and voices as well. No date was set, but no one doubted now that we would be going into the insurgent stronghold soon, that the battle was finally coming.

Lieutenant Kutilek, the fearless Weapons Company platoon leader who I would come to depend on for security time and again in Fallujah, has a favorite picture from our time at the dam. It was taken shortly before we moved on to Fallujah for the assault. In the photograph, Kutilek is standing on a wide barren hill—open desert really, the most desolate hillside you can imagine—next to a little Iraqi boy who's sitting sidesaddle on a small white donkey, a red-and-white-checked kaffiyeh headscarf half covering his face. Kutilek has his helmet off, and the shy little boy and the strong, stern Marine are both squinting into the desert sun. His name was Achmed, a goatherder's son following his family's meager flock. "Unfortunately I didn't meet him until near the end," Kutilek says now. "I would have stopped by and seen that kid over and over." Kutilek and his men gave the Iraqi boy all the candy, food, and water he could carry, and Achmed and his donkey went on their way. "We had three missions over there," Kutilek says. "First and foremost, to kill bad guys. Second, to help any other coalition forces. And third, to help innocent Iraqi civilians. I would have liked to have been able to do more to help that little boy and his family." There wasn't much he could do for Achmed, though. The battalion was due on the outskirts of Fallujah in just one week, and no one doubted what our mission there was going to be.

CHAPTER 8

At the Gates of Hell

W*e suck. I mean, we really, really suck.* That's exactly what I remember thinking as we drove through the gathering dusk along the northern perimeter of Fallujah on November 6, 2004. I had talked my way into joining a reconnaissance run that the battalion command element was taking along the route we would use to attack in two days, and I didn't like what I was seeing.

It wasn't the pissing rain that bothered me, though it was a surprise in Iraq, and it wasn't the sporadic mortar and machine-gun fire we ran into along the way. It was the distance from the rear to the front. This was the first time I'd traveled the route, and it took us a good forty-five minutes to drive from our base at Camp Fallujah to Checkpoint 84, more than two kilometers north of the railroad tracks that run along the northern edge of Fallujah. Checkpoint 84 would serve as our regimental ambulance exchange point. Any casualties we took in the city would be evacuated to Checkpoint 84, and from there transported by truck convoy to the base hospital at Camp Fallujah. And forty-five minutes was just too long. With the kind of injuries we were expecting, an untreated man could easily die in ten to fifteen minutes; five minutes or less if he had a serious arterial bleed. There was no way the system was going to work.

The full battalion had shifted down from Haditha the week before. The 1/8 was assigned quarters adjacent to Camp Fallujah, in a base that had been used in Saddam's day to train Iranian troops who had defected from Iraq's neighbor and bitter enemy. The Iranian Training Camp (ITC) was a decent little camp—bombed to hell at some point, but we sandbagged it up and made it comfortable enough to get by. But that position put us about a mile past the base hospital, coming out from the city. We could set up our Battalion Aid Station there, but what was the use? Our casualties would be coming out of the city and into the regimental evacuation system at Checkpoint 84, and from there straight to Camp Fallujah and Bravo Surgical Company. That would leave us out of the loop, and leave our wounded Marines without serious care for way longer than I was willing to tolerate.

The battle was coming. The presidential elections and the political wrangling in the U.S. were over. The delays and false starts were all used up. The civilian population had been evacuated and the full force of two Marine Regimental Combat Teams (RCT-1 and RCT-7) and an Army regiment were set to start driving the insurgents out of their urban stronghold in just two days. I knew that we were probably facing weeks of intense urban combat. I had looked at the predictions the military puts out for different combat scenarios, including the casualty table.

The estimates were sobering: based on past military experience we should expect 30 to 40 percent of our Marines to be wounded in the coming battle, with a disturbingly high proportion of killed in action (KIA) to wounded in action (WIA). This was going to be close, brutal, and deadly fighting. No one doubted that we were going to prevail in Fallujah, but that wasn't my worry. Victory was beyond my sphere of influence. I couldn't keep men from getting wounded either, but I could sure as hell try to keep wounded men from dying. "Okay, what can I touch here?" I asked myself. "What can I do to keep those KIA numbers as low as possible?"

Chief Folley, Carlos Kennedy, and I got to work, and we came up with a plan. We had to cut down the time it took our wounded Marines to get lifesaving care. We'd move our operation up to Checkpoint 84, we decided, and establish our Battalion Aid Station there, adjacent to the ambulance exchange point. The line corpsmen assigned to the combat units would provide first care to casualties, packing wounds, stabilizing as best they could, and getting the wounded men out of the city. Casualties would come to us at the BAS first, before being transferred into the regimental evacuation system. With our medical tent, we could provide almost everything short of full surgical intervention, and do it forty-five minutes sooner than the doctors at Bravo Surgical could. There would be risks, however. Checkpoint 84 was close enough to the city to take mortar and rocket fire, or even come under direct attack by a raiding party of insurgents. But the trade-off would be worth it if we could keep better track of our own wounded and prevent men from dying en route to the hospital.

Fallujah is a drab town, built on the eastern bank of the

Euphrates River and stretching out to the east for a couple of miles. A market center, it underwent a building boom in the 1980s as Saddam poured money into the region in an attempt to shore up his local support. The result was a grid work of some two thousand blocks of streets and alleyways laid out more or less on a regular north-south grid pattern and bisected by Highway 10, also called Main Street, which ran from Baghdad some thirty miles to the east, through the center of Fallujah, across the Euphrates, and on to Ramadi to the west. Neighborhoods to the north were primarily residential, composed of thousands of two-story cement houses surrounded by courtyards and high walls; to the south lay a large but decrepit industrial area and some of the shabbier residential neighborhoods. The highway would become an important objective for the advancing American forces, and the site of fallback resistance from the insurgents.

Higher headquarters had been working on a battle plan for months by the time we arrived at Camp Fallujah, but those of us on the ground didn't get our first look at it until shortly before the battle. Once the battalion had the regimental plan in hand, our leaders put a battalion operations plan together for the coming battle. Lieutenant Colonel Brandl, commanding officer of the 1/8, called a meeting in a large auditorium at Camp Fallujah, to walk us through the battle plan, with the aid of a huge, eight-foot-by-twelve-foot map of the city they had painted on the floor. It was quite a production, attended by the media as well as the battalion officers, and Lieutenant Colonel Brandl's words were picked up and transmitted around the world. "The Marines that I have had wounded over the past five months have been attacked by a faceless enemy," he said. "But the enemy has got a face. He's called Satan. He lives in

Fallujah. And we're going to destroy him." Strong words, but our CO had a point—we had lost four Marines and had another thirty wounded, and we had yet to face an enemy who would stand and fight.

We would be fighting as regiments in Fallujah, the four Marine and two Army battalions and the various air, artillery, and other specialized units divided into two Regimental Combat Teams. RCT-1, built around Third Battalion, Fifth Marines; Third Battalion, First Marines, and the Second Battalion of the U.S. Army's Seventh Cavalry Division, would take the western half of Fallujah. RCT-7, which included the 1/8 as well as First Battalion, Third Marines, who were reinforcing us from a MEU deployment, and the Army First Infantry Division's Task Force 2-2 battalion, would take the eastern half. There were Iraqi units attached to each American battalion, as well as various support units, and the Second Brigade of the Army's First Cavalry Division—the Black Jack Brigade—would provide a security cordon around the city while the other units pressed in.

The last time Marines had entered the city, the preceding April, they had come in primarily from the south, east, and west. Prebattle reconnaissance indicated that the insurgents were expecting our assault, and that they had prepared the majority of their defenses along the southern rim of the city. We would hope to catch them somewhat unawares by attacking down from the north. Going in, the planners expected to meet the most resistance in the older, Jolan neighborhood, built along a dogleg in the Euphrates, and laid out in the more typical Middle Eastern pattern of twisting roads and narrow alleyways. The neighborhood had been a major insurgent stronghold during the April 2004 battle, and it was home to many of the insurgency and terror group leaders. This time, our strategy was clear: we would push down fast from the north in a line and then enter every neighborhood, every single building if necessary, to root out the insurgents wherever they were. Combined with the Black Jack Brigade's cordon, there would be no retreat for the insurgents, no safe zones, no reinforcement, and no escape. They would have no choice but to fight or surrender.

The vast majority of Fallujah's 200,000 to 300,000 citizens had been evacuated before our assault, and the Iraqi Interim Government declared martial law, imposing a twenty-four-hour curfew on the 10 percent or so who chose to remain. Activities such as holding weapons or using private vehicles were banned. Civilian casualties had cut the April offensive off short; this time every effort was made to avoid injuries to noncombatants, and the public relations fallout they would cause.

With most of Fallujah laid out on a grid pattern, maneuvering would be more straightforward than fighting in the twisting, jumbled streets of a typical Middle Eastern city. Our planners superimposed their own grid system over the map of Fallujah to ease navigation on the ground and tracking of our progress from the rear. The major streets would be our "phase lines," or benchmarks of the Marines' progress through the city. Phase lines running across our axis of attack were given girls' names in alphabetical order from north to south, from Phase Line April, the northern edge of the city, through Beth, Cathy, Donna, and on to Fran. PL Fran was Highway 10, the main east-to-west artery through the city, and it would become our evacuation route out to Bravo Surgical Company at Camp Fallujah once it had been secured. Phase lines running along our north-to-south push would be known by boys' names; before the battle was over, the 1/8 would have seen action all the way from Charles to George.

The main attack on Fallujah would begin on the evening of November 8, 2004. Several units ran feints along the southern edge of the city on the day before, to throw off the insurgents. That evening the Thirty-sixth Iraqi Commando Battalion, supported by American forces, seized control of the two bridges across the Euphrates and the Fallujah General Hospital that stood on the far side of the river from the city. Controlling the bridges would cut off a potential route for insurgent escape or resupply. Securing the hospital on the far bank would allow it to stay open to serve the remaining civilian population during the coming fight and also prevent hospital staff from creating sympathy for the insurgents by inflating civilian casualty numbers, something they had done during the April assault.

The enemy we would face in Fallujah was the hard core of the insurgency. The estimate going in was that some three thousand or so insurgents were waiting for us among Fallujah's tens of thousands of buildings. There were the fanatics, jihadis from across the Muslim world who embraced death as the ultimate expression of their faith in the twisted, deadly version of Islam that underlies so much of the violence and terror around the world today. Joining these would-be martyrs was an even more sinister and deadly knot of trained, professional warriors. Some were Iraqis, former members of Saddam's military machine, but they were joined by many foreign fighters. These were the Mujahideen, Islamic "holy warriors" and veterans of the terror training camps of Afghanistan and of the decades-old rebellion in Chechnya, the ethnic battles of Kosovo and perhaps even the long-ago insurgency against the Soviets in Afghanistan.

Of the two groups of adversaries, it was the professionals who presented the larger problem. The image of an enemy who is as eager to die as he is to kill is frightening, but in reality, suicide attacks are a tactic better suited to killing innocent women and children than to taking on a highly trained and technologically superior force of professionals. You want to be a martyr? The American forces would be only too happy to oblige. But the Muj, the hardened foreign fighters, were another story. They knew their terrain and they had worked out sophisticated tactics to defend it. Ultimately, they must have known that they too were dead-enders, destined for whatever it is that awaits cruel men killed defending mistaken beliefs. But they were ready and waiting to take as many American lives with them as they possibly could. Defeating the enemy on the field of battle was the Marines' job. Robbing them of American deaths would be ours.

And so the battle plan was set, but not the medical plan. Colonels don't spend too much time thinking about medical plans, and maybe that's understandable. They've got a lot to think about going into battle. But neither, too often, do military doctors, and that's inexcusable. The attitude is "You guys show up, and I treat you." But there's more to it than that. Even if you have all your medical personnel and facilities in place, how is that wounded man going to get to you? Is it going to take too long, and if so, what are you going to do about it? How are you going to handle your security? Your communications? What's your evacuation plan? And what's your backup plan for when that route gets taken out by enemy fire?

During combat planning, the operations officers all sat down together, and the battalion commanders all sat down together, and they talked through the plan until everyone knew it inside and out. Unfortunately, doctors tend to be less focused on operational planning, and we never sat down together as officers and leaders to discuss an overall scheme of maneuver for casualty evacuation. Medical leadership at the regimental level didn't discuss the medical and evacuation plan with us either—it was just presented to us and we were expected to follow along. I wouldn't have met the surgeons from the other battalions or even have known who was going to be on my left and who was going to be on my right if Chief Folley and I hadn't made it a point at Camp Fallujah to find the other battalion surgeons and chiefs to introduce ourselves.

Sure, I can take care of my own battalion-level medical operations, but there's a whole higher level of coordination that could have happened, and it didn't. It's such a common problem in Navy medicine. You've got all these doctors who forget that they're officers as well. They forget, or perhaps don't even know, what that should mean in the first place. I had been a regimental surgeon and a MEU surgeon, so I understood the challenges and requirements of those higher-level positions. They're not easy jobs. But to hold a meeting and discuss a regiment-level medevac plan with the battalion surgeons? That shouldn't have been asking too much. We had almost seven days together at Camp Fallujah, and it never happened.

As it was, RCT-7 had established an ambulance exchange point located about two kilometers north of the breach site in the 1/8's zone of attack, at Checkpoint 84. That meant that the wounded would be brought up out of the city and handed off at the exchange point for transport to level-two care at Camp Fallujah. Okay. Fine. What else are you going to have? Would the convoys running back from the exchange point have dedicated security details? Would they have communications on board? What about a doctor? The transport vehicles were seven-ton trucks. If I'm loading up six or seven guys from a mass casualty, who's going to be on that truck to look after them? How many corpsmen are you going to have back there? What about air, if we need it? Can a helicopter get into the exchange point? And what if something gets blown up—my ambulance, my aid station, my exchange point—what's plan B?

I raised my concerns with RCT-7 medical, but they seemed overwhelmed. It was a plan, but it didn't seem to me that it had been thoroughly thought through in terms of how to accomplish our mission—evacuation—with the most effective results possible. My questions went unanswered, and that's what led to my decision: I couldn't trust my guys to a system I didn't understand, a system that might or might not be able to guarantee that they get the very best care we could possibly provide. There was no way I was going to be okay with that, for the sake of my Marines, and honestly, for the sake of professional and military pride as well. I had done too much and come too far, and so had my Marines, to put up with a haphazard, notional approach to casualty evacuation.

So I attempted to apply tactile thinking to the situation. What's my sphere of influence here and how can I improve the situation we're facing? What can I affect, and how can I make it work? You could say that the Marine Corps has an acronym for every situation, and the one called for here was SMEAC: Situation, Mission, Execution, Administration and logistics, and Command and control. It's what we call a five-paragraph order. All the elements needed to identify, plan, and execute a mission, which in this case was saving Marines from dying. The situation was simple: We were going into Fallujah to kick insurgent ass. The mission? To save Marine lives. Execution: Okay, I need to be able to get in to casualties in the city and get them back out again safely. I'm going to station two armored ambulances at the breach point. They'll pick up casualties in the city and evac them to the ambulance exchange point. But they're not going straight onto the trucks. They're making a stop at a full Battalion Aid Station to be thoroughly checked, stabilized, and prepared to make the forty-five-minute trip out to Camp Fallujah and level-two care. We're going to do everything in our power to make sure that if they get to us alive, they're going to get to level two alive, as well.

When a man is wounded on the battlefield, there are three possible outcomes. He can be killed, instantly or within minutes. Or he can be more or less fine—cut, bruised, or punctured in a way that may be debilitating but won't threaten his life, even if he doesn't get medical treatment for hours or more. And then there is the vast middle ground of wounds where timely medical intervention will mean the difference between that Marine flying home in a seat or in a box. That was my sphere of influence, and the corpsmen's sphere of influence. And if we had a duty, a reason to exist, it was to make that sphere of influence as large as we could by increasing our skills and ability and by decreasing the time it took to get care to a wounded Marine. After five months of intensive drilling in Haditha, I was confident that my team had the skill, judgment, and training they were going to need as soon as the battle began. But when I looked at our terrain, and at the regiment-level medical plan, I was not confident at all.

The 1/8 would be pushing down right through the heart of Fallujah. Our initial zone of operations was roughly bounded by Phase Line Dave to the east and George to the west. Superimposed on that grid, I set up a series of predetermined casualty-collection points—phase line intersections that would serve as the meeting places for the mobile wounded and the ambulances or other vehicles that would bring them out of the city and back to our aid station. According to the rules of far-forward medicine that Will Dutton, Joe Langholtz, and I had worked out years earlier, I needed my three key elements—medical, security, and communications—and I ran down the checklist in my mind.

In terms of medical personnel and facilities, we were well covered. We had line corpsmen with every company and platoon in the battalion and they were trained, medically and physically, to do one of the toughest jobs on the planet. Our Checkpoint 84 BAS would be staffed by two doctors, an IDC, and a good, well-trained team of corpsmen. HM1 Lees would be there, too, handling resupply issues and tracking casualties; you never want to lose track of a wounded man, especially in a battle like this was going to be. Think a man is lost when he's really gone up to Bravo Surgical Company and you could waste time, men, and worry looking for him. Think a man, or even a dead body, is safe when he's not, and you could be watching him being tortured, killed or desecrated on some Web site or satellite TV channel the next day.

Security was good to go, too. I had the trust and confidence of my senior battalion leadership in place. The plan of battle called for Weapons Company MAP (mobile assault patrol) platoons led by Lieutenants Matthew Kutilek, Sunny-James Risler, and David Lee to be available for dangerous missions as they came up: emergency fire support for heavily engaged units, medevac runs, whatever it took. I knew those guys already, and I was going to get to know them a lot better. I could count on their help whenever we needed it.

Communications and medevac needed work, but they came together. The air evac question was raised and the regimental surgeon established a secure landing site in behind the ambulance exchange point. And our big break came in the form of two aging M113 APCs, on loan from the Army National Guard. They were Vietnam-vintage armored personnel carriers, tank-like vehicles, which were configured to act as ambulances, with room for four casualties on litters in their rear compartment and crewed by a three-person team: commander, driver, and Army medic. They were ancient vehicles, and their thin armor had been designed for a time before armor-piercing bullets and rocket-propelled grenades had become readily available weapons of choice. The tracks, as we called the vehicles, were far from invulnerable, but they were a lot safer than a rubber-tired Humvee, and smaller and more maneuverable in narrow city streets and alleyways than the Marine Corps tracks—hulking Armored Assault Vehicles (AAV) that the Corps used for transporting troops, supplies, and casualties. The two APCs came under my command, and we would use them to extend our reach deep into the battle zone. They would need a security escort—ambulances carry no guns, of course—and we painted over the large red crosses on their sides. The American forces would be observing the international rules of war, but the men we were fighting would follow no such restrictions. A red cross in that town might as well have been a target.

As we set up, waiting for the battle to begin, my mind wandered back to the reconnaissance run I'd made with the battalion command two nights before. We had a plan now, and I was confident that for our battalion, at least, it was a good one—with our BAS at Checkpoint 84, I had closed that forty-five-minute gap between the edge of the city and lifesaving care for our wounded. But what about getting casualties out of the city? The APCs would be a huge help, but would they be enough? Would we be able to make a real difference if it still took too long to get wounded Marines out of the city and into our BAS? Was there anything else within my sphere of influence, some way to cut that delivery time down, or was I just worrying about things I couldn't help because that was all that was left to worry about? The answers to my questions would become apparent soon enough.

CHAPTER 9
Hard Lessons

November 9, 2004, approximately 1000

We had just finished transferring Gunny Shane, Doc Lambotte, and the other wounded from the cultural center to a convoy headed to the Bravo Surgical Company, when I heard the sound of Humvees roaring toward the Battalion Aid Station at Checkpoint 84. A door flew open and one of my corpsmen, HN Joel Dupuis, came running toward me, screaming, *"Sir, sir, fuckin' Volpe's hit, Volpe's gonna die, sir, Volpe's gonna die."*

Private First Class Paul Volpe was one of Lieutenant Kutilek's dismounts. The third platoon, Weapons Company, had stayed in that ambush intersection at the cultural center until we pulled out in the APC, and they escorted us out to the exchange point. Amazingly, they took no casualties themselves, despite having pulled farther into the open intersection to provide better cover for us as we worked on the casualties. Call it luck, call it skill, call it aggressive tactics. Kutilek says he attributes it to the hand of God and his parents' prayers. Good enough—it all works for me.

But their day was far from over. Kutilek immediately had his Marines stage their vehicles to go back in; he's a huge military history buff, and he knows that you need to keep your men motivated and moving after an intense, emotional experience like they had just come through at the cultural center. For many of the eighteen-to-twenty-one-year-olds, it had been their first real firefight, and it was about as violent as they come. Kutilek's Marines snapped to, though, and set about preparing to reenter the city, resupplying water, reloading ammunition, cleaning weapons. Within fifteen or twenty minutes, while Specialist Cook was still cleaning out his ambulance, another call came in from the cultural center—more Marines had been wounded and needed an emergency evac. "We're goin'," Kutilek yelled, and his platoon pulled out and raced back into the city. And from there, he says, things just kept getting worse.

The insurgents had seen how we were collecting casualties, and realized that it was a vulnerable moment for our forces. They were communicating by cell phone and could move quickly through the city streets and a system of underground tunnels. They could swarm in anytime there was a Marine down. So this time, as Kutilek's team headed back to that same intersection near the cultural center, it was like the insurgents were expecting them. The enemy was holed up in buildings along the route we had just taken and it seemed like the rounds were coming from every direction, and third platoon was faced with an even more intense firefight than the one we had just escaped. They strategically placed their vehicles to provide cover while they loaded up the casualties as well as another fatality, a Marine from another unit killed in action.

They'd barely started back toward the BAS when they got yet another call for a casualty pickup: another 1/8 Marine had been hit just a block away. Kutilek didn't like the idea of leading his train of eight vehicles back into that firestorm again, too many targets. So he decided that it made more sense for him to dismount and sprint across Phase Line Ethan and pick up the guy himself. He ran across the same street where Lonny Wells had just been shot and made it, but then he needed to get the wounded Marine out of there. "Can you run, can you make it back around the corner?" Kutilek asked the young lance corporal, eighteen, nineteen years old, shot in the arm or upper torso, and terrified. "Yeah," he said, and the two of them hustled back to the lead Humvee, where the wounded Marine immediately hit the floorboards, and no one could blame him for that.

Third platoon was ready to get moving back to the BAS, but just as they started pulling out they got yet another call, from Charlie Company this time, with casualties at or near the first house we had been to that morning to extract the wounded Force Recon corpsman. It was like a rerun of that first rescue—they couldn't exactly describe their location. Kutilek got on the radio and started yelling, "Where are they at?" but everybody was on the radio at the same time and there was complete confusion. And in the meantime, they were getting shot at and needed to get the hell out of there. By now, Kutilek's Humvee was at the rear of the line of vehicles because the platoon had executed a "reverse order, reverse route maneuver" as they headed back toward that first house where we found the wounded corpsman. The Humvees were spread out, about fifty to seventy-five meters apart, and they slowed down as they neared the casualty pickup area. Private First Class Volpe, who was in the lead vehicle, and the other dismount Marines had climbed out of their Humvees to walk beside the vehicles, weapons in hand, when a Marine from Charlie Company called out that there were two KIAs near a gray house about two hundred meters off the main road. You don't want to leave fallen Marines out in the open, because you don't want to give the enemy a chance to desecrate them. So Volpe and Staff Sergeant Steven Davis headed toward a wide, soccer-field-sized open space between the houses, with their Humvee following slowly behind.

And that's when Kutilek heard the last thing a platoon commander ever wants to hear over his platoon frequency—*Man down—there's a Marine down!*

"I knew one of my guys got shot," Kutilek later recalled. "And I wanted to be there immediately. I mean, you love these guys. These are thirty-nine of your Marines and Sailors and you care the world for 'em. I didn't know who it was or what was going on, but the immediate thing I wanted to do was get there." Together with his corpsman, HN Dupuis, Kutilek started sprinting up toward the front of his column.

Marines are trained to approach such wide-open areas with caution because they are a perfect setup for an ambush. The gray house was on the far side of the field, so while Davis provided cover from behind a wall, Volpe had started running across the open space. He'd cleared about thirty yards when two men ran out of one of the houses and opened fire with AK-47s. Volpe was hit at least three times, maybe four—his leg was so messed up we were never sure how many bullets made impact.

Volpe was down on the ground, in overwhelming pain and in the open, and still taking fire.

There's a saying, Fire superiority is the only care under fire, and the Marines did everything they could to provide it. The lead Humvee roared up on the field and began laying down a barrage of suppressing fire. Private First Class Harry Johnson, from New York City, blasted away with his Mark 19, firing several dozen rounds into nearby fields and through windows into the surrounding houses. The MK19 fires high-explosive 40-millimeter rounds, and they detonate on impact. Private First Class Johnson was so close in that he was getting hit with shrapnel kicking back from the rounds he fired, but he didn't let it stop him. But the dismounts were still trapped in a 3-D firebox: the field was a blind alleyway surrounded on three sides by buildings, and there was enemy fire coming from above, below, and all around the sides. In a replay of Gunny Shane's courageous rescue attempt at the cultural center earlier that morning, Davis ran out and hoisted the 165-pound Volpe onto his back and started moving out. But he didn't get far. A bullet sliced through Davis's hand, nearly severing one of his fingers, before slamming into Volpe's forearm. As the two hit the ground, Davis threw his body over Volpe, protecting the nineteen-year-old New Jersey native from the ongoing fire.

Staff Sergeant Matthew Smith entered firing. He was shot in the upper arm but shook it off, standing in the open and firing his M203 grenade launcher as well as his M16—he calmly fired and reloaded the single-shot M203 no fewer than ten times. As Kutilek arrived on scene, he saw Gunnery Sergeant Gordon Hill run into the field, throwing grenades at two hot spots, directing machine-gun fire at a third. Kutilek sprinted in, handed off his rifle to Gunny Hill, and started dragging Volpe out of the fire-box, leaving a bloody trail in the dirt. "I remember thinking that I would get psycho strength," Kutilek says; I had thought the same thing lifting Wells over the wall, but apparently that's just how it happens in the movies. Volpe felt plenty heavy, but Kutilek managed to get them both to safety and threw him into a vehicle. By this time, both men were covered in blood. Dupuis and HN Joseph Maston immediately started working on Volpe, applying a tourniquet, packing his wounds, injecting him with a shot of morphine, but the young private didn't look good to the platoon commander. "He was already starting to black out. He was really hurting. His entire lower extremity was saturated with fluid," Kutilek recalled. "You don't think human beings can bleed that much until you see it." The Marines fell back in an Australian peel, a staggered retreat that keeps each man covered on his way out. They loaded up and sped out of the city, toward the BAS, as fast as they could go. Somehow, despite the speed of that vehicle, Dupuis managed to get an IV line going.

Four Humvees came screeching into the aid station flat out. Dupuis, a big, strapping kid from Louisiana, jumped out of the back of one and was running toward me, frantic, rambling that his best friend was dying. I ran to the back hatch of the Humvee, and there lay Volpe, unconscious, his eyes rolled up in his head, in complete shock and bleeding profusely—AK rounds in the arm, the calf, and the killer, the right thigh, the femoral vein. He was fluorescent white. It's hard to imagine that anyone could be that white and still be alive. There was still a feeble pulse, but he was bleeding out, and fast.

My guys sprang into action and rushed the limp and cold Volpe into the aid station. We were moving so fast that Chief, who was helping with the litter, accidentally smacked right into Staff Sergeant Davis's hand, which had been nearly cut in half during the ambush. Davis is a very intense Marine, with a well-developed ability to use very colorful language in the heat of the moment, and he was in a lot of pain. He let out a scream of agony and started yelling at one of the corpsmen, HM3 Hirkala. Davis really needed some morphine, but the focus had to be on Volpe. Hirk's usually pretty timid, but he wasn't taking it that day; he yelled right back and told Staff Sergeant Davis to shut up and wait.

We got Volpe up on a table with IV access and cut away his clothing. Volpe looked bad, as bad as Lonny Wells had or worse. All I could think was: *I can't let this happen again or there's no point in me being here.* Kennedy was already packing the groin wound, and he was doing a good job, but by then I knew—good wasn't going to be good enough. "You fucking pack that tighter than you've ever packed anything in your life!" I barked. "If you have to jam your knee or hand in the wound, do it!" While I held Volpe's leg, Kennedy bore down on the wound like a wrestler going for the pin.

We couldn't get a blood pressure reading on Volpe, and the corpsmen were struggling to get another needle into the private's collapsing veins so that we could get more fluid into him; Dupuis stepped up and took over. Miraculously, he managed it again—he got a wide-bore IV needle started and we pumped Volpe with Hespan, the blood expander—500 cc's, and then another 500. A full liter, which is an awful lot.

And then the most amazing thing happened. Volpe's color started to come back. He opened his eyes suddenly, very weak but alert, and looked around, asking, "What the hell is going on?"

It was like Frosty the Snowman coming back to life. It was the most rewarding thing you ever saw. We were all too surprised to answer. He saw the fear and confusion on his friend Dupuis's face, and I guess he got it then. Dupuis managed to ask, "You doin' all right?" and Volpe came back with, "I'm all right. Hell, I can see your ugly-ass face." Our laughter was a sweet relief on a day of unbelievable pain. I don't know if there was a man in that BAS tent who thought it was possible that Volpe would actually survive, let alone have the grit to crack a joke as he came out of it. Dupuis went almost nuts with relief, and we were all pretty much overwhelmed with surprise—all maybe except for Kutilek. He took a moment and said a prayer. As Kutilek leaned over, Volpe looked him right in the eye. "Sir, did I let you down?" Volpe asked. Kutilek was stunned. Here's this nineteen-year-old kid, who's just been shot three or four times, and that's what he's got to say, he's worried that he let down his platoon commander. Kutilek struggled to maintain his composure. "Absolutely not," Kutilek assured him. "You did more than I could ever have expected of you."

My mind was already wringing the lessons out of the morning's tragedies. Two severe wounds, and two radically different outcomes. The quick initial action of the line corpsmen, Maston and Dupuis, had definitely saved his life, but even so, if Volpe had come in one minute later, just a few seconds more delay, he would have been dead. He'd had absolutely no time to spare. Could I have saved Sergeant Wells if I had gotten to him sooner? Should I have tried to get IV fluid into Wells on the track? Could I have tried harder to stop the bleeding? Specialist Cook says he remembers me in the ambulance, getting deep into Wells's wound, trying to find the bleeding vessel with my fingers. I don't remember doing that, and I wonder why I can recall telling Cook to move on, but not that? Lonny Wells was the first Marine to die in my arms, or die in my care. Not the last, but the first. Under fire, with so many other men to care for, should I have moved so fast? Could I have saved him under more controlled conditions? I don't know for sure, but what I learned from Lonny Wells—seeing how fast he bled out, even though it looked like venous blood, not arterial—had saved Paul Volpe's life. If I hadn't seen Wells, I wouldn't have known to tell Kennedy to pack him harder, and harder, and harder.

Tamponade—that French term again, it just means packing. It's such a simple concept, but so crucial. You can't apply a tourniquet on a groin wound, no amount of blood-clotting agent is going to help, and it's a tough spot—you're trying to pinch off a vessel by pushing it into more soft tissue. Intense pressure is the only thing that can stop a bleed like that. We all knew that going in, we'd practiced it, talked about it. Stuff the wound with gauze; if it's big enough, stuff a whole roll of Kerlix in there like a tampon. Stuff it, cover it, and then apply pressure, everything you have. We all knew that, we just didn't know what "everything" really meant until Lonny Wells.

But there was another lesson, and I was determined we would learn that one, too. Volpe made it by the very slimmest of margins. He was moments, literally seconds away from leaving an agonizing emptiness in his mother's heart. I had come to this war for one reason—to keep as many mothers from feeling that pain as I could—and it was now clear to me what we had to do. *We need to follow the fight into the city,* I thought. *We need to get closer.*

CHAPTER 10
Heading into Hell

It wasn't even noon yet on the first day of the Battle of Fallujah, and I had already seen more than enough to know that
even with our Battalion Aid Station placed as far forward as
Checkpoint 84, we were still too far away from the men we were
there to save.

And it was only going to get worse, because the front line was
moving farther away from us every hour. The Marines were
making incredible progress, pushing south into the city and taking their objectives much faster than anyone anticipated. They
had won control of al-Hydra Mosque by about noon, and continued to press south into the evening. Almost all units from both
attacking regiments would make Highway 10 in central Fallujah
by eight p.m. on November 9, 2004—just twenty-four hours to
take half the city—though the insurgents used the wide roadway
as a fallback point, and kept many American units pinned down
there with sniper fire for hours. There were also concerns that

the Marines might be moving too fast, and leaving too many hidden insurgents behind their advancing line. And the costs of that rapid push south were high—the 1/8, and especially Bravo Company, was meeting the stiffest resistance and suffering the highest casualty rates of the battle. I couldn't control who got hit or where, but I still had my sphere of influence, and I decided that if it was taking too long to get the wounded out of the city, then the only way we could cut that travel time down was by moving ourselves in. That would mean, in effect, setting up an emergency room in the middle of the hot zone.

This was one of the many times I was grateful that I had a good relationship with headquarters and that I kept my ear to the ground. I got wind that our XO, Mark Winn, was planning to head into the city the next day to establish a Jump Command Post in the heart of the city, after Captain Aaron Cunningham and his Alpha Company Marines secured the main government center downtown. It was a whole complex of buildings—the mayor's complex, some people called it—and Alpha Company was assigned to capture and clear it during the early hours of November 10, the Marine Corps birthday. That's where I wanted us to be—right in the middle of the city, as near the front lines as we could get. I asked Mark to let us follow him in later that night and establish an aid station next to his new command post; I wanted to set up a Forward Aid Station.

Winn was an excellent leader and a terrific liaison between our battalion commander and the rest of the battalion, and we had become good friends. But like everyone, he assumed we'd be too heavy, too bulky, to really move in with them. "How expeditionary can you guys be?" the XO asked skeptically, and I think he was surprised when I said that all I needed was security and the men and supplies I could fit in the two ambulances. I didn't even have to explain that if we moved forward, we'd save more of his Marines—he got it. "Roger that," Winn said. "We convoy in on the tenth." That gave us time to get ready, and Winn just needed to clear the move with Lieutenant Colonel Brandl and Major Kevin Trimble, the operations officer. Fortunately, I had a good relationship with both of them as well. Before we left the States, I had made the rounds to make myself known. Too often medical officers keep to themselves and then get frustrated when they need to get something done but don't understand how the overall system works. So I got an early start on getting to know the men who would end up being my companions and colleagues in Iraq. One of the first people I met was Lieutenant Colonel Brandl. He's a large, imposing man, with a brooding, almost moody demeanor, and he takes himself and his position very seriously; we rarely saw him smile, if at all. Battalion commander can be a lonely job, and in the colonel's case I believe he made it even more so than necessary by maintaining a distance from his officers and men. Then again, he was the one man responsible for the entire battalion, for every Marine and Sailor among us, and for the success or failure of our mission in Iraq. That is a staggering responsibility, and one that is beyond anything I have experienced. Lieutenant Colonel Brandl led the 1/8 through what were probably some of the toughest hours in the battalion's long, heroic history, and he deserves a great deal of respect and admiration for that.

A native of Passaic, New Jersey, Lieutenant Colonel Brandl was a big outdoors type and avid hunter. He didn't just make "Hunter" his radio call sign and assign the Latin motto *esse predator*—"be the hunter"—to the battalion; he and his wife,

Mona Rae, named their daughter Remington, after the firearm manufacturer. Lieutenant Colonel Brandl had a reputation as a bit of a showboat, and you could see a subtle shift in his bearing when reporters were around. He was without question dedicated to the care and safety of his Marines. When they needed to be hammered, he saw to that, but for the most part he was appropriate in his leadership and discipline, never over the top. In my experience, he wasn't particularly hands-on in terms of overseeing the medical side of the operation—but then, doctors and medicine can seem a little soft to tough Marines sometimes. But his concern for the good of the battalion was obvious; if I told the colonel that I needed something to help me take care of his Marines, he allowed it, no questions asked. And when I took the initiative, he supported me all the way.

One of the big reasons for that, I think, is that I hit it off right away with Winn and Trimble, and they were able to help me negotiate my relationship with the colonel. The two men bunked with Lieutenant Colonel Brandl at Haditha Dam, and because the colonel spent so much time in their room, the other two spent a lot of time looking for other places to hang out. I like to think we had a pretty good atmosphere at the Battalion Aid Station, so we saw a lot of Trimble and Winn. They became good friends of mine—definitely guys I would hang out with at home—and invaluable sources of information. I was extremely well served by Chief Folley as my HMC, but having a couple of officers on the Marine side I could talk things over with as well would turn out to be a very important part of our success. They would advise me on the colonel's attitudes and plans for certain things, so that when I spoke to him I was able to say I had already run it by his XO or his Ops. O, which I think gave him more confidence in my ideas.

Major Trimble is an interesting guy. When he was awake, he was totally hyper, just zipping off the walls, but when the guy went to sleep, he could really sleep. Nothing would wake him up—he slept right through a mortar barrage in Fallujah in July, shrapnel ripping through the sides of his canvas tent and everything. The colonel had a lot of faith in Trimble and his assistant, Captain Ralph Hershfelt, and they worked incredibly long days and nights doing most of the planning and running of the battalion. The two of them made a great pair; Trimble is a small guy with a nasal voice, a former wrestler from Kentucky, and Hershfelt is as tall and lanky as Lurch from *The Addams Family*, with a very dry sense of humor. About the only thing they had in common is that they both had a dip of Copenhagen snuff tucked in their bottom lips the moment they woke up, and I wouldn't be surprised if they slept with the stuff, too. Add in their senior enlisted man, Master Sergeant Donald Funkhouser—a man of a thousand opinions, many of them absurd, some of them obnoxious, and all of them delivered with the introduction "Boys, let me Funkify things for ya"—and you end up with a very entertaining corner of the battalion. I tried to handle my own ops as much as I could, though, not to avoid the battalion ops team but to give them a break. Those guys had plenty on their plates as it was.

Mark Winn was another story. I met him as soon as I showed up at the battalion, and I saw how he worked right from the first moment. He called me on the phone and asked me to come up to his office, because he was dealing with a young lance corporal who didn't think he was medically fit to go to Iraq. I checked in with the orthopedics department at the Camp Lejeune base hospital and got the story. The kid had patella femoral pain syndrome, or PFS. As the name suggests, it's a pretty painful condition, caused by overuse of the knee joint. But it's a very common complaint in the Corps—I would say that about 75 percent of Marines have it at some point in their career—and it just takes a little rest and a little Motrin to take care of it. But the kid's mother was a nurse and she had decided that the condition should disqualify her twenty-one-year-old son from deploying. The kid's mom was sitting in Major Winn's office with her husband, insisting that her boy was not going to Iraq. You could feel the pain in the room and understand why these people wouldn't want their son to go off to war. But my job, and Mark Winn's job, was to protect the battalion. And that meant that everyone who could go was going to go. I explained the situation to them—that ortho had done a full slate of tests, and there was no reason why their Marine couldn't deploy. Mark just said, "Well, that's what the doc says," and that was it. As soon as the couple left his office, though, Major Winn put his head down on his desk and groaned. "Ugh," he said, "I really had a rough one last night."

Mark enjoys a drink and a good time, and he fancies himself quite a ladies' man, though nobody could ever figure out where that idea came from. His call sign is "Raisin," which came from being told by a young lady he was attempting to charm one night at a bar that "your head looks just like a raisin, all small and shriveled up." For some reason, he was proud of that. Mark isn't a physically imposing man—I don't know if he could lift a notebook over his head, though Mark insists he can handle at least two—but he's one of the strongest runners I've ever met. At forty-one years old, he could probably outrun 99 percent of the battalion, and that's mostly guys in their late teens and early twenties. He was an outstanding leader and a fantastic mentor to the younger officers. He listened, he was decisive, and he had a great sense of humor. He also cared deeply for all the Marines and they knew it. Mark Winn became my primary liaison to the colonel and every other officer in the battalion.

Anyway, with Winn on board, getting permission from Lieutenant Colonel Brandl and Kevin Trimble was largely a formality. Now I had to scramble, because we had a lot to do before we pulled out.

I made HM2 Johns my point man; he's a big, dependable guy from the middle of some cornfield in Monon, Indiana, and he didn't put up with shit from anyone. I didn't know if my corpsmen would want to go in with us, but I did know that Johns would get them rogered up and ready to go regardless. "Get a Forward Aid Station together, get Zimmerman, and get your shit together—we're moving out," I told him. I left it to Zimmerman and Johns to select the corpsmen who would come into the city with us. We needed guys who wanted to be there, but we also needed good people left behind to man the BAS at Checkpoint 84. We would essentially be dividing the battlefield in half, giving wounded Marines two options for treatment rather than just one, and the main BAS would continue to see plenty of action in the days to come, from our battalion and others.

We assembled near the breach point by early evening on November 10 and settled in with Winn's people to wait for the word to move out—through the breach and into hell. We had Johns and Zimmerman, my senior guys, and four young corpsmen: HA

Ernesto Argueta, HA Daniel Avila, HN Collin Stedman, and HN Raymond Masino. We also had the six National Guard ambulance crewmembers plus their commander, Lieutenant Todd Wilson. All of them were Army National Guard medics and Wilson was a civilian physician's assistant as well, so we had a good medical team. We also had a pretty surreal experience. November 10 is the Marine Corps birthday, and a very big deal for Marines everywhere, even in the middle of a battle. At about 0200 on November 10, Mark Winn called us all together so that he could read the commandant of the Marine Corps' birthday message. This was his annual message to all Marines, but there was a part that mentioned Fallujah, and just as Winn was reading those lines, a bunch of enemy rockets hit right beside us, just far enough away not to do any damage.

The corpsmen ended up pulling some guard duty, too. There aren't a lot of trigger pullers in a headquarters group like the one we were traveling with, and Lieutenant Risler, the platoon commander in charge of security for the convoy, was concerned about setting up an effective perimeter with just his eight Marines. We were in a very precarious position, about three-quarters of a mile ahead of the rear line and more or less in the open. We were trying to eat and get some sleep, when Risler's first sergeant came over and asked if I had any guys who could stand watch. *Well* . . . tough call. The corpsmen have M16s, but they're not supposed to take on a combat role. Then again, there were mortar rounds coming in and some heavy machine-gun fire, and there was no telling who might try to sneak in on us—they could at least listen. We sent the four junior corpsmen out to protect our rear, each one with a radio and a Marine.

We were there all day, and by the time we started moving, after midnight. No one was sorry to go. We had been defending a dump site, and our sentries were getting tired of standing up and finding dirty diapers stuck to their butts. Stedman had a very dry sense of humor—"Thank you, Sir. I appreciate the opportunity to lie in a garbage dump in the middle of a war." Masino was a little more animated about the situation, but he was a little more animated about everything. He was brand-new to the Navy, eighteen years old and a former state wrestling champion—he was always trying to get everyone to wrestle with him—and just about as hyper as they come. Masino picked up the nickname "Novelty Item" because having him around was a little like having a bobblehead doll on your dashboard—amusing, but after a while he could get a little annoying. He more than earned his keep, though. Sometime after we got down to the government center, he replaced the wounded HN Joel Lambotte with Bravo Company and did a remarkable job. Those Marines loved him.

We piled into the back of our ambulances in the very early hours of November 11, and fell in with Winn's much larger tracks—the Marine Corps' AAVs, or AmTracs. It was quiet and very eerie as we sat in the darkened interior of our track convoying into the city. The only noise we could hear from inside our ambulances, other than our own engines, was an occasional mortar and the drone of *Basher*—the huge, lethal AC-130 gunship—flying around above us looking for targets and blasting pretty much anything that moved with its 105-millimeter howitzer. We sat there hoping that our glint tape was clearly visible, so *Basher*'s crew could see it reflect in their night-vision system and know that we were friendlies.

As we neared the government center sometime around one or two a.m., we could hear sniper fire and stray mortars going off around us, and it was probably forty minutes before we got the okay to climb out of the ambulances. It was pitch-black. You couldn't see anything. There were tracers going off and lots of gunfire and explosions. They had told us the area was secured, but there were a lot of snipers still running around. Alpha and Charlie companies were engaging insurgents nearby as we began to unload the APCs and a few of our corpsmen, including Johns, were recruited to help with the counter-sniper operation. We were drawing a lot of sniper fire from this one building—not pinpoint sniper fire; it was more for harassment, just to keep us on our toes. Everybody had PAQ-2s and PAQ-4s, infrared lasers, on the front of their rifles, and Johns remembers that someone got on their radio and said, "Hey, with your PAQ-2, hit the building that you think the sniper fire is coming from." If you had your NVGs, or night-vision goggles, on, you could see thirty red lasers come up out of nowhere, all pointing at the same building. *Basher* had been flying overhead, and all of a sudden it was like the sun came out; the top of that roof got hit with *Basher*'s million-candlepower infrared spotlight, and sure enough, there were a couple of insurgents up there. But there were too many friendlies around for *Basher* to safely take them out. Rumor had it that *Basher* had a female pilot who was very attractive, and we all ended up with visions of this super-tough, smoking Angelina Jolie *Tomb Raider*–type flying around up there. We heard her find another "target of opportunity" later that night. Her spotlight apparently picked up twenty insurgents in another part of the city, and she took care of business. She was a real badass, and we were glad to have her on our side providing cover whenever and wherever needed.

Anyway, I guess the insurgents got the message because things finally quieted down a little bit. We hunkered down in a corner of the parking lot, next to an outside wall, to get a little sleep and wait for daybreak.

CHAPTER 11

The Prayer Room

We didn't need an alarm clock to know when the sun started to come up. The insurgents had evidently anticipated our move into the government center and had fallen back into the taller buildings and minarets that surrounded it. That made us perfect sniper bait, and as soon as there was light, we started hearing the *crack . . . crack . . . crack* of slow, careful sniper fire. Damn. We got up and looked around and saw we were much more exposed than we realized. Okay, we'd better get set up and secure. Johns and I took the lead, playing Marine really. He had been in the infantry and I still remembered a few things from my earlier life as a Marine, and we called on those experiences as we scoped out a possible location for our Forward Aid Station. We found a small, one-story cement building containing a prayer room. It looked secure, and we decided that was where we would set up shop. It was small, maybe eight feet by twenty, but it had a center hatch with enough room to put two stretchers on either side. It was located near an opening in the ten-foot-high wall that surrounded the complex; the gate had been blown out by our tank rounds. There was a row of candy stores and coffee shops along our side of a parking lot, so we had good vehicle access without excessive exposure.

So we started cleaning and setting up. The FAS was pretty well stocked for what I would consider level-one-point-five casualty care—somewhere between the standard level-one battlefield medical attention and the sophisticated surgical care at a level-two facility like a field hospital or the surgical company at Camp Fallujah. We had intubation kits and tracheotomy kits, chest tubes, pericardiocentesis catheters, Hespan and other blood expanders, tourniquets of different varieties, Kerlix gauze, Ace wraps and burn wraps, electric and manual portable suction and more—good stuff. We improvised where we needed to: my guys found some metal plates in the street, cleaned them up and draped them with sterile surgical towels so we could use them as trays for scalpels and other tools. We scavenged cement blocks to get the stretchers off the floor. Kutilek came in at one point, looked around, and couldn't believe that we had so quickly improvised a well-stocked aid station with everything you would really need for forward combat medicine. The room had a decent roof, but all the windows had been blown out, so we began hardening up, sandbagging the windows and the porch, anything else we could think of to improve our position. The idea was that we would get wounded Marines who were completely unstable, do what we needed to do to stabilize them, and then medevac them out to the Camp Fallujah hospital by ambulance.

It didn't take long to figure out if the system would work. As the sun rose, the insurgents started pouring it on and we started getting deliveries of mass casualties, groups of eight and ten wounded at a time. We were so close to the action, literally in the middle of it, that we didn't have to send the ambulances in to collect casualties—the Marines were just bringing them straight to us in whatever vehicles they had. Their travel time was usually under five minutes. We didn't have a radio in the Forward Aid Station (although we could monitor the ambulance radios if they were around), so Mark Winn or someone from command would usually run over and alert us if they got a call that casualties were on the way. But if we got a call that three guys were coming, the truck would pull up with something like six; if they said two were on their way, we'd get ten. There was always more, never less. A lot of the time, we'd get no warning at all. We'd just hear the screech of tires outside our door and we'd come running.

We were still being shot at, and there were mortar attacks outside the perimeter, but after a while, we got more or less used to it. The corpsmen had their M16s with them, but they couldn't really carry them while working on the casualties; they just got in the way. So most of us were carrying nothing but our 9 millimeters. No one was specifically assigned to provide us with security, but there was a Marine company stationed at the complex and there was always someone around to provide firepower if we needed it.

The first mass casualty event we handled at the FAS was typical of everything we faced those first few days. Kevin Trimble yelled at me that there were two urgent casualties coming in, and thirty seconds later here they come—two huge Marine AAVs, not just two casualties. They were coming in at a good clip, too, and they spun around on their tracks with a maneuver like a car fishtailing. They dropped their ramps and I went into the first one, to start triaging. There was an absolute flurry of activity in the dark interior, and it was a total mess—ammo and chow scattered all around—and I almost broke my neck trying to get to the four wounded men lying on ponchos and moaning in pain. Zimmerman and the corpsmen came up with stretchers and took the four men in the first track; I headed to the second vehicle, where I found two more wounded Marines. One was upright with a lot of blood on his shoulder; the other was on a stretcher with blood in his groin. A lot to deal with all at once, but we had it covered—get that groin wound taken care of first, pack it like we now knew we had to. Get Zimmerman on the next most urgent casualty; make sure everyone is getting what they need.

We had all the casualties stripped and stable and were hitting them with Ancef antibiotic and morphine for the trip up to Bravo Surgical when a pair of Humvees tore in with two more wounded Marines. One was hit and bleeding from the neck and left shoulder and arm, the other had a leg wound and maybe a fractured femur. I have no idea if they were from 1/8 or not, but it didn't matter; we got them stable, too, and evacuated everyone to Camp Fallujah. We were wiped, but pretty pumped, too—we had handled it and it looked like all the casualties were going to be okay. What we didn't know is that we would be keeping that pace up for the next seventy-two hours.

We always took the most urgent casualties into one of the four stretchers inside our FAS. The less urgent guys went to a treatment area we set up on the front porch just outside. Zimmerman usually took on the most serious cases inside, and I would move around and help out as needed. We had a corpsman on each "bed" inside and another manning our supply store, which was just a shelving unit we pulled out of a nearby building. He would pitch us whatever we called out for—gauze, Hespan, tourniquets, predrawn syringes; we'd just yell it out and the item would be sent via air to the table. The corpsmen actually practiced this when we had downtime, and they got so good at it that they could have found whatever we needed with their eyes closed.

Once we had our casualties stabilized, we transferred them into one of the waiting ambulances and sent them on their way to the surgical center. If there was any downtime between deliveries, we'd restock supplies and clean up the FAS, using bottled water to wash out the blood because that was all we had. And we were always looking for ways to improve our position, sandbagging windows and the porch area out front, setting up sleeping quarters, whatever we could do to make things a little better.

But there wasn't a lot of downtime, certainly not during the first several days, anyway. Sometimes the waves of casualties would come in so close together we didn't even have time to resterilize our instruments. We'd just have to throw some alcohol on the stuff and use it again. I didn't get a chance to wash my hands a lot, either. I wore gloves as much as possible, but they'd get all torn up, and my body would just be covered in blood.

I worked hard to keep my corpsmen focused; the emotional toll could be significant, especially when they were working on guys they knew. Staying on top of them helped me keep my own emotions under control, too, most of the time. After a particularly heavy round of casualties, I remember stepping outside for a moment, to collect my thoughts and have a rare cigarette, even though I don't usually smoke. When I looked down, I saw that I was leaving a trail behind in the dust, a trail of bloody footprints. My boots were so full of blood that it would squish out with every step.

The corpsmen were working great, and so was the system, even better than I had hoped. During the first four days in Fallujah, we saw scores of wounded, so many that their faces and injuries became a blur after a while. We worked pretty much nonstop, got almost no sleep, and were under fire on a regular basis. There were times when we almost ran out of supplies, and we'd have to get on the radio and call out to RCT-7—or, if they didn't respond, to MSSG-31, the MEU Service Support Group, who never let us down—for another corpsman or more bandages, Ace wraps, or Mylar space blankets, to keep the casualties from losing body heat. It was truly hell, but consider this: We didn't lose a single man in our first two days at the FAS. Everyone who came to us alive left us alive.

The only guys who didn't survive were those who died before they made it to us. Captain Aaron Cunningham and his Alpha Company were fully into the fight now, and both they and Bravo lost good men that first day. First Lieutenant Dan Malcom, a twenty-five-year-old Marine from Brinson, Georgia, who had been a classmate of Kutilek's at the Citadel, was shot on a rooftop by a sniper, but that was still on the tenth, while we were preparing to go in, so I didn't see him when he was brought to the BAS. He was the only KIA Marine from the 1/8 that I didn't see. Malcom was a hard loss; he was the Weapons platoon commander for Alpha Company and he was someone we knew well. He had played chess with a lot of the corpsmen and it was hard for us, knowing that we hadn't been able to help him. Bravo Company

Corporal Romulo "RJ" Jimenez II, twenty-one, an energetic and popular Marine from Belington, West Virginia, who loved the outdoors and his 1992 Ford Mustang, was killed that day as well, shot in the neck by a sniper. Jimenez had just been promoted to the rank of sergeant but died before finding out the good news. HM3 Milton Jones, the line corpsman, worked on him hard, but there was nothing he could have done.

There's a lot of talk in trauma medicine about something called the "golden hour." The idea is basically that if someone survives an initial trauma, you've got about an hour to intervene before losing them. Well, that may hold true to some extent in the civilian context—car accidents, falls, that sort of thing—where survivable events tend to involve blunt trauma. It might even have been true in previous military conflicts, but it is no longer true. Ironically, this is because of the protective gear American troops now wear. Outfitted with a Kevlar helmet and Kevlar-and-ceramic-plate body armor, the modern Marine is protected from many impacts that would otherwise be lethal—head shots, chest shots, and so on. But that tends to push the wounds we do see outward from the core and into other areas of the body. We saw a lot of guys get shot across the breastplate and live; the insurgents would fire their AKs in a burst, raking across the chest, and our guys would end up with wounds in their arms, but clear in the chest, a very survivable situation. We're seeing a lot of amputations in this war, too. These are often men who would have been killed outright by very heavy fire or close-proximity explosions had it not been for their protective gear.

But we also saw a lot of precisely deadly wounds resulting from insurgent sniper fire. These snipers were most often trained warriors, posted in the upper floors of buildings and the minarets of mosques. They had the patience and the skill, some of them, to shoot for the neck, groin, and upper thigh—all unprotected areas that are packed with high-volume blood vessels. A shot there won't kill as fast as a round to the chest or the head, but hit a major artery and a man has no more than five minutes to live without care; hit a vein and survival time might stretch to ten. On today's battlefield, survival time is measured in mere fractions of that "golden" hour.

The traditional approach to battlefield medicine was developed over hundreds of years, and it made sense for earlier times. The line between KIA and WIA was more absolute then— wounds fell more easily into the categories of lethal or nonlethal, and corpsmen or medics with the units served as much to provide comfort to the dying and transport to the dead as to intervene with lifesaving medical care for the wounded. Both of those roles are still an essential part of the job, but today we have more wounds that could go either way, and we have vastly improved higher-level care that can help even severely wounded warriors survive and rehabilitate off the battlefield.

The interesting thing is that the technology and techniques of battlefield medicine have not changed much since Vietnam. There are a few exceptions; the colloidal carbohydrate blood expanders like Hespan are the big ones, but even they are just more efficient replacements for older resuscitative fluids like lactated Ringer's solution. There have been huge advances in level-two care and beyond—lifesaving and reconstructive surgeries, and the extended care and rehabilitation. But that system starts beyond the edge of the battlefield, in field surgery units, and really kicks in once you get to the Thirty-first Combat Surgical Hospital in Baghdad and the American military hospitals in

Landstuhl, Germany, and back in the United States. Out there on the battlefield, any corpsman will tell you that 90 percent of their interventions were made with Kerlix gauze rolls, Ace wrap bandages, and Hespan IV fluid. Add in one gram of the antibiotic Ancef for everybody who came in, treat for shock, and that was about it, that's what it took to save lives. The difference we made out there didn't come from sophisticated techniques or high-tech gear, it came from aggressive tactics, tactics like extending our operation into the heart of the battle.

As we moved into the evening of the eleventh, exhaustion was becoming an issue. Just about everyone had had only a few hours of sleep in the last four days and were desperate for some sack time. Things tended to be a little quieter at night, so guys would try to grab an hour or two whenever they could. A lot of animals had been left behind in the city when the residents evacuated, and they were getting into fights for food and shelter. Their nighttime screams could jolt you out of the soundest sleep. At one point, two scroungy cats came running into the FAS at night while a corpsman was sleeping there and climbed up on his sleeping bags, while he was still inside it, and started battling away. Then another big tomcat joined in the fight, and by the time the poor guy got rid of them he was a mass of scratches. What was more common was that you'd have barely gotten to sleep before someone was waking you up because more casualties were pulling in. You'd think, well at least I got a couple of hours in, and then you'd glance at your watch and realize it was only five minutes later.

Zimmerman and I worked out a system where one of us would take watch at the aid station and the other would head back to where the corpsmen were bunking down. My first night back there, on the fourth night of the battle, I crawled in kind of late, after the corpsmen were all asleep. I settled into my sleeping bag on the floor with the corpsmen all around, and I was thinking, *Hey, this is way too cozy.* I was just about to pass out when I heard one of the corpsmen—no, I'm not going to say which one—just going to town on himself, masturbating. Okay, coziness shattered. "Damn it, I think I am going to be sick!" He looked at me like it was my fault for interrupting. "Sir, it's two o'clock in the morning, you shouldn't be awake, and I need personal time." Well, you can't really argue with that, I guess. I got up and cleared out—everyone needs their moment of peace.

Despite the lack of sleep and the constant stream of casualties, life at the government center wasn't so bad all the time. We had our group and we had our system, and we tried to keep things together and running smoothly. After Ray Masino went out with Bravo, I brought in two more corpsmen, HM3 David Lester and HM3 David McArdle. Weapons Company had a mortar pit set up across a field from us, so we'd see their corpsman from time to time as well, HM3 Thomas Stahura, a good kid who we called Crackhead. (He kept his head bald, and he'd been in a car accident as a kid and ended up with a huge scar running across his scalp—so, Crackhead.)

Lester's main job was to get the corpsmen together and get our position sandbagged and hardened. He's a good-natured guy, nice kid, maybe not quite as much hustle as I'd like to see sometimes, though, so we'd get into it once in a while. It never stuck, though, and soon we'd be covering the same ground again. Lester has a wandering eye, strabismus, like me. So one time I started in on him with, "Dammit, Lester, I guess we just can't see eye to eye." The whole aid station cracked up. You do what you can for a laugh in wartime.

I had actually been giving Lester shit about shitters, of all things. Once he got the FAS hardened down, we put Lester to work building us a decent place to relieve ourselves. The basic principle is that you need a seat with a hole in it and a plastic bag underneath, something you can take out and throw in a pit to burn. At first, we improvised with plastic bags and empty MRE (Meals Ready to Eat) boxes, but that wasn't a long-term solution. Lester started out trying to use some plastic lawn chairs he had found, with the plastic latticework seat punched out for a hole. I was sitting with Gunny Ramos from Alpha—a hard, hard man—who was in for resupply, and we were critiquing Lester's design. He presented the first prototype. No way, Gunny said, that'd be like sitting in a bear trap, too many little plastic spikes sticking out. So Lester came back with the edges taped up, and I shot that one down—too sticky, too unhygienic. Lester was looking despondent already, but Gunny Ramos looked at him and barked, "Lester! Sandbag shitters! Pack 'em!" So Lester was back to packing sandbags, and we ended up with a sweet set of very secure, hardened heads. He stacked those bags up like a throne, with a back and armrests on it. People from other units would come by just to use them. It's actually impressive just how much a quality shitter situation can help out with morale; if you have a good place to relax and do your business, it makes just about everything else seem better.

But I don't want to gloss over the fact that as successful as our far-forward medical system was, aggressive tactics can also make you more vulnerable. We took quite a lot of sniper fire during our time at the government center; you could hear the incoming rounds sort of clinking around the place as you worked.

I remember one morning, we had a couple of Marines, Corporal Dewalt and Sergeant Emick, working with us to keep track of the casualties as they came in, to make sure that we always knew where every man was. It was crucial work and they were both outstanding. But Corporal Dewalt did tend to be "on his own program" from time to time. We looked around that morning and we couldn't find him, and I started yelling and cursing when I saw him coming back around the corner. "Where the hell were you, Dewalt?" I demanded. "You've got work to do in here." Turns out he had gone on the roof with one of the machine-gun teams and they had targets directly outside our gate. "Well, some guys were trying to come across, so we shot them," Dewalt said. Okay, pretty good excuse. I let it go.

On the second or third day there, we had received another mass casualty and were just finishing up. McArdle was working on a patient outside and he started having trouble, so I ran over to help. Mark Winn was right there, almost standing over me as I knelt down, and I looked up for a moment and saw a muzzle flash coming from a building across the street, maybe a hundred meters away and directly over his shoulder. I usually took my helmet off when casualties came in, because it got in the way—I actually lost it a few times, and had to pick out a new one from the pile we collected from our casualties—so I was standing there bareheaded. Having rounds going off around us wasn't new. We'd gotten to the point where we barely noticed them. But this was different. This guy was clearly aiming right at us.

"Hey, Mark, muzzle flash," I said, and saw it again, perfect little points of flame in a circle, direct fire, not off to the side. "I think they're shooting at you."

"Oh yeah?" he asked. "Why would they want to kill me? I'm a nice guy."

"Well," I answered, "there was a picture-perfect muzzle flash, and I know they don't shoot at doctors."

Okay, not true—these guys would love to take out a doctor. But that wasn't my main concern right then, I had a casualty to deal with. Just then a bullet hit the ground right next to us. I felt more irritated than scared. "Mark, would you please go kill that guy?" I said, and got back to work. We pulled McArdle's man inside to stabilize him, but we weren't going to be able to move any of the casualties into the ambulance and up to Bravo Surgical until the sniper threat was neutralized. Mark went into his XO mode, marching across the parking lot to Lieutenant Risler's Mobile Assault Platoon and pointed in the direction of the sniper. Winn had them mobilized in a second—they fired a TOW Missile, they fired .50-cal rounds, they fired Mark 19 grenades. I looked up just in time to see the sniper come falling off the rail and drop to the ground. Wow, okay, threat neutralized; we sent the patients out safely.

There's a struggle sometimes that happens with a doctor on the battlefield. Your job is to save people, but sometimes you find yourself in a situation where you end up if not actually shooting enemy fighters yourself, then at least causing them to be shot. I had made the decision long before I got into this scenario that that's what I would do. But the reality is that it's not so easy when you actually have to do it. I don't think I killed anybody, but I guess I wasn't too far from it, either. Ultimately,

I'm not going to die and my patients aren't going to die because I'm afraid of killing somebody who's shooting at us. I remember thinking at the time, *This kid I'm working on is not trying to kill anybody, so why are you shooting at me?* The insurgent sniper had made his choice already, and unfortunately I couldn't just subdue him—he needed to be stopped and he was. Mark likes to talk now about how much courage and wisdom I displayed under fire, but no, I just don't like people shooting at me. Or in my direction, even if they're trying to kill Mark.

But there were real dangers, and that raises the issue of whether by going in to establish the FAS myself I put an important battalion asset—me, the doctor—needlessly at risk.

I think that's looking at it all backward. By putting me forward, I thought we were maximizing our assets. First, there was the leadership issue. A battalion surgeon isn't just a doctor, he's also the leading officer of a medical platoon, and no self-respecting platoon leader anywhere is going to send his men in to do a job he wouldn't do himself.

And, of course, there were the medical issues. I had trained my corpsmen hard and well, and they were a crack team. But there's a big difference between training and experience. I knew this stuff cold and I was the only guy who had actually done most of it before. Not under combat conditions, but my time at the Cowley Trauma Center in Baltimore wasn't that far different. Would a corpsman have been as likely to pick up on the things that I did from losing Lonny Wells and have been able to apply them to the next patient, Paul Volpe, immediately afterward? I don't know, but I did, and that helped us save a life. And to top it off, I was able to share that new knowledge with my corpsmen. Talk about a teachable moment.

We also were seeing plenty of casualties that a corpsman probably could not have handled. The more aggressive interventions, advanced trauma lifesaving stuff, take a lot of training and experience to perform, let alone recognize when they're appropriate or necessary. Inserting chest tubes and surgical airways, putting in central lines and doing cricothyroidotomies and pericardiocentesis—I had mastered them at Cowley. They're tough, invasive procedures, and you have to know when to do them and how to do them. Done right and in the appropriate situation, they can save a life; done wrong or on the wrong patient and they can just as easily take it. And that means more training than you can realistically give a corpsman, even an IDC. If the idea of far-forward battlefield medicine includes getting some advanced life support up front, and I think it should, then you really have to have a trauma-trained doctor as far forward as you can.

And if I went down, well, the guys at the front would be no worse off than they would have been without me. They would still have had access to another doctor, a highly trained physician's assistant, and the best corpsmen I'd ever seen.

I'll also admit that I wanted to be there and I thought I deserved to be there—I wasn't a liability to anyone. I'd had more combat training than most of the corpsmen, and I hadn't lived the life I'd lived up until that point just to sit back and sip tea with old ladies over the far side of the horizon.

But I wasn't giving any of those issues a whole lot of thought at the time; we just had too much work to do, and I had more immediate concerns, like how I was going to handle all of the casualty traffic. With so many wounded coming in, we often had to send both our armored ambulances out to the ambulance exchange point at the same time. They would hand off the guys we had stabilized there, and then cycle by the BAS to resupply our needs, and do their own resupply and refuel as well. That was leaving us without vehicles sometimes for a couple of hours at a time, creating a potential bottleneck—what happens if we get a casualty who needs to get up to surgical immediately?

The next time Lieutenant Wilson came in with one of the tracks, I asked him how things looked back at the BAS. All good with my guys, busy but staying on top of it. How about the rest of his platoon, the other two tracks? They were assigned to another battalion, but they weren't getting any use; the other battalion hadn't even set up an aid station and was just evacuating casualties straight to the surgical unit at Camp Fallujah. That meant that Lieutenant Kennedy and the team at our BAS were covering a lot of their casualties, and it meant that those two armored ambulances were just sitting around idling at the rear. But if they weren't going to put those tracks to use, I figured someone should. I still can't quite believe that it worked out this way, but Lieutenant Wilson was okay with us using them, and the crews were up for it too—they were tired of doing nothing and they wanted in. So they convoyed in with Kutilek providing security, and for the next three days I had a full APC ambulance platoon at my disposal. I could evac eight casualties at a time and still have two ambulances sitting there in case we needed them.

I didn't even get in much trouble over it—you're not really supposed to borrow another battalion's assets—though I did have to give them back when their colonel finally noticed they were missing three days later. My battalion commander, Lieutenant Colonel Brandl, was cool with it, though I don't think he knew that the requisition was unofficial. But he did look around one day and ask me if I was trying to run a tank battalion. "No, Sir," I said, "but we need 'em." I have to be honest— there are a few pimples on Lieutenant Colonel Brandl's ass in my opinion. He was maybe a little too fond of the media attention, and he almost never came into the FAS. But then again, his focus was very much on winning the battle, and he had an incredible number of responsibilities—he had to keep his emotions in check, and that probably meant not focusing too much on casualties. The colonel had the overall mission covered, and I had the casualties covered, so it worked out very well. And when it came to taking care of his Marines and his battalion, Lieutenant Colonel Brandl never hesitated. So when I told him that my pilfered ambulances were going to help us save 1/8 Marine lives, he didn't balk. I was a little more concerned, though, about informing him that the team three medic, Specialist Christine Knight of the North Carolina Army National Guard, was in fact a female. "Well," the colonel said, "build her a separate shitter." That was his answer, and God bless the man—not every commander would have been okay with it. I liked the fact that he made the call that would help his Marines the most and that, when I said I needed the extra tracks, he trusted me.

And boy, did we need them. I said before that most of the care we provided in Fallujah was pretty straightforward, basic stuff—pressure, Hespan, treat for shock, and move 'em on up to the next level of care. But that doesn't mean there weren't harder cases, where you try all your tricks but you don't know going in whether you'll be able to affect the outcome, and you don't always know coming out whether you did the right things. As the surgeon and as the boss, those were my cases, they were my responsibility, and they were my pain. I didn't ever have to crack a chest at the FAS, and I doubt a man could have survived the trip out afterward if I had. But we had some very, very damaged Marines come in, and I was doing some significant interventions. It was all working out okay until the early hours of November 12.

CHAPTER 12

The Going Gets Tougher

The cumulative brutality of the injuries we were seeing was starting to have an effect. The corpsmen were no older than the Marines we were treating—eighteen, nineteen, maybe twenty-three years old at the most—and they were seeing things that would floor an experienced trauma surgeon. And the corpsmen were often treating people they knew well, friends they had trained with for years in some cases, an emotional punch that civilian medical personnel rarely have to face. Sometimes, wounded Marines would be carried in and the corpsmen wouldn't even recognize them; they were coming in so messed up, covered in blood and gunk and mud. Then they'd see the man's name on his dog tags, and you could see the pain in their eyes as the realization sank in.

That moment of recognition was the hardest to handle for all of us. But these kids, my corpsmen, they handled it with real courage, guts, and professionalism. I was old enough to be their father, if I'd started young, or at least their big brother, and I tried to help them learn to do the things that they had to do. But those guys outplayed their potential to the extreme: they took on incredible challenges, they saved a lot of lives, and even in the heat of battle they remained deeply compassionate. If it would help, they would hold a guy's hand. We'd certainly make fun of them for it afterward, but out there they did whatever they could think of to provide comfort and they weren't afraid to do it, didn't think twice. That's not something I taught them. They just did it.

We'd gone a few days without a KIA and Johns and a couple of the guys got it into their heads that the way to keep our luck going was to stop shaving, like we were some kind of superstitious baseball team afraid to jinx a winning streak. I put an end to that pretty quickly. "This is fuckin' medicine, there's no luck," I told them. "If it happens, it happens. You're gonna shave." We were having a hard enough time keeping the FAS clean without a bunch of unshaven corpsmen staffing the place.

Right after that, on November 12, we lost another Marine, Corporal Nathan R. Anderson, 22, of Howard, Ohio. The Bravo Company Marine, known as Nate to his friends, took great pride in serving his nation, and in fighting for the good of the Iraqi people. Known for his compassion and drive to be the best Marine he could be, Corporal Anderson was one of the men who helped rescue Gunny Shane from the street during the ambush at the cultural center. This tough, popular Marine was killed by a group of insurgents who had disguised themselves in the "chocolate chip"–patterned uniforms of the Iraqi National Guard, and his death shook the remaining members of Bravo Company hard. And then things got worse.

We were getting ready in the early hours of November 13 when we heard a truck pull up in front of the FAS, and a corpsman, HM3 Milton Jones, yelled out, "He's not breathing!" I ran outside to the vehicle that had pulled up. I thought I had seen it all by this point, but seeing Corporal Jacob Knospler stopped me cold. His lower face—his entire lower maxillary apparatus, his jaw, his tongue, his teeth—was gone. His windpipe was just there, exposed to the night air.

Bravo Company had been fighting for four days straight by this time, and Knospler, a squad leader from first platoon, had been on his feet nearly the whole time. He'd fought hard and fought bravely; he was another of the guys who had saved Gunny Shane from the ambush in front of the cultural center. So it must have come as a relief when, at about two a.m. on the thirteenth, he received an order to enter a small house near Phase Line Henry, a major north-south route, and hunker down for a few hours before a planned daylight assault on a nearby mosque. The Marines moved in, clearing rooms on the ground floor with grenades before moving for the stairs. Knospler was first up—as squad leader, he could have sent one of his Marines, but he went himself—and he took an insurgent grenade full in the face. Another two grenades bounced down the stairs past Knospler and exploded, sending shrapnel into another six Marines, causing mostly minor injuries. Not so the corporal—the explosion and shrapnel had sheared his face away, from his left cheekbone to the lower-right-hand side of his jaw. He stumbled out of the building on his own power and collapsed.

Knospler was unconscious when he got to us, and suffocating on his own secretions. We got him into the aid station and tried to get his airway opened up. In a hospital you would use a suction hose to clear the mucus and fluid from the opening of the trachea; fortunately I had brought some "turkey basters"—medical equipment, but they look just like turkey basters—and was able to get Knospler's windpipe unplugged. I was getting ready to insert an airway tube down his throat, when he gasped—a big rush of air in and all of a sudden he's completely alert.

Quick decision—do I intubate now or not? It would be the simplest way to keep his airway open, but what kind of unimaginable pain and discomfort would he experience, hard plastic pushing into his shredded trachea? Knospler couldn't talk, of course, but he was crying, or trying to scream maybe, I don't know. "We're going to ride back together to the ambulance exchange point," I told him. If I went with him, I thought there was a better chance that he'd make it there alive. We got Corporal Knospler bandaged as well as we could, gave him a good dose of morphine to try to dent the pain a little, and I brought the rapid sequence intubation kit in case I had to use it.

We rode in, Specialist Knight and I with Corporal Knospler sitting between us on a stretcher. All I did was hold his head in the dim red light of the track, keeping him upright so the fluids he was leaking could drain. He kept trying to touch the bottom of his face, where it had been, and I had to hold his hands back. I actually held his hand, kept talking to him, kept sticking him with morphine, as much as he could tolerate, though I don't know how much it helped. He knew something was wrong, but he didn't know what and he couldn't talk, couldn't ask. It was a thirty-minute ride, I'll never forget it. We got to the exchange point and I grabbed the young doctor from regiment who was there; we'd radioed ahead, but I needed to be sure he could handle the situation. "Someone needs to ride back with this one," I said, and his eyes got huge—Knospler's bandages were slipping away and the doctor was as stunned as I had been. "Are you going to be okay with this?" I asked him, and he got it together. "Whatever you do, you do not let him stop breathing," I said as I left. Knospler hit Camp Fallujah and the surgical company immediately flew him up to Baghdad. He was at Bethesda Naval by November 16, 2004, after a stop in Landstuhl, Germany—still alive but facing years, if not a lifetime, of excruciating recovery.

By November 14, the American forces had swept through almost the entire city of Fallujah, killing an estimated one thousand or more insurgents and capturing several hundred more. It had been hard going—some three dozen American troops had been killed and two hundred or more wounded by that point. The insurgents took good advantage of defensive positions and their mobility as they fell back into the city. They managed to pin the American forces down time and again, firing AK-47s, RPGs, and sniper rifles from mosques, water towers, windows, and in the street. The official term is an "urban 3-D environment," and it explains why the Marines avoid urban warfare if they can, and prepare themselves for the worst if they can't. A city like Fallujah is a defender's dream. Each house was a potential firebase, hiding place, weapons cache, and booby-trap site, and Marines could be attacked from literally any angle, left, right, front, back, or above. The insurgents even took the fight underground, using a series of tunnels to move from building to building, while coordinating their movements by cell phone. They could fall back when pressed, swarm in to concentrate fire on vulnerable American units, and then fall back again to rest up, resupply, and wait for their next chance. Eventually, they had nowhere left to hide and holed up in houses throughout the city, waiting for a chance to kill a few more Americans as the Marines and soldiers started to move back and forth through the city, clearing it of remaining insurgents house by house.

Bravo Company was still pressing south, though. They held up momentarily at about seven thirty a.m. on the fourteenth, along with some members of Scout Sniper platoon, waiting for forces from the Army's 2–2 Task Force to link up for a joint advance. The Marines went firm, posting security at the perimeters and along rooftops. The sun was just coming up as Corporal Nicholas L. Ziolkowski—everybody called him Ski, one of the friendliest, most popular guys in the battalion—raised his head above his high-powered scope for a moment. A skilled sniper, the twenty-two-year-old from Towson, Maryland, was scanning the surrounding area for movement; in a firm situation like that your snipers are one of the most important aspects of force protection. Maybe it was the glint from his scope, or the movement of his head—I don't know. But something attracted the attention of a counter-sniper on the other side. One crack, one shot, and Corporal Ski went down.

HM2 Kevin Markley, Bravo Company's senior company corpsman, was there on the roof with him right away, and he saw, he knew, there was no way with a head shot like that. But you do everything you can, always. First Sergeant Whittington wanted to get his wounded Marine off the roof, so Markley did what he could to stabilize the man, and they moved him down, called in the medevac, and got started on their way in to us. Lieutenant Kutilek happened to be nearby when the AmTrac rolled into the FAS. I don't know if there's ever been a more eager platoon commander, and he had come into the command post to try to pick up another assignment. Kutilek helped me unload Corporal Ski into the aid station, and HM3 David Lester came into the FAS with us. I told the rest of the corpsmen to take off—they didn't need to see this, and we had no other casualties.

We settled Ziolkowski onto the cinder-block platform we had built to support our stretchers, and I took his helmet off, carefully. One look and I knew I couldn't save him. The power of a Russian Dragunov sniper rifle round can be amazing, and Ziolkowski had suffered overwhelming trauma. I could feel the plates of his skull moving under my hands as I tried to hold his neck aligned to place an airway. The smell of brain tissue was overwhelming, and I had to work hard to keep going. I remembered back to the operating room at the Washington Hospital Center trauma department, seven years earlier, and to the scruffy homeless guy who had tried to kill himself with a handgun, my first serious headshot. It wasn't fair—we put so much effort into saving that man, and he hadn't even wanted to live. Here I was with this brave Marine, a guy with the whole world to live for, and there wasn't a damn thing I could do for him. But we tried everything anyway—fluids, bandaging, I put a trach tube in— but there had never been any hope, and he passed quietly. I don't think he suffered from the time he was shot. We sent him home, and today he's buried in Arlington National Cemetery.

After that, I had to send Lester back to the BAS. We had already been through so many casualties, and this one, it was just too much. Lester had to bear the brunt of it, but we all felt Ski's loss deeply. I was glad to have Kutilek there. I think we helped each other hold our emotions in check in front of the men. He recalled the last time he had seen Corporal Ziolkowski; it had been at chapel service back at Haditha Dam. Ziolkowski had come in wearing a T-shirt and shorts—you were supposed to wear a uniform, but who cares, right? The guy came to church. Kutilek says Ski had a prayer request that week, for his sister's baby who had just been born. I don't know why, but I like that. It helps.

Somewhere toward the middle of that first week at war, I lost my composure one night. With all the casualties, discarded equipment was piling up around the FAS and our own supplies were starting to get thrown around and ending up out of place; there was just a lot of potential for chaos and squalor to arise. Zimmerman and Johns did a terrific job of keeping that from happening; they really kept the FAS very well organized and functional under the most extreme conditions imaginable. But after dealing with scores of casualties—probably something short of a hundred in the first four days—the blood, the smell of gray matter, it was there all the time, it just kind of lay in the air. This particular night, we had just gotten done dealing with another mass casualty and the place was a mess, and understandably, everyone was pretty down. I snapped a little. I guess I was cursing as much to keep us all moving as anything else. "I don't care how tired you are—get your fucking heads in the game now or go home," I barked, or something like it. Everyone rogered up, and we started getting the FAS back into shape. There was blood all over the floor, and Masino—Novelty Item—said, "Sir, there's blood on the floor, how we gonna get this out?" I completely lost my temper. "If you fucking guys can't figure out—dammit, that is the most absurd thing I've ever fucking heard from a Sailor in the United States Navy! You don't know how to get blood out of a room? What the fuck are you doing here?"

Okay, Masino did have a knack for pissing me off. But I wasn't just annoyed with him; it was the blood on the floor that made me crack. We had lost too many good men and the blood was like a rebuke, like an accusation of failure. It wasn't just blood, it was the lifeblood of Marines who had come to us for help, and sometimes, no matter what we did, we could not provide it. That blood meant that we had failed in our mission and let our Marines down. If I hadn't had Masino to blow up at, I don't know what I would have done.

It's dangerous for a doctor to get too used to winning, we start thinking that we've got some special power to change events. But you can't change them all, not in a makeshift FAS in Fallujah, and not in the most modern OR in the world. You can forget that lesson for a while, but that just means greater pain when you do lose the competition with death. It's not just the pain of failure; it's the pain of knowing that you're sending a patient home to his family in a box, and that they are going to have terrible Thanksgivings or terrible Christmases for years to come as a result of your failure. For me, that's the worst, knowing that I couldn't save these families from that grief as a doctor any more than I could save my own family from the grief of losing my brother Gregory as a nine-year-old. I tried to keep that misery to myself in Fallujah, as a doctor and as an officer, that was my duty. But once in a while, some of it escaped.

Later that night, I took a moment to lay down the law. I told the corpsmen that they were adults, they knew their jobs, and they knew our plan. Figure out what needs to happen so things work smoothly, I told them; fix what needs to be fixed and don't rely on me for every little decision along the way. It was good advice, I thought, and most of the time, it worked; they found shelving units, reworked the sandbagging, and set up a system for tracking daily chores, as well as rigging up a sort of squeegee/ mop out of a piece of two-by-four and an old broom handle that worked well enough for clearing blood out of our little prayer room. But they may have taken it too far on occasion as well. We had our FAS set up, and a secure sleeping quarters nearby, but I realized that we needed a call room; either Zimmerman or I was on call at the prayer room all the time, and dammit, you want a place to sack out if you ever get the chance. I suggested that there must be a couch or something around somewhere, and that it might be nice to have one. I guess they were trying to show me that they were really trying, because it didn't take long before they came trotting up with this nice, big black velvet couch, with gold embroidery, that they'd found in the high-rise building across the way. True, I did tell them to get a couch and to work things out for themselves, but I didn't think they'd sprint across a sniper field to get it. "Oh yeah, we got shot at a little bit," they said. "But we got the couch." Their hearts were sure in the right place, even if their brains sometimes weren't. But, hey, we had a couch, we were improving our position. We put it on the porch, and if we ever got a moment of quiet, we hoped to be able to sit down and relax.

I shouldn't give them a hard time, though, without mentioning that they were in good company. Mark Winn, the battalion XO, is a terrific commander and an unbeatable runner, but he's also a hard-core junk-food addict, and his number-one drug of choice is Coca-Cola or the closest thing to it he can get. We were standing at the open gateway near the FAS on our first night at the government center, talking about how we could make it more secure, harden it up a bit, when Mark spotted a single two-liter bottle of Pepsi sitting on a countertop in a candy store across the open area. "Just shoot this in the air if you hear anybody shooting at me," he said, handing me his M16. And then he was off, running, doing the zigzag. Well, he made it there and went through the open door—no snipers, no booby traps—and he got his prize. He grabbed the bottle and managed to run back without getting shot. With great satisfaction, the XO twisted off the top and was about to take a chug of it, when he detected an unfamiliar stench. That's when he realized that the bottle was filled with a green, nasty-looking and bad-smelling mold. He poured some on the ground and it was like pond water. We both started laughing as he said, "Well, I guess if that's the worst thing that happens, we'll be okay." It wasn't, of course, not by a long shot. But it was still a funny moment—we didn't have enough of those.

Around the thirteenth, an Iraqi unit came down and set up near us in the government center. We had found a Holy Quran in the prayer room we were using for our aid station, and we had set it aside, not quite sure what to do with it. When the Iraqi unit came in, Johns took it over and presented it to them. They were thrilled—very, very grateful, I guess because Johns was showing respect and consideration. I'm not quite sure how he learned how to do that, growing up in an Indiana cornfield, but time after time I saw him just step in and know the right thing to do. Someone else might have looked at that Quran and thought it would make a sweet war memento, but Johns, and all these guys really, seemed to have a real sense of care, concern, and respect for the Iraqi people and their customs and religion. The embedded Iraqi troops were okay, much better than their counterparts at Haditha Dam. We got along fine for the most part, and they did their thing, mostly going out with our line companies to sweep mosques. A lot of it was photo-op stuff, honestly, but at least they showed up for the fight. A funny thing, though: we did requisition a few items—Mark's Pepsi, my couch, a bookcase, and those cinder blocks we used to prop our stretchers up on—but the Iraqi troops started treating the shops across the street like they were their own personal canteen. The shops were all padlocked down, but when the Iraqi unit came in, they cracked them open and just helped themselves to whatever they wanted—coffee, candy, whatever they could get. We didn't do that, we were very careful not to do that, but how do you tell somebody in their own country that they can't do that?

And I have to admit, I was somewhat sympathetic. You really do need whatever small comforts you can get when you're living under the kind of extreme stress we had at the government center. That couch, for example. Even with all of the work, all the gore and brutality, the constant stress and responsibility, I still managed a few moments of quiet contemplation from time to time, usually sitting out there on that couch on the FAS porch. I had to spend a lot of my nights in the aid station; Zimmerman or I had to be there all the time, and you couldn't sleep outside in the open air, it was just too dangerous. Our setup worked great when we had casualties, and that little room made a good, safe aid station—it was the lifesaver for a lot of people. But at night, alone, it felt more like a morgue to me. I hated being in there by myself, in the pitch dark, with the smells. It was still warm during the days, and there was only so much we could do to swab it out. Having that couch outside gave me a place I could go for a few minutes, just to clear my head and my lungs. A moment's peace.

Sometimes, however, you needed a distraction more than peace. That's how the tradition of "story time" began; just before we were about to turn in, I would start telling a story. We'd hunker down behind the sandbags at the aid station, smoke some cigarettes, and I'd tell them stories about my past. I would like to be able to report that these were stories about my good deeds, previous glory and early sporting triumphs, but hey, we were at war. The young guys, all their stories were about the gorgeous women they'd supposedly been with. "Well, boys, lemme tell ya . . ." I'd start, and proceed to dredge up the most sordid, drunken, despicable episodes from my hooligan past that I could recall, some of it stuff I hadn't thought about in years, all of it stuff that any decent officer, husband, or father would have kept buried as far down in his psyche as he could get it. One of their favorites ended with my college roommate saying, "Dude, you got a problem."

What can I say? I was a huge hit. Story time became a nightly institution, and the audience kept growing. I was amazed, and just a little horrified, at how many of these stories I had. I'd tell a different one every night, and I didn't have to make anything up. On that first evening, there were just three or four of us sitting out there, the corpsmen and me. The second night, Sergeant Kelly Starling from the CO's mobile security unit showed up—"Sir, I hear you tell a pretty good story," he said, and settled in, so we had a group of five or six. By the next night, when Sergeant Major Anthony Hope came running up and asked, "Sir, is it seven o'clock? Are you telling a story tonight? I heard they're pret-ty foul!" I started to think that my college roommate probably had had a point. But what are you going to do? An officer has to look out for his troops' morale, no matter what the personal sacrifice.

CHAPTER 13
Finishing the Fight

As the battle wore on, there were whole days that were a blur, but there were always moments that remained crystal clear in my memory. The memories from the middle days of November 2004 are rough. There was Corporal Ziolkowski's death, and on the same day Alpha Company lost another Marine, Lance Corporal Travis R. Desiato, nineteen, the son of a doctor from Bedford, Massachusetts. Alpha Company's first squad had come under fire, and entered a house with the intention of clearing it, so it could be used as a base for counterattack. But as Desiato, an outstanding athlete with a gentle streak and a soft spot for little kids, moved through the house, he was met with a hail of gunfire from six insurgents who had been hiding there. During the ensuing firefight, Desiato's unit tried repeatedly to reach him, but by the time they did, he was dead. Desiato had joined the Marines with his eye on Iraq, saying that he wanted to go where he was most needed. If he didn't make it back, Travis left a message with his family: "For anyone who asks, say 'I did my job.'" Lance Corporal Travis Desiato did his job, and then some.

The next day, November 15, Bravo Company suffered two more fatalities. Lance Corporal William L. Miller, twenty-two, of Pearland, Texas, was killed by an insurgent hiding in the minaret of a mosque. Lance Corporal Miller and several other Marines were climbing the stairs into the minaret—Miller, as brave and gung-ho a Marine as there is, was in the lead, right where he always wanted to be—when the enemy above fired down, killing Miller and forcing the others back down the stairs. Sergeant Samuel Williams and the rest of the squad kept fighting their way back up the stairs under heavy fire until they finally managed to recover Lance Corporal Miller's body; the minaret was destroyed with a five-hundred-pound bomb shortly afterward. Lance Corporal Bradley L. Parker, nineteen, of Marion County, West Virginia, died the same day, killed instantly after being hit with an exploding IED. A very likable young Marine and a high achiever, Parker was known for his sense of humor and his contagious smile. He had wanted to be a Marine from the age of six, and learned about life in the Corps from an uncle who was also a Marine. Lance Corporal Parker had known exactly what he was getting into, and he died doing it with honor and courage.

These deaths were a blow to all of us, and the bare outlines of these Marines' final moments could never do justice to the lives they lived—as one of the 1/8 "Gold Star" mothers says, "It wasn't how they died that made them heroes, it was how they lived." Some of the fallen Marines I knew personally, and others I just got to know more about later, but I can say that they were heroes, every one. By the end of the first week of the battle, the 1/8 had lost eight brave Marines, and we must have treated almost 150 casualties. But the Marines had done an incredible job of fighting through the city, and I thought the worst must be over. I was tragically wrong.

By the eighteenth, the open firefights in the street were pretty much done, and the flow of casualties had slowed to the point where I felt I could take a break and get out into the city a little. It would be the first time I left the FAS since I had gone out with Bravo, earlier in the week, to help a pregnant civilian who was going into labor and was having some trouble. There weren't many civilians left in Fallujah but some of those who stayed were people who couldn't get out for one reason or another, and we ended up helping quite a few. We got that lady transported up to the "Jordanian" hospital on the eastern edge of the city.

But on this day, my mission was to check in with my line corpsmen who were out with Alpha Company, seven guys in all. I took along my medical bag, but my main goal was to boost morale, let the guys know they were not alone. The Marines were now focused on the dangerous job of clearing the remaining nests of insurgents from the buildings where they had holed up. There were something like twenty or thirty thousand buildings in Fallujah, and there weren't many that the Marines didn't enter, search, and clear. The problem was that these houses were like pillboxes—perfect fire platforms and defensive positions for a handful of insurgents to hole up in or booby-trap. To clear them was nerve-wracking work.

Alpha Company's Gunny Ramos came in to pick me up— and probably to visit Lester's sandbag shitters—and we headed out. Alpha had pushed all the way to the southern extreme of the city by this time. It felt good to get out into the city and away from the government center and the FAS for a while. First, I went to see Alpha's senior company corpsman, HM3 Casey Moody, and to say hello to Captain Cunningham, the company CO, to let him know I was there. "Man, Doc, you just show up everywhere," he said, and that felt good; it was always my goal to let the Marines know that we really were everywhere with them. I watched Alpha Company clear some houses and get in some gunfights, and thankfully nobody on our side got wounded. The worst thing that happened to me was that I froze my butt off sleeping out there with them. It had turned cold quite suddenly about halfway through November, which helped from the standpoint of hygiene and odor around the FAS, but it made the nights pretty chilly.

I was feeling upbeat when we pulled back into the government center on the morning of the nineteenth, but that feeling didn't last long. HM2 Markley, the senior company corpsman from Bravo, was back again; he'd been through everything by that point: Lonny Wells and the ambush at the cultural center, Jimenez, Anderson, Ziolkowski, Miller, Parker, and scores of wounded. He was a tough kid, a twenty-two-year-old Navy brat and a first-rate corpsman, but I think this last round of casualties was his limit. He was yelling when he came in, calling out that Brown was shot, that he needed help.

First platoon had been clearing a house near a mosque at the intersection of Phase Lines Grace and Frank. First squad lined up in a stack, breached the front door, and poured into the hallway, only to be met by a spray of AK-47 fire from a single occupant. Three men went down immediately, two Marines and an Iraqi interpreter who had inexplicably joined the stack at the last moment. Lance Corporal Demarkus Brown, shot in the chest, struggled back into the courtyard and out of the kill zone; the other two men were unable to move on their own. Lieutenant Andrew Eckert hustled the rest of his platoon onto the roof to breach the house from above and hopefully avoid the enemy fire. The occupant had holed up in a ground-floor bedroom and popped out to fire another AK burst into Dimitrios Gavriel, a burly twenty-nine-year-old lance corporal from New York City who lay wounded in the front hallway. The Marines on the roof dropped a stun grenade down the ladder well and stormed after it into the hallway. They were met with an exploding fragmentation grenade, tossed from behind the bedroom door; three Marines were wounded, three others made it into an adjacent room; from there they breached the back bedroom with a frag grenade of their own. The one insurgent had inflicted six casualties on his own. When the Bravo Company Marines recovered his body from the bedroom, they recognized him as a man they had exchanged fire with on the other side of the block not long before.

HM2 Markley and Lance Corporal Brown were close—they were the same age and had trained together for years, and they used to spend a lot of time BS-ing about their cars. Markley drove a Toyota MR2, Brown a Nissan Skyline, and they'd spend hours talking about how they were going to soup them up once they got back, who was going to beat who in the ultimate race. Stripping off Brown's vest and uniform, Markley saw the wound in his friend's chest—bright red and frothing, a sucking chest wound. But Brown was alert, more than alert, he was talking. The corpsman got an Asherman chest seal bandage on Brown's wound and piled him into the waiting AmTrac. The aid station wasn't far, Markley thought, so they should be fine.

Brown was still talking in the back of the cas-evac vehicle, but he was starting to fade. The Marine was losing blood fast, so much blood that Markley had to keep changing out his chest bandage, the damn thing wouldn't stick in all the fluid. The corpsman laid his friend on his side, with the wound down so the one good lung could breathe, and he kept talking, trying to keep Brown awake. "Come on, Brown, fight for it," he shouted. "I don't want to have to put a tube in you if you go under!" Brown was in and out by then, but he laughed when Markley slapped him awake, laughed and said, "I'm gonna die," just like that—no fear, no anger, just sort of "Why are you so worried, can't you see what's happening here?" Then the lance corporal got quiet. "Hey, Doc, come here," Brown whispered. "I leaned in and he kissed me," Markley said later. "He kissed me and said he loved me. I told him he was a big fag and told him to keep fighting, but if I could take that moment back I would have told him that I loved him too."

It wasn't the largest mass casualty we had, but in terms of the severity of the wounds, it was bad. I don't remember the order they came off the Marines' AmTrac. I just remember being grateful that Carlos Kennedy and Russ Folley were there to help out; we were starting to rotate guys out to the BAS, and Carlos and Chief had come in to take over for Zimmerman and me. I started triaging, and it was painful. There was nothing we could do for Lance Corporal Gavriel, he had suffered severe gunshot wounds to the head and chest. He was twenty-nine, a graduate of Brown University, and a former Wall Street financial analyst who had joined the Marines after friends were killed in the

September 11 terror attack on the World Trade Center. Gavriel had already been sent to the rear once with a minor wound, but he insisted on going back in to continue the fight. (That's not surprising. The former Division I college wrestler had dropped forty pounds and overcome old knee and ankle injuries to get into the Corps in the first place—no way was he going to let anything keep him from the action.)

The interpreter—a very nice guy the Marines called either Moo, after his first name, or Blue, like the character from the movie *Old School*—was attached to Bravo and he had been shot in the arm and in the back, just below his flak jacket. He was very unstable and was screaming in pain. He needed help fast. I sent him into the FAS and Kennedy got to work on him.

I assigned corpsmen to the other wounded, and took Lance Corporal Brown myself. He was still alive, taking breaths and looking around, his eyes open, but the shot in his chest was a bad one. "Don't let him die," Markley said to me, desperation in his eyes, and to Brown he said, "Don't worry, you're here—you got Doc, you're gonna be okay." Mark Winn was there too—he was always there when we had casualties—and he gave me a look. "Don't worry," I told them both. I thought we had it. But as I started examining Brown, I discovered that he had lost a lot of blood, a lot more than I expected. We couldn't get an IV line in to give him Hespan—you need some pressure in the veins to get a needle into them. His status plummeted. He got shocky and was losing consciousness and his pulse was getting weak and thready. *Damn*—tension pneumothorax, maybe hemothorax, I figured, air or blood filling up inside his chest and keeping his lungs from expanding. I moved to the side of his rib cage and tried to decompress his lungs with a needle, but it quickly clotted up, so I slid a chest tube between his ribs and into the space around his lungs. I got the tube in and blood rushed out—a lot of blood. Brown perked up for just a moment like he could really breathe all of a sudden, and then collapsed back and went under completely, his breathing stopped.

We tried to get an airway tube in, but couldn't get it down past his voice box—laryngeal spasm, his throat closed off. I had to do a cricothyroidotomy. While Winn held the lance corporal's legs, I cut down into Brown's windpipe and inserted a tube so we could breathe for him. *"C'mon, Brown, don't give up on me!"* I was yelling. But nothing was working. I looked over for a second and saw Kennedy struggling with his patient, the interpreter. This was his first big one; he had a month of trauma training and he'd handled casualties at the BAS, but he was on his own on this one and the interpreter was losing pressure fast. He wouldn't stabilize. Kennedy was slightly shaking. I saw the fear in his eyes and I recognized it. Not fear for himself, but fear for his patient, fear that he might not be able to do enough for him. I knew that fear all too well. I was driven by it. I actually think it's a big part of what makes a good trauma doctor so long as you can keep it under control. The Iraqi interpreter survived long enough to get into the ambulance, but he died the next day or so. I believe he was the only person who left the FAS alive who later died from his injuries. No one will ever know what prompted him to go into that house.

Brown didn't have a choice but to go in—it was his job and he did it bravely and well. Now I was trying to do mine, but we still couldn't get fluids into him, and nothing I tried was helping to revive him. Todd Wilson, the ambulance platoon commander, was with us, and he started in on a saphenous cut-down. The guy's a cardiothoracic physician's assistant. He does this all the time, slicing down through the skin above the ankle bone to get at the saphenous vein, the vessel cardiothoracic surgeons use as graft material for heart bypass operations. Wilson got in and got his fingers around the vein and he worked a cannula, a long thin tube, right up into it—dry, nothing came out, no blood. Brown was literally drained. We worked on him for forty-five minutes, but eventually there was nothing else to try. It was a crushing loss. I put my arms around Markley, both of us crying. "I'm sorry," I said. "I didn't do it, couldn't do it. I'm sorry."

Lance Corporal Demarkus D. Brown had come into the FAS just two days earlier; you could still see the stitches where we had patched up his lip, after he got tagged with a piece of shrapnel. He had a tooth knocked out too, but Brown was smiling and trying to laugh, even while Zimmerman was sewing him up. He was a tough kid, but cheerful. He wanted to go back out and we said sure, fine, there was no reason for him not to. "Hey, Doc," he joked when he heard he could rejoin his unit, "do I still get a Purple Heart for this?" "Sure you get one," Zimmerman said, and we all laughed. But now that he was dead, I found myself wondering if we should have let him go. I know it was the right call, but it still bothers me, and I know it still bothers Zimmerman, too. Brown wanted to go back out, he was medically fit and it was his job—and it was our job to send him. But when he came back in with that chest wound, I couldn't save him; that was my job too and I failed. I don't know if we ever had a chance—if I had had blood for a transfusion maybe, but we didn't have the facilities. Should I have cracked his chest and cross-clamped his aorta to try to boost the blood flow? Maybe, but hell, I'm in the middle of freaking dirt and dust, and how would he ever survive the trip up to surgical with a cracked chest and no life support? I probably let Wilson work too long trying to get access, and maybe I should've just gone for a central line, punched an IV catheter right into his subclavian vein, a big fat vessel up near the heart. I didn't have a central line kit, but I could've figured some way to get in there. Did he not have blood because he had pericardial tamponade? I didn't tap his heart, but it didn't hit me, didn't look like that was the problem. I don't know. I just don't know. Demarkus Brown, Lonny Wells—when they come in alive and then they die, you question everything you did, time and time again.

You don't always have time for that right away, but the losses still affect you. I looked around and there was blood everywhere; it may have been the bloodiest day we'd ever had in the FAS. Almost immediately after we got the rest of the casualties evacuated up to regiment—no time to clean up, no time to get my head back, no time to check on Markley, who had gone off in a rage—another Marine came into the FAS with a kind of confused look on his face. Zimmerman and Avila had brought him in. "Doc, I got a headache," he said. I looked up and saw that his helmet had a hole in the front. "Holy fuck, dude, you got shot!" I said. We carefully took his helmet off and discovered that he had taken a high-velocity sniper round right through the Kevlar and across the crown of his head. He had a graze wound that parted his hair right down to the skull. But that was it. He needed to be stapled back together, but there was no real damage and not even much blood, just this incredible split down the middle of his scalp. Avila and Zimmerman closed him up and then sent him to the rear. I probably could have sent him back to his unit, but there's a point where it's just enough— maybe this guy had used up his luck for the day.

CHAPTER 14
The Pickle Factory

The 1/8 had penetrated all the way to the southern edge of Fallujah by November 15, 2004, and then started pushing from east to west. The game had changed. American forces controlled the open spaces now, posting security teams along the major roadways and occupying important buildings. But hundreds of insurgents remained, armed, cornered, and facing certain death or capture. Some people have compared Fallujah to Vietnam, but as Bing West says in his book *No True Glory*, it was really more like Iwo Jima. Both sides were willing to fight to the death to take control of this strategic "island." To finish the job, our troops had to go into the houses where the insurgents had holed up and pull them out. It was an enormously dangerous task that gave the insurgents every advantage: from the time the Marines blew the lock on the outer metal gate, went through the front courtyard, up to the front door and into the entryway of the typical Fallujah house, the Marines were forced to pass through narrow "funnels" without cover, while the defenders had dozens of angles to fire from, options for booby traps and corners from which to launch final, desperate grenade and AK-47 attacks.

It was a brutal task for the Marines, and it changed the pace and tempo of our work as well. Central Fallujah was largely pacified by that time, and the Civil Affairs Group was planning to move their operation into the government center to get ready for the time when civilians would return. Most of the action by this point had shifted south, so we shut down our government center aid station when the battle space was reorganized and the battalion left, and we established a new position deeper in the city. I left that up to Lieutenant Kennedy, Chief Folley, and the crew of corpsmen they brought in with them and I convoyed up to the rear for a few days. I went out with the National Guard crews and their ambulances; the Army wanted them back, and we figured we were probably done with the mass casualties they had been so essential for. It was hard to see them go, though—those twelve men and one woman were fearless soldiers and skilled medics, and they played a huge role in saving as many Marines as we did.

I stopped in at the Battalion Aid Station, but it was quiet there now, so I headed on to Camp Fallujah. It was a huge base, with a lot of civilians and contractors. It was just a few miles away from the battle, from the Marines who were still fighting every day, but it was like a different world. I visited some of our wounded who were recuperating there, but I also got to spend some time by myself. I took showers—a lot of showers—and got some clean utilities. I only had two sets of cammies when I went into Fallujah, and both of them were completely caked with blood. My boots had become so stiff with blood that Lieutenant Colonel Brandl had given me his extra pair. I even took a couple of aerobics classes—it was surreal. I was glad to have some rest, but I wanted to get back in. I returned to the city on Thanksgiving Day, November 25, 2004.

Some people will tell you that I'm hard to please. Well, okay, yeah, I'm always looking for ways to improve things, and I guess that can be a pain in the ass. Plus, it's kind of fun to ride the corpsmen a little—*"Aw, Sir, you never like anything we do, you always want something different."* They did find a good spot for our new Forward Aid Station—it was in the industrial area in southern Fallujah—and they set us up in a building I called the pickle factory. I don't know if it was really a pickle factory, but they were definitely putting something in big jars and I like pickles, so . . . pickle factory. Anyway, the building was good. There was a warehouse area at the back with a loading dock, which was handy because we no longer had our ambulances and had to use Humvees to load and unload casualties. As soon as I'd said hello, happy Thanksgiving, I told them we were going to change it all around. I wasn't just yanking their chains, either—they had set up the aid station in a smaller anteroom off of the loading dock and taken the larger space for their sleeping quarters. That left room for only two stretchers in the aid station proper. These guys hadn't had any casualties while I was gone—remarkable—and they didn't know that we were going to need a lot more space than they had allowed themselves. They found out real quick.

I was back for maybe a minute, just long enough to spoil the corpsmen's Thanksgiving by telling them they'd screwed up everything, when things got worse, fast. A casualty call came in over the radio, six wounded, and we had only the two beds set up. Now I was pissed for real. "Dammit, you fucks are making this real difficult!" It wasn't their fault we had casualties coming in, wasn't their fault that it was Thanksgiving or that it happened the minute I got back. And it wasn't their fault that two of the casualties were coming in deceased, that for the rest of their lives their families would now dread Thanksgiving Day instead of looking forward to it. But I didn't have anyone to yell at for all that, so I yelled at the corpsmen instead, and we hustled fast to get set up.

It was Bravo Company again. They were hard into clearing operations now, and the work was getting confusing. RCT-7 had started running a food and water distribution point for civilians near a mosque in Bravo Company's area of operations, and that brought noncombatants out into the streets. That increased tension levels, but the men persevered, and everyone was looking forward to Thanksgiving and the promise of their first hot meal since the battle began. But there was work to be done first—third platoon Bravo had located a large weapons cache in a house, and the area had to be secured. First squad headed out to get Explosive Ordnance Disposal (EOD, the bomb squad) while third squad investigated the area.

Five Marines—Corporal Gentian Marku along with Lance Corporals Thomas Hodges, Jeffery S. Holmes, Michael Rodriguez and Blake Benson, a combat engineer—were approaching a neighboring house when machine-gun fire erupted through the front door. *Ambush*. Holmes, a twenty-year-old lance corporal from White River Junction, Vermont, was the first hit and he went down, in the building's courtyard. The others scrambled for cover, but Hodges, Rodriguez, and Blake were hit as well. Marku, a twenty-two-year-old Albanian citizen who had immigrated to

Sterling Heights, Michigan, with his family at age fourteen, opened up on the insurgents in the house, giving the other men a chance to find better cover and help return fire. Hit hard, Corporal Marku fell near the door of the house. Benson, though shot in each leg, stood and rushed in to retrieve Marku, but was shot in the head and barely managed to escape to cover. More Marines—Corporal Dominic Esquibel and Lance Corporal David Houck—rushed into the area to assist, and managed to get Benson, Hodges, and Rodriguez to safety while they returned the insurgents' fire. Again and again the Marines pushed in to try to recover Holmes and Marku, but the enemy was firing from too many vantage points—windows, the door—and rescue was impossible. For Holmes, it was too late already, but Marku, though seriously wounded, was alive briefly. Unfortunately, the insurgents noticed this too—and literally sent everything they had into the two fallen men. The Marines continued to fight to retrieve their bodies for forty-five minutes.

When Bravo pulled in to our new Forward Aid Station, I knew right away that it was bad. The wounded Marines needed help fast, but the corpsmen were seasoned veterans by that point, and I knew they could handle everything that came in that day. My role was starting to change then—from overseeing the treatment of the wounded to taking care of the guys who didn't make it. My corpsmen had enough to cope with treating the living, I figured, so I tried to spare them that final grim duty if I could—let them be part of the wins instead of the losses. I guess that probably started with Gentian Marku and Jeffery Holmes.

The insurgents in that house had been ruthless with Holmes and Marku, and their bodies arrived at our FAS in very rough shape. Matthew Kutilek happened to be there at the time, preparing to head out on a patrol, and news of Marku's passing hit him hard. "I had known Marku for over two years and thought him to be an outstanding Marine," Kutilek says. "He gave his life for a country he could not even call his own. It was the first and only time in Iraq that I had trouble looking at a dead body, friend or foe." Corporal Marku loved America and died defending our country—and he was very proud of being a United States Marine. But it was his wish to be buried in his family's village in Albania. He was awarded that country's "Golden Medal of Eagle" for "sublime sacrifice in the fight against terrorism, for the protection of the values of democracy, peace and freedom, by glorifying the honor of his nation." Gentian Marku was a remarkable young man and Marine, and a credit to his native land and his adopted home alike.

If Marku's body had been in bad shape, I knew that Holmes was going to be even worse. The Marines brought his body in wrapped in a sheet, and even though the Marine stood six feet, two inches tall—he had wanted to be an Air Force pilot but felt he was too tall—the bundle could not have measured more than three feet long. The corpsmen, thankfully, were busy with the wounded, so I asked Lieutenant Dennis Cox, the Navy chaplain, to help me. I don't know if it was his job or not, but Lieutenant Cox never hesitated when I asked for his assistance with a fallen Marine. Even if it was just help getting a man into a body bag, these Marines were now in a place where a chaplain was of much more use to them than a doctor, and I was always glad for his help. Lieutenant Kutilek joined us, and together we pulled back the sheet that contained Jeffery Holmes's body. The Vermont Marine was a great guy, with an infectious sense of humor and easygoing nature, and all I can say is that it was a blessing that he had already passed when the RPG struck his body. We worked in silence, arranged the lance corporal's body as well as we could, and decided that it was time to establish a morgue. I don't know if I've ever felt more inadequate in my life.

We spent the next day shifting things around, moving the aid station into the larger space, setting up four stretchers, and spreading the sleeping quarters around a little to make enough room for everybody. I had a couple of concerns. One was that with the ambulances gone, we had to rely on Humvees for transport in and out. That was fine in terms of security: the insurgents who were left had gone to ground, holed up in houses and buildings just hoping to cause some damage to the Marines who would inevitably be coming to get them. I couldn't always get more than one vehicle at a time, though, and I didn't want to evacuate wounded men and bodies at the same time if I could help it. We needed a morgue.

The pickle factory site had pretty good resources for that sort of project, and I got busy creating a suitable area. I walled off an area at the back of our larger space with an L-shaped stack of crates. I found a cot and mattress at the back as well and put those in the new space, too. The prayer room back at the government center had felt like a morgue sometimes, and now I was sleeping in one for real. I never shared the room, though; I always made sure that we evacuated the bodies out of the city before sleeping myself, not because I wouldn't sleep in the presence of our fallen brothers but because they had done enough, given enough, and if I couldn't help them in any other way, at least I could speed their bodies on that long, last journey home to their families.

It was important to me, as it is to all Marines and corpsmen, to be sure that the deceased Marines were treated with respect and dignity at every step on that final voyage. I made sure that we had room to lay them out individually and in a careful manner, and I looked at every man who came in. You have to do that to an extent. You have to go through their pockets to see if they're carrying any ammo or secure materials, things like maps or operational orders. But there's more to it than that. I made sure to look every Marine in the face; there's something about seeing their faces. It's too easy to start thinking about our deceased service men and women as numbers—one thousand killed, two thousand killed, and so on—and forget that each one was a vital human being, a son or daughter, often a mother or father, and someone who will be missed desperately at home.

We laid the men out in body bags when we had them, but we didn't keep many around—just part of not wanting to have to use them, I guess. But we also found some bolts of white cloth nearby, I forget where, and we were able to make decent shrouds to cover the deceased Marines. It wasn't a lot, but it was the best we could do to show our respect for these young men who had sacrificed so much.

And so it was back to work. The temperature had really dropped by this point and it was regularly below freezing now, twenty-seven, twenty-eight degrees or so at night. That became a major concern for us, and not just for our own comfort. In the initial phase of the battle, we saw a lot of penetrating trauma and deep bleeds, the results of sniper fire and open-range firefights. Now the wounds were shifting toward more percussive injuries, shrapnel blasts and burns, the results of opening up a house to be met with a booby trap or a barrage of grenades. Any trauma patient needs to be kept warm; the body is trying to go into shock and low body temperature will only speed that process. But we still had big bleeds, too, and that made warmth a particular issue. There's a point in the progression of blood loss where the body starts to go into crisis. Doctors call it exsanguination, or hypovolemia, Marines call it bleeding out, but what it comes down to is that there's a lot more involved in bleeding to death than blood just sort of draining away. Blood is a pretty complex fluid, and when you lose too much of it you start to get into three specific kinds of trouble. Trauma specialists call it the "lethal triad"—hypothermia, coagulopathy, and acidosis. The cycle starts when blood levels in the body drop to a point where the tissues aren't getting enough of the oxygen blood carries, so the metabolism starts to shut down and body-heat generation goes with it. That kicks off hypothermia, a drop in core temperature, which can be hell on the heart and circulation. Hypothermia also messes up the blood's ability to clot, or coagulate—coagulopathy—so you lose one of the body's major natural defenses against bleeding. And it doesn't take much time in an oxygen-deprived state for your cells to start producing lactic acid, which drops blood pH and messes up the heart even more. A lot of other things can go wrong along the way, but the three physiological factors feed back on each other. Once the body enters this triad, it tends to spiral out of control rapidly; the heart spasms and gives out, the vessels relax, and the fluids release—"declamping syndrome," some people call it—and the patient dies. Trauma care for massive bleeding focuses on preventing the cycle in the first place—you've got to plug the bleeds, of course, but you also have to keep your patients warm.

We had been using Mylar space blankets all along to help the wounded men hold on to their own body heat, but with the dropping temperatures, that was no longer enough. The warehouse space we were in had been impacted in the battle and the roof had partially collapsed. Light discipline—making sure that no light escaped so we didn't give our position away—wasn't as important now, so we got aggressive about improving the temperature. I had the corpsmen construct makeshift fireplaces out of rubble in the window wells that were set into the external walls. We would keep embers going in them, and every time we had casualties coming in we would stoke up the fires with busted-up shipping pallets. It was crude and it made for a pretty ominous atmosphere—the bombed-out ceiling, the light from the fires, the smoke and the condensation from our breath—but it worked. The other concern was our IV fluid. Even at body temperature, it presents a lethal triad risk because the fluid dilutes the blood cells. But if you put cold fluid into a wounded man, you might just as well declare him dead on the spot. The corpsmen came up with a brilliant solution, though, and spent the rest of the time at the pickle factory with a couple of 500cc bags of Hespan taped to their thighs under their utilities.

The Marines continued to sweep back and forth through the city, clearing houses, destroying weapons caches, and securing mosques and major buildings. And the casualties kept coming in. We lost two more Marines on the twenty-sixth. Alpha Company's Bradley M. Faircloth, a twenty-year-old lance corporal from Mobile, Alabama, earned his nickname—Barbarian—the hard way. The former high school football player had a defensive lineman's aggressive instincts, and he always wanted to be point man when his squad was entering a house to secure it. Faircloth had already been wounded twice in the Battle of Fallujah when he was killed by RPK fire while entering a house occupied by several insurgents. He was almost as dedicated to his high school football program as he was to the Marine Corps, and Lance Corporal Faircloth made an unusual request before he deployed to Iraq: if anything happened to him, he said, he wanted a memorial fund set up to help pay for a statue of his high school's mascot. The result—an impressive half-ton bronze panther—was unveiled at Murphy High School in Mobile in April 2006.

Bravo Company Marines Dominic Esquibel and David B. Houck had played key roles in rescuing three of their wounded brothers the previous day, but they were distraught over the two they lost—Marku and Holmes. Lance Corporal Houck had been particularly close to Corporal Marku, and was angry and heartbroken as Bravo pushed on with the mission—clearing more houses just like the one that had claimed his friends' lives. Maybe that was why he went in first this time, angry, with just his rifle, when he could have let a SAW (squad automatic weapon) gunner go first with heavier firepower. The front door had been open, and the first room was clear, but Houck noticed a towel stuffed under an inside door, and he must have known that meant insurgents. He went anyway, first, and though the blast of gunfire wounded him mortally, he managed to pull the door shut and block the insurgents' attack. The Marines pulled back, and the house was destroyed by a D9 Cat bulldozer— there had been eleven enemy fighters in that room. Lance Corporal Houck was twenty-five, from Millbridge, North Carolina, and the son of a Navy vet and one of five children all home-.

schooled by their mother. Houck had joined the Marines just two years earlier, but he had gained a reputation as a man who really believed in the mission, and who would never hesitate to put himself on the line for a fellow Marine. He was awarded the Navy Commendation medal with a combat V for valor posthumously, for his courageous rescue on Thanksgiving Day. Dominic Esquibel was awarded the Navy Cross for his part in that rescue, but he thought he didn't need to be rewarded for doing his duty and decided to decline that honor—second only to the Congressional Medal of Honor.

The clearing operations were lethal for our Marines, and they also meant that we were starting to see a lot more wounded insurgents coming through our aid station. The day after Thanksgiving, we took some insurgents, including one of the big shots. He came in with a fractured femur. That is a brutally painful injury to have, but we couldn't give him any morphine until after he had been interrogated by intel—morphine dulls the brain every bit as much as it does pain. But we splinted his leg and made sure he was stable. We had treated insurgents back at the government center, too, but there were more now. Some would come in subdued and almost apologetic—I'm sure they were scared as all hell—but some of them came in defiant and aggressive. One of them even tried to bite HN Roger Millhouse, the smallest, youngest corpsman we had out there. The insurgent came in with a hood over his head and zip-tied from behind. Millhouse moved the hood because he was trying to redress the guy's wound, and *chomp!*, the captured man really tried to take a chunk out of the corpsman.

We also treated some civilians who had been caught up in the cross fire. It wasn't always easy to tell the difference between the combatants and the innocents, actually, and sometimes, there wasn't much difference. An Iraqi fighter could put down his AK and take off his ammo belt and claim he was just another Joe Fallujah out for a stroll. The interpreters could spot the foreign fighters easily enough, and intel had gunpowder residue kits they could use to see if a person had fired a weapon recently. The martial law rules laid down by the interim government in Baghdad made any firearm use in the city illegal, but some civilians actually got wounded defending their houses from the insurgents, so it was hard to be 100 percent sure if you had a good guy or a bad guy.

Treating your enemy adds a couple of layers of complexity to a medical operation. You've got a security problem there in the aid station, and you've got a moral struggle going on in your heart. These were the guys who had killed my guys, and we all knew it—they were responsible for the blood, pain, loss, and death we had been living with for three weeks by that point. They were not honorable men or worthy opponents—they were cowards and terrorists. But we gave them care as good as any Marine got, and a lot better than what we could have expected if they had gotten ahold of one of us. I treated the insurgents because that's what a doctor does, and also because that's what a United States Sailor or Marine does—that's what an American does. And I'm proud of how well we managed to do that.

We knew there was another issue as well. Some of the guys we were facing in Fallujah weren't the real hard-core elements. Some of them were just guys who got paid to stay there and fight us while the leaders—the rabble-rousers, the torturers, and the kidnapping murderers—cleared out of town. We found guys who had their kids, thirteen, fourteen years old, holed up with them in buildings and shooting at Marines. Most of the Iraqis I interacted with were not like that, not at all, and my heart goes out to a country and to a people who have to live with that going on in their midst. With the civilians especially, I always thought it was very important to treat them with respect and dignity, and help them out if I could.

With the insurgents it was a little different—you're never going to change a radical's mind, let alone his heart. They've been taught since they were kids that we're evil, the Great Satan. But I can't help but hope that somehow, in some small way, giving them good medical care might have helped a little. I don't know, maybe one of these guys that we patched up, maybe somewhere down the road, that will mean something to him. I know he's not going to start loving Americans, but maybe if nothing else, if he goes back out there and captures somebody, one of our guys, maybe he'll treat him with just a little more decency. Poison spreads poison and hatred spreads hate. Maybe that's a cycle we can interrupt, if just a little bit. If nothing else, you need to be able to go home at the end of the day and live your life. I know that's a lot easier to do if you're not carrying a lot of hate around with you.

Still, that's not always easy to avoid when you're fighting men who are consumed with hate for you and everything you stand for. You see them kill and maim your friends and your countrymen, and they try to kill and maim you. It's hard to come out of that without some hatred and a desire for vengeance in your heart. But you keep that in check and you treat the guy and save his life—I don't like you, dude, but I'm gonna do what I gotta do. And maybe with the real hard-core radicals, that actually is a form of vengeance. These are guys whose whole goal in life is to get themselves killed while trying to kill as many of us as they can. So you know what? If I can use my abilities to mess with that goal and hand them the failure of surviving, I'm okay with that, too. I guess that was my vengeance—making sure these guys would have a good, long time to sit there and think about how they didn't get to be a martyr.

We had the new FAS running smoothly now, and we were working steady, but not overwhelmed. Not by wounded, anyway. On November 27, 2004, for the third day in a row, we took two more KIAs, along with several more wounded Marines. Lance Corporal Joshua E. Lucero, a nineteen-year-old combat engineer from Tucson, Arizona, came in with a single bullet wound to the upper left chest. I remember looking at him for a long time, because he looked so quiet and peaceful. It was hard to believe that he had come in deceased. There was no blood and very little apparent damage, and I couldn't understand why that one shot had killed him. Lucero had been a skinny kid growing up, but he packed a lot of heart in his five-foot-two-inch frame, and earned a reputation as a loyal friend and very determined Marine. On the same day, we suffered another difficult loss. Scout Sniper Corporal Kirk J. Bosselmann, a fearless twenty-one-year-old Marine who grew up on a farm near Frederick, Maryland, had been jumping from rooftop to rooftop with his partner, securing the approach below for Bravo Company as the Marines worked their way through the city at street level. Corporal Bosselmann was a skilled and careful sniper but it's as dangerous a job as there is, and an opposing sniper's bullet found him before the Marine could neutralize the threat. Like a true Marine, Kirk Bosselmann put his own life on the line to ensure the safety of Bravo Company Marines below.

We pulled back in the first week of December, all the way out to Camp Fallujah, and the companies were given assignments outside the city. Fallujah was changing. The Civil Affairs Group came in and really had no use for us, and while clearing activities would continue on into late December, the 1/8 lost no more men after Bosselmann and Lucero. (But that doesn't mean the danger was gone. Lance Corporal Jason E. Smith, a twenty-one-year-old from the First Light Armored Reconnaissance Battalion, had been assigned to the 1/8 since Fallujah. The Phoenix, Arizona, Marine was driving from Abu Ghraib to rendezvous with Mark Winn at the ITC on New Year's Eve, 2004, when his Light Armored Vehicle hit a powerful IED made of two anti-tank mines. He was killed instantly, and like Ziolkowski, Malcom, Houck and Gavriel, Lance Corporal Smith now rests at Arlington National Cemetery.) I don't think a one of us left that city with regret, and even though our Marines had triumphed, our mood was somber. There was one more thing I had to do before I left, though. Kutilek and his Weapons Company platoon were clearing houses in the industrial district, and I asked him to take me along. Not as a passenger, either. I wanted to see what those guys had been going through. I can't imagine what he must have thought, but we'd been through enough together by then for him to keep it to himself. Kutilek's jaw squared a little, his brow dropped just a touch, but he said, "You wanna go, Sir? I'll take you."

So for two days I did the job of a lance corporal. Kutilek's platoon followed along with Charlie Company, providing security as they went into the houses, and I followed along with the Weapons Marines and the corpsmen who had saved Paul Volpe, HNs Dupuis and Maston. We didn't do the clearing, but I dismounted the Humvee and posted security with an M16 at the ready—scared, tired, anxious, just like everybody else. They captured a few insurgents and bulldozed a few buildings, and I suppose I was still the doctor if something had happened, but nothing did. For those two days, I got a small sense of what all these brave young men had been going through for three long, brutal weeks. Nothing happened while I was out, and still I was scared to death every minute. Imagine what it must have been like for the Marines who were doing it in the face of constant attacks.

CHAPTER 15

What Comes Home

We pulled our operations back to a small firm base completely outside the city. It was even farther back than our old Checkpoint 84 position. We set up a small aid station there and kept it staffed—one doctor and a few corpsmen in case anything happened—and we rotated out to our quarters at the Iranian Training Camp adjacent to Camp Fallujah. We didn't take any more casualties and there were no complaints about that at all. We played cards, caught up on our sleep, and started thinking a little about going home. The 1/8 was scheduled to rotate back to Camp Lejeune at the end of January 2005. Fallujah belonged to Civil Affairs and the Army now, and by December 23, 2004, the city's residents would slowly start returning to their homes. By the time our battalion headed back to home soil at the end of January, some 30 percent of eligible Fallujahns would even have voted in the first free democratic elections of their lives. But we weren't thinking about that then. Our time in Fallujah was done.

I can't begin to describe what a huge transition it was for us to be out of the city—forty-five minutes from hell, but a world of difference. It was incomprehensible. One day you were immersed in the smells of fresh cordite, old fires and stale sweat, blood and fear, and keyed up to face the ever-present prospect of more casualties. We were in a hyperalert state all the time in Fallujah, always aware that someone was trying to kill us, and then, suddenly, it was just . . . over. All of a sudden, it was nothing to get a hot meal, or to sleep in and take a long hot shower when you got up. It wasn't like being back home in North Carolina, but it was nothing short of jarring. And there were a few surprises in store for me, too. Joe Langholtz, the command master chief of II MEF and my old buddy from Sixth Marines, had managed to finagle a trip over to Iraq for a predeployment survey—he would be coming back over with the rest of II MEF soon—and his top priority was a visit to our crew with the 1/8.

Back in the spring, when I had originally signed on to deploy to Iraq with the 1/8, I tried to convince Langholtz to come along. It was unrealistic; he was the big boss on the enlisted side and was essentially running the bulk of East Coast operations, in terms of Navy involvement with the Marines. But I figured if I was stepping down to the title of battalion surgeon, he could step on down to battalion chief and join me at the 1/8. I even suggested that he deliberately piss off an appropriate someone and get himself demoted, but he wouldn't go for it. "Richie," he said, "those days are done, dude."

Now, not only had he managed to get to Iraq, he managed to show up right when the beer did. Lieutenant General John Sattler, commander of all the coalition forces in western Iraq, had banned drinking in his theater of operations, out of respect for

Muslim custom. The one exception was for November 10, the Marine Corps birthday. We were a few weeks late for the customary celebration, but hey, we had been busy. And, boy, were we happy to find that our birthday beer was still waiting for us when we got out. As for Joe, well, he always shows up for beer, so maybe I shouldn't have been surprised to see him. We situated ourselves at the ITC, toasted the Marine Corps, and got an update on how our wounded were faring back in the States. Joe had made a point of checking on them. Then we performed a Navy ritual: the distribution of our Fleet Marine Force warfare devices. A military uniform isn't just decoration, there's a lot of meaning tied up in all the stars and anchors that we wear. Many of these symbols represent competencies, they demonstrate that you have been trained, tested, and certified to a particular level. You have to *earn* your decorations, in other words. And one of the most coveted for an FMF corpsman is called the Fleet Marine Force warfare device, which indicates competency in the Marine Corps—basically, that you know as much about the Corps as a Marine does. Our corpsmen had been studying and preparing for their FMF warfare devices ever since our time at Haditha Dam. All they had to do was "get boarded"—to pass an oral examination—and who better to administer it than the II MEF Command Master Chief?

Langholtz went into his tough-guy mode, snapped them to attention, squared his shoulders, and picked out our most junior corpsman, HN Millhouse, to go first. "Hospitalman Millhouse," Joe said when the questioning was done, "you know your shit pretty good. Now *you* hold the boards on the rest of these guys." And Joe and I sat back and watched this tough little kid who the other corpsmen called Bubbles—not long out of high school and a veteran of the most brutal American battle in two generations—absolutely grill the other corpsmen. "HM2 Johns! Tell me what types of rounds will go in this machine gun! HM3 Lester! Tell me what the cyclic rate of fire is for this machine gun!" Millhouse had all the confidence and command of a Parris Island drill instructor, and he had earned it the hard way. Take a test? No sweat. These guys had been through hell on earth. They all passed their boards with ease, and never had a group of corpsmen deserved that FMF warfare device more.

It was a sweet ending to our time in Fallujah, and for me it was very near the end of my time in Iraq, as well. The battalion was scheduled to return to Camp Lejeune at the end of January, over several days, but my second pleasant surprise was that I would be leaving a little earlier than that. I can't say that I had been giving my future a whole lot of thought during the battle, but when I came out of Fallujah, there was a letter waiting for me from the Medical College of Georgia, and it was good news—great news, really. I had thought that I had used up my very last chance for a urology residency when I decided to go to Iraq rather than join MCG's program in July—the paperwork came through after I'd already taken on battalion surgeon duties with the 1/8—but now it looked like there was a chance left.

There was only one problem: the residency was supposed to start on the first of the year, January 1, 2005, and we were not scheduled to leave Iraq until the end of January. The early start date would have suited me fine; I knew that our work in Iraq was done, and I really wanted to get back to the United States, back to Melissa and MacKenzie. But now that I had what I thought was a pretty good excuse to depart early, I didn't think I could wrangle a seat on a flight out of the war zone that quickly. I called back to MCG to explain my predicament. I was more than a little anxious, but it turned out they were very reasonable and flexible; they talked to the higher-ups and said they could hold the position open until February 1, but that was the latest. I spoke to Lieutenant Colonel Brandl about it, and he clearly knew that this part of the show was over, too, and that he wouldn't be needing me again on this trip. "Yeah, Doc," he agreed, "if you can figure out how to get out of here, you can go."

So a few weeks later, I flew out. It was a little strange leaving before the rest of the battalion started shipping back home, but in a way it seemed almost fitting. I had joined them at the last minute, and we had accomplished what we all went there to do—we had performed our jobs, we had paid our price, and now it was up to the bureaucrats, the politicians, and the Iraqis to do their part. The fate of Fallujah, let alone Iraq, was far beyond the spheres of influence of me and my men, and my own responsibilities with the battalion were covered. Carlos Kennedy was more than capable of taking on battalion surgeon duties, and really, the corpsmen and the Marines were all busy doing nothing but gearing down to get back home. So we were all in the same boat. I was just setting sail a little early.

The trip was anticlimactic. I flew to Kuwait and sat there for a couple of days, and then flew home. If Camp Fallujah had seemed like another world a million miles away from the battle, I can't even tell you what it felt like to step onto a civilian aircraft. The trip was extremely long and tiring, and oddly, it was both relaxing and at the same time stimulating to be surrounded by civilians, especially on the flight coming back from Europe. I hardly knew how to act. Lieutenant Cox, the Navy chaplain, and I were traveling together, and it was so strange. We were all sitting there, the business folks in their suits, families with kids, just regular Janes and Joes going about their lives, just like we were going about ours. Cox and I just happened to be wearing uniforms instead of jeans or whatever. But I guess it wasn't that interesting. I was also amazed at how little time it took me to be annoyed with the lack of leg room, the lousy food, and the long, boring trip.

When you fly home with your unit, there's a lot of fanfare and excitement; later, I went to meet the 1/8 when they were coming in and it was terrific. All the families were waiting for them, the community, with banners and balloons and a great big celebration, which is very cool. But I came home alone, so I didn't have any of that. What I had instead was the sight of my wife holding our daughter. MacKenzie had been just four days old when I left for Iraq. Up until I stepped off that plane, I had mostly only seen pictures of her. Now, she was seven months old and it was like I was meeting her for the first time, and she was this wonderful little person already, not much of a baby any-more. Just sitting there in her mother's arms, a tiny perfect little girl, and it seemed so unbelievable. I realized suddenly how much of her life I had missed. MacKenzie wasn't quite as bowled over as I was, but she seemed to put up with me okay at the time and she doesn't seem to mind having me around now.

Seeing Melissa, holding her again after so long, well, that was wonderful, that's what men at war dream about, that's what keeps us going through it all. I couldn't believe how natural it felt, almost like I'd never left. It was like right at that moment, the entire time in Iraq was put away and we started right back up from that moment seven months earlier when I left Melissa and MacKenzie standing in the driveway. Missy was so beautiful that day, and she made the transition home easy for me. It was like I just put the deployment away, and we became each other's best friend again with no elapsed time in between. I've got a lot to be grateful to Melissa for, and that moment, that transition, is one of the best.

Since I've been back, I've tried to stay focused on my work and my family. But Fallujah is never too far away from my thoughts. I've gone back to Camp Lejeune a couple of times. I was there when the rest of the battalion returned, but I just went up to see if I could help out in any way; the guys were reuniting with their families and it was pure joyful chaos, and I didn't want to take up anyone's time. In February 2005, I returned again to attend the memorial for the fallen of the 1/8. It was a deeply moving event, conducted with a great deal of dignity and respect, and it was very difficult for me to see the families of our deceased Marines. I had imagined their grief and loss every time we had a fallen brother, and now I was witnessing it in person. Those Marines put their lives on the line for their country, and they paid the ultimate sacrifice. But their families pay a steep price as well, and they deserve all the respect and gratitude this nation can give them. Most of the wounded Marines were there as well, and I talked with many of them. Paul Volpe made a point of coming over to talk with me; he thought I might not remember him, but how could I forget? I asked him how he was doing. He said he had massive scars on his legs, but he was recovering. Finally, in January 2006, I went back to accept a Bronze Star, with a combat V for valor, from Brigadier General Joseph J. Mc-Mennamin. I was touched and proud when I was told that I was the only Navy doctor who had earned that combination thus far in the Iraq war, but at the same time I didn't want a big production. It was a small ceremony in the conference room, with just a few of the guys I deployed with, and that's the way I wanted it. Mark Winn and Lieutenant Colonel Brandl had nominated me, and I felt pretty emotional when I read what they had written about me in the citation. But they really got it when they pointed out several times that I was just one part of a team effort, what they called "the heroic lifesaving efforts of the medical team." Without the corpsmen, nothing would have been possible—they are the heart and soul of any medical team. Zimmerman, Lees, Kennedy, and Folley were the brains and leadership, and without them, everything would have fallen flat. Me, I just came up with the idea and set this thing in motion.

The Marine Corps and the Navy are good at conducting memorials and ceremonies. They know that these rituals are an important part of honoring the service and sacrifice of their Marines and Sailors, living and dead. But we all have our own ways of remembering, too, our own personal memorials. Almost everyone who goes to war seems to bring something back with him from the battlefield, some small reminder of where he was and the men he was with.

Matthew Kutilek, who's a captain now, and is doing a two-year stint as the Junior Marine Officer Instructor at the Citadel, returned from Iraq carrying a single rifle slug. It is a small thing, a chunk of lead core and brass jacket bent into a claw on impact and scarred by the barrel of the Dragunov sniper rifle that sent it slamming into his friend and fellow Citadel graduate, Lieutenant Dan Malcom of Alpha Company. If losing a patient on the table is the worst thing that can happen to a doctor, then losing a man on the battlefield is the worst thing that can happen to a platoon commander. Kutilek and his platoon made it through Fallujah without a single KIA, which, given the amount of fire they took and the places they went, really is a miracle. But none of us made it through without losing someone we knew and cared for.

Kutilek says that the slug that killed Dan Malcom is a reminder of all the men who aren't coming home—a reminder for himself, but also for the country. "I bring it out on certain occasions and try to convey to people the importance of this," he explained not long ago. "That this United States Marine gave his life, and this is the bullet that took him, and he died on November tenth, the Marine Corps birthday, for your protection. My goal is to never let these guys die in vain—Lieutenant Malcom, Houck, Marku, all of them—to keep these guys fresh in our memories and never, ever forget." Kutilek oversees roughly 110 Citadel students who want to become Marine officers, and I know he does his best to prepare them for what they'll be facing as new officers. He's also working hard to honor the memory of the men who served before them and didn't come back by raising money for three different Marine cadet scholarships at the Citadel, including one in honor of Lieutenant Malcom, and trying to establish a memorial to the Citadel's war dead in Iraq on the campus as well. Our motto in the Marine Corps is *Semper Fidelis*—always faithful—and as Kutilek knows well, that means staying faithful to the memory of our fallen brothers as well.

Shawn Johns chose another way to record the bravery and sacrifice of the battlefield. He has given over most of his upper left arm to a tattoo in their honor. It's a remarkable flesh-and-ink memorial, complete with the al-Hydra Mosque, where the

Marines met so much resistance, a trio of UH-60 Blackhawk medevac helicopters representing the large number of casualties, and a full-action portrait of Gunnery Sergeant Shane, HN Lambotte, and the late Sergeant Lonny Wells, fighting to get each other to safety under enemy fire—the ultimate expression of the brotherhood and sacrifice that the 1/8 displayed in Fallujah. The tattoo is surrounded by twenty-one stars, one for each of the twenty Marines from the 1/8 who gave their lives during our deployment in Iraq, and one more for Marine Sergeant David M. Caruso of Naperville, Illinois, a Force Recon Marine supporting our battalion who passed at our Checkpoint 84 Battalion Aid Station on November 9, 2004. Much like our National Guard ambulance crews, Sergeant Caruso and his platoon from Second Force Reconnaissance Company had been assigned to our battalion just before the battle for Fallujah began. He was killed while his team was protecting 1/8 Marines from encroaching insurgents—he died protecting his team from machine-gun fire and was awarded the Bronze Star with combat V for valor—and both he and his family have been adopted by the 1/8 Marines and their families.

I'm not sure what drives the impulse to take something home from the battlefield, or to leave its marks on our bodies somehow. I suppose it could be something as simple as a trade. No one goes through that experience without leaving something of themselves behind—their blood, a fallen friend, or just an immeasurable piece of their own spirit or soul—so maybe taking something back with you is one way of creating some balance.

For me, I brought home just one memento: a dirty, crumpled piece of paper that for some reason I picked up off the ground outside of the Forward Aid Station at the government center. In some respects, it's nothing special. In fact, it's standard issue—there's a National Stock Number printed on the bottom so you can reorder them by the case—and I don't know what drew me to it, but I picked it up out of all of the debris and trash that was scattered around. I had seen similar cards and read the words many times before:

The Marine's Prayer

Almighty Father, whose command is over all and whose love never fails, make me aware of Thy presence and obedient to Thy will. Keep me true to my best self, guarding me against dishonesty in purpose and deed and helping me to live so that I can face my fellow Marines, my loved ones, and Thee without shame or fear. Protect my family.

Give me the will to do the work of a Marine and to accept my share of responsibilities with vigor and enthusiasm. Grant me the courage to be proficient in my daily performance. Keep me loyal and faithful to my superiors and to the duties my Country and the Marine Corps have entrusted to me. Make me considerate of those committed to my leadership. Help me to wear my uniform with dignity, and let it remind me daily of the traditions which I must uphold.

If I am inclined to doubt, steady my faith; if I am tempted, make me strong to resist; if I should miss the mark, give me courage to try again.

Guide me with the light of truth and grant me wisdom by which I may understand the answer to my prayer.

I found this card almost immediately after Demarkus Brown died. I was frustrated, tired, and angry—thoroughly deflated. I had come to Fallujah to make a difference. And during those first couple of weeks in the FAS, I felt like I did. It was like everything I'd done in my life up to now, everything I had learned as a Marine, everything I had learned as a doctor, was meant to get me ready for this moment in time. You know, like I was the right guy in the right place at the right time. But after Brown died, I was doubting everything. I wouldn't say that I was angry with God exactly, but I was feeling a little abandoned that day. So I went out to the heads to take a piss, and it didn't strike me until I was on my way back that it was an almost perfect day outside, bright and sunny, warm but not hot, with just the slightest breeze blowing through. I took a moment, and looked up into the sky, and then looked down and saw the card on the ground, surrounded by all the dirt and litter and chaos.

I'm not a particularly religious person and I'm not much given to prayer or church, but I have always believed in God, and Christ, and life after death. I'm a Methodist, and typically enough I don't believe that God is necessarily an active presence in our everyday lives, answering prayers and offering protection—there are just too many things done in this world with evil intent and without protection or punishment. And yet, when I read the words on that piece of paper, I decided that the prayer card had come out of Demarkus D. Brown's pocket that day, and that I was meant to pick it up. He may have been trying to tell me it was okay, that he knew I did all I could. Or maybe it was God telling me not to worry, even if I didn't understand everything that was going on around me. Or maybe it was just another piece of trash in the street. I put it in my pocket, and I brought it home.

I think that I will always carry some part of Fallujah with me—in my medical work, in my home life, in my heart. And I don't think I'll ever stop thinking about the men (and the one woman) who I worked with there. I've had the pleasure of serving with an awful lot of very good people over the years, but there is something about bonds forged in the heat of battle that makes them very, very strong. And I know I'll never stop thinking about our Marines—not the ones we saved, and never the ones we lost. I've already said it, that the worst thing that can happen for a doctor is to lose a patient on the table, and that is certainly the case in combat; your job, the only reason you exist, is to be the guy who steps in and interrupts that wounded man's demise. And I can't overlook the fact that we lost men in Iraq, men who came to us alive looking for help, who we couldn't save. Lonny Wells. Nicholas Ziolkowski. Demarkus Brown. I can't help thinking, over and over again, is there something I could have done, something I should have done differently? What would have happened if I'd made just one change in the whole long chain of events leading to their deaths, would it have changed the outcome? I don't know, and I don't think I'll ever know.

We all have our own ways of dealing with the things we saw in war, and as Melissa can confirm, I had some rough nights after I came back. Having MacKenzie to take care of and throwing myself into my work helped to keep me moving forward and focused on the future. I've heard that it's easier to make the transition if you come back to a military base for a while, because everyone there understands, and you're surrounded by people who went through the same thing you did. I didn't get to do that. I went right to work, splitting my time between the Medical College of Georgia and the Augusta Veteran's Administration Medical Center across the street. I've made a lot of friends there, but I'm not sure that anyone could really relate to what I had experienced just a few weeks before I arrived. So it was with some relief that I went to visit Joe Langholtz, who lives just about a half-hour drive from my parents' home, near Camp Lejeune. It's a strange neighborhood— all the streets in the subdivision are named after the characters from Robin Hood—but Joe and his wife, Ida, have a great family there, with five boys, and it was really good to see him. It was a warm, pleasant spring night, and Joe had been working on an enclosed porch at the back of his house. Or actually, he was supervising; it's hard on a tough guy like Joe, but he's forty-two years old, and after almost a quarter century of hard living, he finally managed to tear his back bad enough while serving in Iraq that he had to take some time out for surgery. Anyway, we were out back and it was just a roof, two guys, and a couple of beers.

Joe is real typical Navy enlisted in some ways. He loves the old war movies, and he looks the part of a chief, small, wiry, and strong as an anchor chain. And even though he can bark like a rottweiler when he wants to, he's actually got a heart of gold, and he was probably a little concerned about me. Neither one of us is the kind of guy who's going to be comfortable with a lot of touchy-feely stuff, but that one night, we kind of had our moment. It wasn't a big deal, just sort of checking in.

"Are you okay?"

"Yeah, I'm okay."

I kind of like the way Joe describes it: "We didn't fucking hug and Kumbaya and have tears streaming or anything like that. Maybe a little bit of mist, and a little bit of 'Dude, I know where you're coming from.'"

I think Melissa knew my time in Fallujah hadn't exactly been a picnic. But she didn't press me about what had happened, and that was the best thing she could have done. I knew she suspected I was dealing with some tough issues, because one night, when I was still in Fallujah, she got a quick look into that world. It was during that first week at the Forward Aid Station. There was a rare break in the action, and I took a chance and called her on a satellite phone. I was sitting outside, and we were talking, and it was completely quiet when all of a sudden here comes *Basher* overhead, the big AC-130 gunship, and just as I was saying, "Yeah, nothin', we're doing fine, no big deal," they opened up with the howitzers and started just blasting away at insurgent positions right around us. *Bam! Bam! Bam!* I quickly disconnected the phone; my instinct was that it was better for her to think we'd just lost the connection. I didn't want to add to her worry. But I don't know if I did her any favors.

I love my wife, and she loves me, and I think we just sort of get each other. We're not real sappy though—we're much more likely to tease each other about stuff than do the whole lovey-dovey thing. But Melissa has shown her love and support for me in ways that I could never have anticipated. Just after I got home, she set up the best homecoming gift I could have ever imagined: tickets and a trip to see a Philadelphia Eagles playoff game. All I had to do was show up. My whole family has been fans forever, and I couldn't have been farther from Fallujah than I was in that stadium. It was perfect. We were together, the game was about to start, and I think I was teasing Melissa about her not shelling out for better tickets as we were making our way to our seats—a perfect, happy, loving moment.

But then the national anthem came up and they flew a couple of jets over, and I lost it. I mean, I just fully, completely lost it. We hadn't even gotten to our seats yet. But when the "Star-Spangled Banner" came up—*"And the rockets' red glare, the bombs bursting in air . . ."*—I stopped in my tracks. A lot of people have died for that song, and I was at least going to stand still and take my hat off. And then I just completely broke down. Standing in that crowd of people, I couldn't stop crying. And Melissa stood there and held me. People around us were asking, "What's wrong with him?" But my wife just held me and never asked. And I'm okay with that. I am very, very okay with that.

Life After Hell

People ask me all the time if I'd ever consider being a battalion surgeon again, and I find it a hard question to answer. I still owe the Navy another four years of service for my residency, and at some point, I'll have to decide if I'm going to stay in once that debt is paid. In my opinion, being a battalion surgeon is one of the most vital and rewarding jobs there is, and there's a big part of me that wouldn't mind doing it forever. But that's probably not going to happen, and not just because Melissa might kill me if I deploy again. I've found that family is becoming more and more important to me. I've always been close to my family, but as I get older, most of the things I really want to do seem to involve being around them more. I'm not saying I've lost my taste for challenge, but right now, being with my family is very much where I want to be. I like what I'm doing. My colleagues at the Medical College of Georgia and the VA Hospital across the street have been great, and I have found among them the camaraderie I always valued in the military. I also really like being a urologist. I like the fact that for a large number of my patients, I really can change the course of events in a very positive way. Urology is one of the few medical fields where you can consistently cure cancer, for example. It fits my temperament and my Marine attitude—identify the problem, neutralize it, and move on. I especially like treating our veterans; it's an important part of showing our appreciation for their service and sacrifices.

But I have to admit I worry sometimes that if I go into private practice and become a gentleman urologist, I might get bored eventually. I don't want to ever become one of those doctors who are just going through the motions. So who knows? Maybe there's a way for me to combine my love of medicine and my love for the military well into the future.

No matter whether I stay in the Navy for the long haul or not, I am committed to doing my part to bring about some much-needed changes in military medicine. The truth is that most Navy doctors don't want to be battalion surgeons, and frankly, most Navy doctors are not suited or qualified for the job. I think that's a situation that has got to change, and to me, that means making some significant adjustments in the way the Navy recruits and trains its doctors.

These aren't new thoughts for me. But they took on a new urgency after what I saw on the streets of Fallujah and what I saw of the regimental-level planning for medical operations during the battle. The estimate everybody seems comfortable with is that during the fighting we managed to save thirty Marines who would have died if we had held back at the Iranian Training Camp, as the plan dictated. No one can say for sure if that is true, but whether it was thirty lives, or fifty, or ten, we know we made a difference, for the 1/8 as well as other units. That message came home to me while I was at the rear in Camp Fallujah, just before Thanksgiving. I ran into a good friend of mine, Lieutenant Colonel Rob Kosid—we had gone through The Basic School together when we were both Marine Corps second lieutenants—and now he was the executive officer for RCT-7. As XO, Rob reviewed all PCRs—personal casualty reports, which are issued for everyone wounded or killed in action—for our regiment. And he was confused: why had he been getting PCRs from the other battalions with my name on them? The answer was simple—the injured were taken to the nearest aid station, and that was often my FAS, or the BAS at Checkpoint 84, where Lieutenant Kennedy, Chief Folley, and others were stationed. If they went to either place, the PCRs would have my name on them, because I was the senior medical official for both places.

I suspect that our KIA-to-WIA ratio was significantly lower than would have been expected, despite the 1/8's taking some of the most intense resistance of the battle, if not the most intense. And again, I think the fact that both the FAS and BAS were closer to the action than most aid stations gets the credit for that—as does the outstanding efforts of the corpsmen in the 1/8.

I point this out not to attack the Navy or other Navy doctors, or to suggest that the other teams didn't work every bit as hard as we did. In fact, I think it's pretty obvious that I'm a company man. I love the Marine Corps, and I love the Navy. But like any other institution, they're not perfect, and if you want to make something better, you can't be afraid to pick at the blemishes. The men and women in the service deserve everything we can give them. If that means sending doctors—including me, for another tour—out on the front lines, I'm fine with that. I believe that when you sign up for the military, you agree to do whatever is required to fulfill their needs at the time. And there are some simple corrections that could be made in how medical support operations are run that could start saving Marine lives today if they were implemented across the Fleet Marine Force. For example, more trauma training for corpsmen and doctors, as well as better medical, tactical, and logistical planning from the regimental level on down.

On a more fundamental level, I believe the Navy has to rethink the way it recruits and trains its doctors in the first place. There are basically two ways to become a Navy doctor: you can attend a civilian medical school on a Navy scholarship, or you can attend the Uniformed Services University of the Health Sciences (USUHS) in Maryland, which is the military's own medical school. And I hate to say it, but graduate medical education in the military just isn't producing the kind of doctors we need. The men and women who come out of USUHS and the Health Professions Scholarships program may be excellent physicians, but by and large they're just not great officers. If my experiences in Iraq taught me anything, it's that the Navy's medical officers often need a lot of work on the second half of their title.

The point is, there's a lot more to being a medical officer than just the medicine—there's leadership, there's logistics, there's even the knowledge and understanding of military life and culture. And that means everything from how you interact with the Marine Corps staff to your physical abilities. Even if you're a doctor, you can't be a shitbird, unable to keep up with the troops on a hike or a run, because in a Marine's eyes, a lot of times you're measured by the level of your physical fitness. It might seem trivial, but it's really a trust issue, and a lot of what we achieved in Fallujah wouldn't have been possible if the corpsmen and I didn't have the trust of the Marines. And to an extent, that also means being "one of the guys"—not that medical officers can afford to fraternize, any more than other officers can, but there's no need to be aloof and distant, either.

There's a tendency for battalion surgeons, and medical officers in general, to put on airs and place themselves above the men they serve with. Just one example: people in the Marine Corps tend to call corpsmen "Doc," in the same way they call gunnery sergeants "Gunny." It's more than a rating or a rank, it becomes part of their name and their identity. Doc Lambotte, Doc Markley, Gunny Shane—you could know these guys for months and have no idea what their real first names were. Well, a lot of the Navy doctors who work with the Marine Corps get very uptight if anyone should call them "Doc." They think, *Hey, that's what they call an eighteen-year-old kid with three months of training, and I'm a doctor.* Well, I've seen that eighteen-year-old corpsman run out under fire and save a man's life; I've seen that thirty-one-year-old IDC run sick call for a thousand Marines for months at a time; and I've seen that forty-year-old chief covered in blood to his elbows, cheating death day in and day out with not much more than his hard-won experience. I've also seen battalion surgeons sitting back at the rear, listening to the sounds of battle in the distance. The point is, you aren't something different and above what they are; corpsmen are the heart and soul of Navy medicine and you're all part of the same team. So what if a Marine calls you "Doc" and that's the same thing he calls a corpsman? If anything, that should make you feel proud.

Frankly, one of the reasons I wrote this book was to deter certain people from taking the Navy medical scholarship. If you don't want to be in the military, you shouldn't be accepting the scholarship. And if you don't want to deploy overseas, and go to war if that's what's required of you, well, then you shouldn't be in the military, it's that simple. At the same time, what I really hope is that these stories might also draw some readers to the Navy and Navy medicine, because they see what the job is and actually want to do it. Now, is that going to be your typical medical student? No, I don't think so. But maybe it will be some of your prior service types, men and women who have already served their country in a combat or support unit and are looking for a new way to make a contribution. Maybe it'll be some medically minded people who want the challenge of deploying, who want to serve their country and their fellow Marines or Sailors, or soldiers on the Army side for that matter. The military would be wise to consider those already in their ranks and identify prospects who have the ability and desire to become effective battalion surgeons.

Our men and women in uniform deserve doctors who want to be in the military—not just doctors who want to get their tuition paid—and I have no doubt that we have the raw material in our ranks already. Why not put some effort into identifying corpsmen or others from the enlisted ranks who might have what it takes to be doctors? I realize that not all of them are cut out for it, but some of them are. You could provide incentives for them to get through an undergraduate degree, and then give them a couple of chances to take the MCAT and see if they can make it into medical school. If they want it bad enough, they'll do it. I'm a big believer that heart and motivation can take you a long way. At the very least, there could be more trauma training for corpsmen, and more of a push toward having them become IDCs, with a trauma specialty. The key point is, we should be doing as much as we can to train battalion surgeons who know medicine *and* tactics.

Trying to get more attention on this topic is where I'm focusing my efforts these days. It helps me make sense of my experiences in Iraq. But I know a lot of the guys I served with are also trying to figure out ways to make their own sense of what they experienced. One thing is certain, no one goes through something like Fallujah and comes out unchanged. Different people end up dealing with the experience in very different ways. For many of us, the difficult times started as soon as we pulled back from Fallujah.

I feel a great deal of support from the men I served with in Iraq. We stay in touch and we look out for each other. But some are doing better than others. It's not just the men with physical wounds who brought challenges home with them. Realistically, I suppose that all of us had PTSD—post-traumatic stress disorder—to some extent or another by the time we were done, and more than a few had real trouble when we got back. Most of us are fighting through it pretty well two years later, some are just getting started on the journey back, and some are still struggling. There's been a lot of talk about the psychological fallout of this war, and with plenty of good reasons: the brutal, pressure of knowing you've got a target on your back all the time, of never being able to tell a friendly civilian from a suicidal enemy, and of never knowing when the vehicle you're rid-ing in is going to be engulfed in the flames and shrapnel of an IED attack. Not to mention the horror of seeing your buddies shot and bombed and ambushed beyond the point of recognition. For me and my corpsmen, that was a particularly harrowing and constant struggle. As I pointed out earlier, civilian medical personnel generally don't treat their friends and family. The emotional strain is just too much—the pressure to help them, the fear of failing them—and gets in the way of clear thinking and decision making. But we faced that every day.

My corpsmen did an unbelievably tough job in Fallujah, and they did it incredibly well, far exceeding even my very high expectations. But the work took its toll. Men have to harden themselves to get through battle, and they drive their emotions down deep. Kevin Markley, an HM2 now, says he shut down his emotions on November 9, 2004—right after the Bravo Company ambush at the cultural center—and he's still struggling to find them again. "I'm cold," he says now. "Everyone tells me I have no emotions anymore, but once you've turned them off it's hard to turn them back on again." His company commander, Bravo's Captain Read Omohundro, says that acknowledging the pain of losing men was a luxury he couldn't afford during the battle. "I did not allow myself to fixate on the casualties at the time or I wouldn't have been able to focus on everything else," he says now. "I knew that if I survived, I would be able to mourn later." It's a common reaction, a basic survival response when emotions get too high and there's still so much work to be done. But men suffer for it when the combat is over, and even mourning can become nearly impossible. No matter how tough you are, those demons are going to find a way to come out and haunt you.

Like many of the men going through PTSD, Markley says he has sought help in the form of counseling and drugs, "the full meal deal" of antidepressants, antianxiety meds, and sleeping pills. And like most of the men, he's trying to get off them. "They help somewhat," says Markley, "but they just keep you numb. You're still going to have to deal with everything later."

HM3 Jason Smith, who played a critical role in running the Checkpoint 84 BAS when we went in to set up the FAS at the government center, has had some of the hardest times since coming back. He broke his neck in a car accident just six days after returning to Camp Lejeune, and his friend who was in the car died. Like a lot of guys returning from combat, Smitty started hitting the bottle pretty hard. "I didn't realize this was what I was doing at the time," he says, "but I started self-medicating myself with alcohol. I met my fiancée right after I broke my neck, and for the first two and a half, almost three months that we'd known each other she hadn't seen me sober for a full day." His alcohol abuse led toward serious trouble at the base and in his personal life, Smitty says, but his brothers looked out for him. The tough love came from HM2 Johns. "When he came back to the base after his neck was healed, I punched him in his chest and said, 'You're coming with me, motherfucker,'" Johns says. "I took him right over to get help, told 'em this kid has a drinking problem and they put him in a program." HM3 Smith hasn't had a drink since, and he's finding it easier to transition to civilian life. He left the Navy in the summer of 2006.

Johns has had his hard times, too. "I had a long road to recovery," he says. "I still have problems, and some of them I'll probably be dealing with for the rest of my life. I've had a lot of friends that turned to drugs and got caught, friends who found the bottle and are getting in a lot of trouble with it, but I don't drink that much, so that's something. If you talk to my wife, though, she'll tell you I've got a problem with fishing." They live in a house down on the water near Camp Lejeune, and Johns spends a lot of time now just casting off into the channel. But he's moving forward, too. Before Fallujah, Johns thought he would eventually settle into civilian life as a firefighter and paramedic, but his experiences there have left him feeling like he's seen enough of trauma medicine to last a lifetime. It's a shame, too—he was very good at it. When we first returned from Iraq, Johns wanted to go back over, badly; it's a pretty common reaction, because dedicated guys like him don't like the idea that they've left a job unfinished. Things worked out differently, though, and he recently accepted orders to report to the Navy's Survival, Evasion, Resistance and Escape (SERE) school in Brunswick, Maine, where he'll become an instructor, teaching Navy and Marine personnel in "High Risk Capture" jobs—Navy SEALs, Navy and Marine Corps pilots, Force Recon Marines and Sailors—how to deal with survival and capture situations.

It might be surprising, but many of the corpsmen do plan to pursue careers as paramedics and EMTs when they leave the Navy. HM3 Smith is one of them, despite the painful memories of Iraq and the friends he lost there that still haunt him. His list of symptoms is impressive: "Severe anxiety attacks, depression, a stutter, frickin' mood swings—I've gotten away from the big ones but now my memory is really shitty," he says. Except for when it's all too clear, like the time he was instantly transported back in time from the Camp Lejeune orthopedics clinic to the hot, dusty roadside in Iraq where H&S Company lost Lance

Corporals Michael J. Halal and Cesar Machado-Olmos in the vehicle rollover. "I was fine," Smitty says, "and then all of a sudden I'm down on my knees doing CPR. I'm looking at Halal's chest to see if it's rising when I blow in, I could taste the fluid and blood and stuff coming up from his lungs." But he thinks that working as a civilian paramedic will be completely different, because the accident victims he'll try to help there will be strangers. "I'm still planning on specializing in trauma medicine," Smith says. "My shrink looks at me, he's, like, 'Well, how can you wanna do that after the problems you're dealin' with because of this?' But he doesn't get it. These were brothers. Even if I wasn't there and I didn't have to treat 'em and I didn't have to see their bodies, I went through it and experienced it still, and it ripped me open every time I heard about one of these guys takin' it."

I've been very impressed by how hard the corpsmen are working to confront the symptoms they're dealing with, and to get on with their lives. These are not guys who are going to be okay with sitting around feeling sorry for themselves forever.

HM3 Hirkala—HM2 now—says he puts a lot of his effort these days into staying motivated. "I try and tell myself that there are two kinds of attitudes to have in life," he says, "and that's positive or real positive. There's no time for negativity." That doesn't mean it's always easy to do, he says, "but seeing what we saw out there, you know what's good and what's bad and you can keep the good. And if you keep a positive attitude I think you affect more people than you do with a negative attitude." Hirkala quit smoking about a year after returning from Iraq, and says he's spending a lot of time running now. "Running is kind of how I vent my stress," he says. "If I feel pressured or I want to make a negative remark, I go run instead because I know there's guys out there that can't run that would enjoy it. So I try and do it for them, in a sense. And that's pretty much it." Hirk says he doesn't regret his time in Iraq, but he's not quite sure what will come next for him. "I was real unsure what I was going to do after the deployment," he says, "and a lot of the guys really helped me think it all through." He paused for a moment before he added, "You know, 1/8 was the place to be. And I'd give anything to go back right now. I mean, if I could go back with the same guys. I learned a lot with those guys, and I guess that's kind of a good thing and kind of a bad thing. It was an expensive learning lesson. Very expensive."

HM2 Markley is in Rota, Spain, now, stationed at the U.S. Naval Station there. His wife is in Rota, too; she's also a corpsman, and works in the maternity ward at the base hospital. Markley works in the hospital also, caring mostly for the dependents of active-duty personnel, but says that if he were single, he'd try to go back out with the 1/8, with Bravo Company if he could. "It's lonely," he says, "because nobody can really understand what we went through. I miss the camaraderie and brotherhood that you can't really get anywhere else but the Marine Corps. We all suffered through the same thing." The company stays in touch, though. Markley visited with some of the Marines who are still on active duty when they passed through Rota on their way to Beirut in the summer of 2006, and Bravo uses the social networking Web site MySpace to keep tabs on each other. He talks with his father, too, Markley says. "My dad was in Vietnam, and he used to tell me not to join up, not to go into combat. But I was young and dumb and I couldn't wait. Well, it's not like you think it's going to be, it's not like it is in the movies.

They don't tell you about the emotions and the garbage you have to carry around afterward. They don't tell you about everything it wrecks." Like Pinocchio, he says, someday he's going to "be a real boy" again. It's a sense of humor his friend Demarkus Brown would have loved.

I've been able to keep up with some of the senior guys as well. Lees is now at the Naval Hospital at Camp Lejeune; Folley at the hospital in Corpus Christi, Texas. Zimmerman has moved up to chief, and is heading to the Newport Ambulatory Care Clinic in Rhode Island. Kennedy is at Bethesda, doing an orthopedics residency.

As for the Marines we treated, they're all dealing with the fallout of Fallujah in their own ways, too. Many, of course, are still with the 1/8, and the Beirut Battalion continues its proud tradition of brave, selfless service. After helping out in New Orleans following Hurricane Katrina in September 2005, the 1/8 prepared to deploy again, this time with the Twenty-fourth Marine Expeditionary Unit. They set sail in June 2006 for a scheduled six-month "float" at sea. As with any MEU, there's no telling exactly where they'll go or what they will be asked to do. And as with any Marines, there's an iron-clad guarantee that they'll be up for the mission, no matter what.

Mark Winn was promoted to lieutenant colonel and volunteered for a second tour in Iraq. He became the Team Leader of an eleven-man team that advises, trains, and mentors the Iraqi Border Forces that guard the Iraq borders with Syria, Jordan, and Saudi Arabia. He hopes to be back in the States in the spring. Trimble is at Quantico, Virginia, training brand-new second lieutenants at TBS, the Marine Corps training venue. It is a very important job, and almost all the majors who go there are handpicked by the commanding officer. Pretty impressive. Colonel Brandl received a Bronze Star with a combat V for his time in Fallujah. In July 2005, he transferred to United States Joint Forces Command (JFCOM) in Norfolk, Virginia. He's been selected to command the 22 MEU, and will take over sometime next summer.

Even some of those with the most severe wounds have found ways to stay with the Corps. Jacob Knospler, remarkably, not only survived his grenade wounds but has been promoted to sergeant and remains on active duty; he's stationed at Henderson Hall in Arlington, Virginia. Sergeant Knospler remembers very little of what happened in November and December 2004, and that is almost certainly a blessing—his journey from battlefield wound to medical recovery has been grueling at every step, but those first two months were unbelievably rough. There was emergency brain surgery in Baghdad, a medically induced coma in Germany, and a bout with meningitis when he reached Bethesda Naval Hospital. He was surrounded by family there— his wife, Janna, for the night shift, his mother, father, stepfather, and brother during the day—and received his Purple Heart personally from President Bush, but still, he says, his time at the hospital was just miserable.

Knospler returned home to East Stroudsburg, Pennsylvania, on New Year's Day, 2005—a big relief. (He still lives there and travels to Henderson Hall several times a month.) He has undergone over twenty surgeries on his face so far—a plate inserted to repair his fractured skull, tissue from his shoulder grafted to his cheek to repair his facial wounds—and still has many more to come. The process is slow, he says, because his doctors must leave time for his flesh to heal between surgeries. "The surgeons tell me that they don't know how much more they will be able to do because they don't usually get patients with so much bone missing in their face," Knospler says, "but I am making progress." Knospler says he relies on his family to help him cope with the new realities of his life, including a significant loss of short-term memory. "Life is getting better every day," he says. "There was a long time where I could barely walk, and now I'm running again and working out. I still have very bad back pain, but everything is getting better, even the back pain."

Paul Volpe stayed with the Marines and the 1/8 initially as well, but has since left the Corps and is moving forward in his life. He left Germany just two days after Knospler, on November 18, 2004, and he too got a visit from President Bush at Bethesda. Volpe was discharged on December 13, 2004, and after a couple of months recuperating at home in New Jersey, and a return to Bethesda to remove more shrapnel from his leg, Volpe reported to Camp Lejeune. He had his heart set on rejoining his unit, and did his utmost to make that happen. But his leg injuries were just too severe; there was no way he could handle the physical training and field exercises. He left the Corps as a lance corporal in October 2005, with a permanent 40 percent disability. And in the fall of 2006, he started college at San Diego State University, in California, where he plans to study communications and eventually get into sports marketing and advertising. Volpe says it's going great; he's a little rusty on academics after three years away since high school, but it's coming along fine and he's meeting new people and having fun. As for his leg, Volpe says it still gets sore after exercising, "but I can work out, I can play flag football, I can play basketball—I'm moving around pretty good, and I've got no complaints."

Gunnery Sergeant Ryan Shane was awarded the Bronze Star for his heroism in Fallujah, and thanks to a series of photographs showing his rescue attempt, he has received a lot of attention in the press and on the Internet. But he's quick to point out that, as Admiral Nimitz said of the Marines at Iwo Jima, "uncommon valor was a common virtue" in Fallujah. "I was just a small part of something bigger than all of us, trying to do the best I could," Shane says. "There were a lot of other great people who did a lot of phenomenal things, and I was just a small dot on the map. I don't think I was a lot different from any of the fellas." And he's solidly focused on the future. "I thought I did a good job of not taking things for granted before, but now . . . A great guy that I tried to help didn't make it, and there's a lot of brave guys who came and got me out of that street, and I'm not going to waste it. I've been given another shot, so to speak, and I'm definitely not going to piss it away."

Despite his injuries, Gunny Shane worked hard to get healthy so that he could stay in the Marines. But his injuries continued to cause him so much pain a year and a half later that he knew he wouldn't be able to return to the kind of work he loved. "I had been accustomed to operating at a certain level, physically, and I didn't want to be a charity case," Shane says. "I didn't want to be that broken gunny that's sittin' at some desk, and everybody's saying, 'Oh, there's that gunny that can't—he can only do like forty sit-ups before he starts to say that he's in pain." Shane was medically discharged on June 30, 2006, and moved to Indianapolis, Indiana, with his son and daughter. He's working there with his former platoon commander from the Third Battalion, First Marines in his outsource staffing business and executive placement company, 3D Global Solutions.

It's not the Marines, Shane says, but it's not bad, especially since it puts him in the position to help a lot of former military personnel find good jobs. "I was in the infantry for fifteen and a half years," Shane says, "and I miss the fellas, man. I miss 'em bad." But he's following his own advice as far as moving forward goes: "Sittin' around cryin' about something is not gonna solve a fuckin' thing, man. Pick your ass up and keep movin'. As long as you're not dead, as long as you've still got a breath in your body, you got no reason to fail, especially as a Marine."

Life after Fallujah has had highs and lows for many of us. I thought I knew what my life was going to be like—long hours as a hospital resident, family time with my wife and daughter. The last thing I expected was to end up on the cover of *Newsweek* magazine. That happened by pure chance. A *Newsweek* reporter, Pat Wingert, saw a little news clip about my Bronze Star while she was working on a story about the wounded of Fallujah. She called and asked for an interview. I hadn't really talked much about what happened in Fallujah since I'd been back—and I sure didn't expect to go into detail about it with a total stranger. Opening that door was easier and harder than I expected. It was almost like I had a need to talk about what we had been through. Over the course of the next several weeks, we did hours of interviews, squeezed into any spare time I had between surgeries or after a shift or on one of my rare days off. I tried to be as brutally honest as I could. In some respects, it was a relief to talk about it. Other times, I would end up pacing the floor for hours after an interview. Awakening all those memories made it hard to sleep. There were times when I wanted nothing more than to shut up and never talk about it again. Melissa could see that the interviews were upsetting me, and asked if it was really worth it to put myself through this again. But I grew to trust Pat, and my hope was that the story might do some good. I knew she and other reporters at *Newsweek* were talking to a lot of people I had served with in Fallujah, and that some of the wounded would be featured in the article. The bottom line was that I thought this was a story that needed to be told.

I didn't know that my picture was going to end up on the cover of the magazine. The only thing that surprised me more was the response the story got after it hit the newsstands: calls from CNN and the *Today* show and even publishers and movie agents. People started calling and asking me to speak, including the National Security Council in Washington, D.C. And I even got invited to throw out the opening pitch at a Baltimore Orioles game—and Chief Folley went with me. Now that was cool.

But what was even cooler was hearing from many of the guys I had served with in Fallujah, now scattered across the country and around the world, and getting updates on how they were doing. I got amazing letters from strangers all over the country. The widow of one West Point grad, having read about my being rejected from the academy because of my wandering eye, even sent me one of her husband's alumni hats.

I heard from many military families who had lost someone in Fallujah. I tried to answer every one of their letters and e-mails and phone calls, and it was an honor to do so.

Among the e-mails was one from the mother of Demarkus Brown. That was a hard letter to receive, and a hard letter to answer. I told her what I could about her son's last days. I also told her about the prayer card I'd found in the dirt after her son's passing, and my belief that it had fallen out of one of his pockets. She is a warm and understanding woman, and corresponding with her has helped me make my peace with that time in Fallujah. But I found myself wishing that I could offer her more than words. And then it hit me. There was one more thing I could do. I pulled that tired-looking prayer card out of my wallet. It had become kind of a talisman for me. Since I'd been back, I'd unconsciously started reaching for it when faced with a difficult decision. But that day, I stuck it in an envelope and sent it to Demarkus' mom. I knew she was the one person who would value it even more than I did.

APPENDIX

II Marine Expeditionary Force (II MEF) is based out of Camp Lejeune, North Carolina, and is one of the Marine Corps's four primary fighting forces (I MEF is in Camp Pendleton, California; III MEF is in Okinawa; and IV MEF is the reservists). The **Second Marine Division** is the ground combat element of II MEF. The **First Battalion, Eighth Marines (the 1/8)** is one battalion within the Second Marine Division, but it was sent to augment I MEF's forces in al-Anbar province of Iraq from June 2004 to January 2005. Within the 1/8, there is one **Headquarters and Service company** and four **line companies:** three **rifle companies—Alpha (A), Bravo (B), and Charlie (C)—**and one **Weapons company.** Each of these four line companies has three numbered platoons of about forty-five Marines and six to nine corpsmen.

1/8 INFANTRY BATTALION MEDICAL PERSONNEL

Headquarters and Service Company (H&S)
Battalion Surgeon Lt. Cmdr. Richard H. Jadick
Assistant Battalion Surgeon Lt. Carlos C. Kennedy
HMC Russell W. Folley
HM1 Richard E. Lees
HM1 Bryan P. Zimmerman
HM2 Shawn J. Johns
HM2 Steve Meszaros
HM3 Jobriath Burn
HM3 Martin Graves
HM3 Clifton H. Hinds
HM3 Ryan D. Hirkala
HM3 David Lester
HM3 David McArdle
HM3 Jason M. Smith
HN Uriel Garcia
HN Raymond Masino
HN Roger D. Millhouse
HN Ricky J. Peterson
HN John Paul Rosales
HN Collin Steadman
HN Justin Troyano
HA Ernesto Argueta
HA Daniel S. Avila

1/8 INFANTRY BATTALION MEDICAL PERSONNEL *(continued)*

Alpha Company (A)	Bravo Company (B)	Charlie Company (C)	Weapons Company (W)
Call sign Avenger	*Call sign Beowulf*	*Call sign Cajun*	*Call sign Wolverine*
HM3 Casey T. Moody*	HM3 Kevin M. Markley*	HM3 Aaron Pines*	HM3 Thomas J. Stahura*
HM3 Reinaldo Aponte, Jr.	HM3 Jeff M. Gregus	HM3 Raul M. Cervantes	HM2 Justin B. Sutton
HM3 Manuel G. Cortez	HM3 Milton L. Jones	HM3 Anthony Lopez	HM3 Christian Rueda
HM3 Duncan Fraser	HM3 Lucas Q. Jushinski	HM3 Michael C. Martinez	HN Joel E. Dupuis
HM3 Ryan Turner	HM3 Luis E. RuizPopo	HM3 David Nadermann	HN Joseph Maston
HN Jordan Holtschulte	HN Rex A. Goodman	HN Luis Lopez	HN Kouji Touya
HN Julian C. Mask	HN Joel Lambotte	HN Ether Maldonado	
		HN Randall McLain	
		HN Barry L. Womack	

*Senior Company Corpsman
HMC = Chief Hospital Corpsman
HM1 = Hospital Corpsman First Class
HM2 = Hospital Corpsman Second Class
HM3 = Hospital Corpsman Third Class
HN = Hospitalman
HA = Hospitalman Apprentice

ACKNOWLEDGMENTS

Of all the things I've done in my life, I never thought writing a book would be one of them, and I know I never could have accomplished it alone. I was very fortunate to receive help and encouragement from dozens of friends, colleagues, and family members, and I owe them all a large debt of gratitude. I'm especially indebted to the families of the fallen Marines of the 1/8, who all took the time to share stories of their sons. Karen and Charlie Fredrickson, whose nephew Sergeant Samuel Williams served with Bravo Company's first platoon in Fallujah, were important liaisons with these Gold Star families, and tireless advocates for the legacy of the fallen Marines. I also want to extend my thanks to the wounded Marines who took the time to tell us about their experiences in Fallujah and their challenges on the road to recovery since.

My biggest debt is and always will be to my loving, beautiful wife, Melissa. She understood when I knew I had to go to Iraq with the 1/8, even though it meant that I would be leaving her just as our daughter, MacKenzie, came into the world. And now she has done it all again, putting up with the long hours, late nights, and nonexistent weekends that went into making this book a reality. In addition, I want to thank my parents, Richard and Barbara Jadick, for a lifetime of love and support and for standing in for me, for being there for my wife and daughter, while I was gone. Thanks, also, to my brother Chris and sister, Denise, for all their great help with the book. As for MacKenzie, a wonderful daughter who has seen too little of her father for the first two years of her life, I can only apologize and promise that I'll be there whenever she needs me, no matter what.

I was never alone in Iraq. Throughout our time there, Lieutenant Carlos Kennedy and I always knew we had fifty-four U.S. Navy hospital corpsmen on the job, ready to take on any task and overcome any challenge. The corpsmen of the 1/8 were the true backbone of our medical operation there, and their bravery, dedication, and skill were at the heart of our success. I could not have asked for, or belonged to, a better team. And I owe special thanks to HMC Russ Folley, who trained, led, and inspired the corpsmen, and helped keep me sane throughout the deployment.

Although Joe Langholtz did not deploy with us to Iraq, he played a special role in both the book and the stories it contains. He has been a good friend to me and my family for years, and he has inspired, challenged, and encouraged me perhaps more than any other colleague in my military career. His influence on my thinking about battlefield medicine was an important element of our success in Fallujah, and his advice, guidance, and suggestions have been a great help in the writing of this book.

The stories in *On Call in Hell* are not all mine, and even in situations where I was present, I was often too busy, or too exhausted, to remember all of the details. Many corpsmen and Marines generously gave their time and photographs, and turned their minds to sometimes painful memories to help ensure that this book is as complete as it can be. I can't thank them enough for that, and I can't emphasize enough that whatever errors remain are mine and mine alone. I would especially like to recognize the efforts of HM2 Shawn Johns, Second Lieutenant Paul Stekatee, Captain Matthew Kutilek and Captain Read Omohundro, who not only devoted an exceptional amount of time and energy, but also shared valuable documents that helped to re-create many of the stories in this book. Lieutenant Colonel Mark Winn read large sections of the draft manuscript, and his comments added depth and clarity to the finished product, and saved it from any number of embarrassing mistakes.

Even with the help of dozens of participants, Marine families, official documents, media reports and other written sources, and my own memories, no account of intense battle can tell the whole story. Readers interested in learning more about the context and events of the Battle of Fallujah and the actions of the 1/8 may find books such as *No True Glory* by Bing West, *Fallujah, with Honor* by Gary Livingston, and *Fighting for Fallujah* by John R. Ballard useful. Many reporters were embedded with American forces during the battle, including *New York Times* reporter Dexter Filkins, who accompanied Bravo Company into Fallujah, and their accounts provide another source of information for interested readers.

My colleagues in the Section of Urology at the Medical College of Georgia's Department of Surgery all deserve special recognition as well, for accepting me into their ranks and for supporting me during the writing of this book. In particular I would like to thank Dr. Arthur M. Smith, who pushed me to write this book, and Dr. Chris Hathaway, who covered for me when I had book deadlines and should have been in clinic. Kim Miller of MCG's Media Relations department first wrote about my wartime experiences for the publication *The Pulse at MCG*, and helped obtain medical releases from the wounded Marines. Michele Rhee, a Research Study Coordinator at MCG, generously transcribed many hours of my dictated notes and read the entire manuscript, offering fresh eyes and an editor's instincts.

I'd also like to thank Rafe Sagalyn, the master agent who did an extraordinary job putting together all the pieces to a very complicated project. This book wouldn't have happened without you. I'd also like to mention Beth Nolan, my attorney, who gave wise counsel throughout.

I'm very grateful to the amazing team at the New American Library/Penguin and especially my editor, Mark Chait, who was passionate about this book from the beginning and has been a source of intelligence and sanity throughout the writing and editing process.

I'd like to thank my writing partner, Thomas Hayden, who brought to life my story and the stories of the 1/8—and helped make this book the great read that I believe it is. Tom is an extraordinary talent and it was a pleasure to work with him. Throughout the process, I was struck by his remarkable patience and intelligence and attention to detail.

This book had its beginnings in a series of stories published in the March 20, 2006, issue of *Newsweek*. Pat Wingert, a Washington correspondent at that magazine, first contacted me about telling my story to the media, and worked tirelessly for several months to make that idea a reality. Pat has been involved with *On Call in Hell* ever since, first encouraging me to write the book and then helping me navigate through the unfamiliar world of book publishing. She has been an invaluable editor, advisor, and consultant during the entire process, and her efforts are visible throughout the book. Finally, Pat and her *Newsweek* colleagues Martha Brant, Jonathan Darman, Andrew Murr, and Evan Thomas generously made their research and reporting available for this book; that material served as a valuable starting point for writing and a guide throughout the process. I'm also grateful to Brian Kelly, executive editor of *U.S. News & World Report* and part-time book doctor, who helped put this project on the right course.